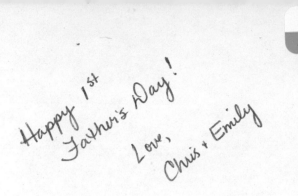

Happy 1st
Father's Day!
Love,
Chris + Emily

P9-ELV-006

Books by
RAY BERGMAN

JUST FISHING
TROUT
FRESH-WATER BASS

These are BORZOI BOOKS
published by ALFRED A. KNOPF, *New York*

Books by
EDWARD C. JANES

THE STORY OF KNIVES
WHEN MEN PANNED GOLD IN THE KLONDIKE
WHEN CAPE COD MEN SAVED LIVES
A BOY AND HIS BOAT
CAMPING ENCYCLOPEDIA
FIRST BOOK OF CAMPING
FRESHWATER FISHING COMPLETE
TROUBLE AT CLEAR LAKE
WILDERNESS WARDEN
HUNTING DUCKS AND GEESE
A BOY AND HIS GUN

FISHING WITH
RAY BERGMAN

Edited by

EDWARD C. JANES

With decorative headpieces by BETTY FRASER

A Fireside Book
Published by Simon & Schuster Inc.
New York • London • Toronto • Sydney • Tokyo

FIRESIDE
SIMON & SCHUSTER BUILDING
ROCKEFELLER CENTER
1230 AVENUE OF THE AMERICAS
NEW YORK, NEW YORK 10020

COPYRIGHT © 1970 BY ALFRED A. KNOPF, INC.

ALL RIGHTS RESERVED
INCLUDING THE RIGHT OF REPRODUCTION
IN WHOLE OR IN PART IN ANY FORM

FIRST FIRESIDE EDITION, 1989
PUBLISHED BY ARRANGEMENT WITH ALFRED A. KNOPF, INC.
FIRESIDE AND COLOPHON ARE REGISTERED TRADEMARKS
OF SIMON & SCHUSTER INC.
MANUFACTURED IN THE UNITED STATES OF AMERICA

1   3   5   7   9   10   8   6   4   2

LIBRARY OF CONGRESS CATALOGING IN PUBLICATION DATA

BERGMAN, RAY, 1891–1966.
FISHING WITH RAY BERGMAN / EDITED BY EDWARD C. JANES ; WITH
DECORATIVE HEADPIECES BY BETTY FRASER. — 1ST FIRESIDE ED.
P.   CM.
REPRINT. ORIGINALLY PUBLISHED: NEW YORK : A.A. KNOPF, 1970.
"A FIRESIDE BOOK."
ISBN 0-671-66898-6 (PBK.) : $8.95
1. FISHING.   I. JANES, EDWARD C.   II. TITLE.
SH441.B449 1989
799. 1'2—DC19
88-24724
CIP

Contents

CONTENTS

Foreword

There is beautiful justice in the appearance of *Fishing with Ray Bergman*. It is an unexpected bonanza both for the multitude of Bergman fans and for newcomers to the writings of this greatest of all angling editors. And it is a fulfillment of a Bergman desire.

I felt despair in 1959 when Ray Bergman told me that he felt he must retire from *Outdoor Life* in six months. I knew the decision had to come soon because Ray, a gentleman and a man of integrity in his personal affairs as well as a genius in his calling, had given me plenty of forewarning.

Nonetheless, knowing what a monumental task I'd face to replace him, I tried to dissuade him. "Can't we go on a little while longer, Ray?" I asked.

"But, Bill," he said, "I was sixty-eight on my last birthday and, remember, my father died last year."

Since Ray's father, a fishing companion from his youth, had lived to ninety-four, and even in his last years had walked almost daily the few blocks that separated their homes in Nyack, I couldn't resist reminding him of the gap between sixty-eight and ninety-four, even though I knew a heart attack had complicated Ray's recent years.

My resistance dissolved when Ray said he was tired and wanted to fish for a while without writing about it and worrying about deadlines, as he had been doing monthly for twenty-six years. "Those were happy years, Bill," he said, "but, you know, the column I could write in a day or two in those years now takes me almost a month to do. First, I want to rest, and then I want to do one more book."

FOREWORD

Thus it was that out of this meeting came his last monthly angling column for *Outdoor Life*, "Ray Bergman Says Goodbye—Until I Write Again" (See Chapter XXXIV). Ray fully expected to do an occasional story for *Outdoor Life* in the future. He never did. He did start on the book he wanted to write, but it was only a start. To his wife, Grace, who typed his manuscripts all those years of his writing and who was the constant companion of his travels, he said one day: "I can't do it, Grace. I wanted to so much, but I can't do it."

On my desk is a beautiful leather-bound volume of Bergman's famous *Trout*, one of 149 copies of a limited first edition. Grace Bergman gave it to me following Ray's death in 1967. It was one of two copies Ray had kept for himself and used as a reference. It has the well-worn but well-preserved look of the library treasure it is for me.

Perhaps most meaningful to me are the notes in Ray's handwriting scattered through the pages. They look like the notes of an author who was planning another book. What did he have in mind? It seems likely that it was a volume of the essence condensed of all the knowledge he had gained from a lifetime of fishing.

So it is poetic justice that the book Ray Bergman couldn't do has been done by another dedicated fisherman and lifelong lover of the outdoors who learned his lessons from the pages Bergman wrote and the streams he fished. Ted Janes, Eastern Field Editor of *Outdoor Life*, author of a dozen books, including one on freshwater fishing, and a winner of a Freedoms Foundation Award for an article on Plymouth, Massachusetts, has extracted pulsing life from the store of experience Ray Bergman recorded in the more than three hundred stories he wrote for *Outdoor Life* as Angling Editor.

These are the words and knowledge of Ray Bergman in a new book that he might have written himself.

WILLIAM E. RAE
Editor-in-Chief, *Outdoor Life*

Introduction

In every century there have been expert fishermen, some of whom have enjoyed writing of their experiences for the instruction and entertainment of their fellow anglers. Izaak Walton is perhaps the classic example, but there are a number of others equally skillful if somewhat less widely known. Nearly two thousand years before *The Compleat Angler* was published, Greek and Roman writers such as Oppius and Suetonius were providing detailed information on the tackle and angling methods of the day. Thomas Best, Robert Howlett, and Dr. W. C. Prime contributed to the growing store of angling lore through the years, and in modern times the names of Edward R. Hewitt, George La Branche, and Theodore Gordon come to mind, along with Ray Bergman, one of the outstanding angler-writers of the present century.

Ray Bergman was born July 15, 1891, in Nyack, New York, and hence, as he tells us in his classic *Trout*, his angling career spanned the transition years between "the old-fashioned ways of the latter nineteenth century and the rapid-fire changes of the twentieth." It began beside the Hudson River and the foaming trout streams that tumbled into it from the adjoining Highlands. Here, at first with his father, and later traveling by bicycle, train, and vintage automobile, he learned the art or craft of angling and in so doing laid broad and deep the foundations of his later career.

Many men are anglers; some of them are naturalists as well. Ray Bergman was one of these. "As far back as I can remember," he says, "I have been passionately fond of the outdoors. Memories of childhood are mostly vague and dreamlike but I have some recollections of these early days which have survived the years. Oddly enough they are of rainstorms and in them I am either fishing with a handline from a long stone dock jutting out into the Hudson River or else I am wandering along the rocky shores of the river in the vicinity of Hook Mountain, that isolated northern rampart of the Palisades.

"With startling reality I can feel the sting of rain on my face, blown against it by the eastern gale. Vividly I can see the angry waters of the river buffeting the dock and the shore, the border of gray light along the eastern horizon and the restless black clouds which seemed to form directly on that border of light and then rush madly across the sky, finally to bank in huge masses against the western horizon.

"During such periods even the village streets were deserted and quiet. To me this condition was ideal and I could not be kept indoors. Wild storms appealed to me, transported me back through the ages to primitive days, brought me thrills which made my body quiver with sheer physical delight. I would rather face the storms at the river's edge or from a mountain top than to have many dollars' worth of fireworks on the Fourth of July, and in the eyes of youth this was a mighty comparison indeed.

"Somehow I feel that the elements and all life, whether human or otherwise, are directly related, so much so that anyone who is sincerely enraptured by the wonders of nature stands very close to the great beyond. To such souls fishing is an outlet to the feelings, a surcease from life's trials. Being so closely attuned to nature's whims I drifted naturally into out-of-door pursuits, and fishing seemed to be the one sport which best gratified that innate craving for an intimacy with those forces of which I knew so little. Is it any wonder that I made the study of fishing my life's work?"

The studies began early, even while the young student was still in the original bait-fishing stage of his career. Using worms, he learned where the fish sheltered and how to present the bait to them in a natural manner. Then, after everyone else in the community had given up trout fishing for the season, this dedicated angler kept on trying and questioning. Where did the trout go in summer? Why would they no longer take worms with the same greedy abandon they had evinced in early spring? Was there some way to catch them in the clear, shrunken streams of summer? The answer to this latter question came on a memorable July day on Crumb Creek when Ray Bergman met an unknown benefactor who demonstrated that trout could be caught at that time of year and opened up to him the fascinating world of fishing with artificial flies.

The studies continued during ensuing years with the keeping of copious notes on weather and water conditions and the habits of fish. "I find that these trout of the Crumb Creek meadow cannot be taken during July and August," he wrote, "unless I use extreme care, not only in the approach but in the cast and the selection of flies. The flies must be of subdued coloration, they must alight on the water softly and sink immediately and the retrieve must be made slowly and with deliberation. It takes from fifteen to twenty-five minutes to work to a suitable casting location and the slightest misstep on the way is fatal to my chances."

So through the years of boyhood and early youth, Ray Bergman continued to fish and to study. Then, all too soon, it was time to leave these halcyon days behind and to begin the more mundane task of earning a living. And what could be more natural than that this young man should open a sporting goods store in his native town of Nyack? The business prospered and the shop became a popular rendezvous for local fishermen and hunters.

Illness ended this first venture, and after recuperation there followed a period of employment with a New York tackle firm and a stint of running a mail-order business in Nyack. It was during his illness that Ray Bergman began to write articles on fishing, articles which came from his typewriter in increasing numbers each year. And from the start it became apparent that here was angling writing that contained a freshness and an authenticity which set it apart from the run-of-the-mill material of the day.

INTRODUCTION

Here was a man who knew what he was talking about and who had the ability not only to entertain his readers but to teach them his skills as well. In 1932 the popular volume *Just Fishing* was published, the first of four angling classics, and Ray Bergman had embarked upon his true career.

What are some of the factors which distinguish Ray Bergman's writings and what is the source of their continuing appeal? First and foremost, I think, is the honesty and reliability which speaks out from each page. To paraphrase the advertising slogan, "You can be sure if it's Bergman." No advice is given, no theory set forth that has not been thoroughly and painstakingly tested and proven in Ray's laboratory of the lakes and streams. It was Ray's conviction that no angling theory or item of fishing tackle could be properly evaluated without subjecting it to at least thirty days of testing under actual field conditions. Some of his theories were several years in the making. Some angling writers, too, are prone to skip over details, but not Ray Bergman.

"I like to fish the pockets with a cast of three wet flies," he explains. "For the end fly I like a rather large and meaty-looking job, say a No. 6 Montreal. A minnowlike fly such as a Wickham's Fancy or a Silver Doctor is also a good end fly. This end fly should be tied on a heavy wire hook, so it will sink readily.

"For the middle dropper I like a size 10 or 12, using one of the following patterns according to the stream being fished and my thoughts and whims at the time: Gold-Ribbed Hare's Ear, Leadwing Coachman, Blue Dun or Blue Quill, Quill Gordon, Cahill, Light Cahill, Ginger Quill, March Brown, and either Coachman or Royal Coachman.

"The flies just mentioned are all acceptable for the top dropper also, but here I usually use one of the Coachman patterns because a gaudy Coachman is more visible to me, thus aiding me in fishing the cast properly. . . ."

Ray doesn't just tell us to use a cast of three wet flies. He names the best patterns and sizes for end and droppers and even the correct weight of wire.

Again in discussing fly fishing, he advises, "Another point

[xii]

should be stressed here. When using size eighteen and twenty flies, you'll remember that I had a ten-foot leader tapered to 8X or .005 calibration. When I changed to the larger variant, I fished it on a 7½-foot leader tapering to 2X or .009—a much shorter and heavier leader. I did this because a long-hackled fly is very difficult to cast with a very long and finely pointed leader. The air resistance on a large, fluffy fly calls for a heavier leader. I bring that point out to show that using a leader that fits the fly is of more importance than having one extremely long and thin. A big fly doesn't act right on a spider-web leader."

Another facet of Ray's writings is the enthusiasm which shines forth from the pages of his books and articles and which transfers itself to his readers.

"Before I'd finished my sandwich, I heard the rod and reel bang against the side of the boat. My quick grab barely saved the tackle from going overboard. It was too late to set the hook in the big bass that swirled to the surface and spit out my artificial bug.

"Lunch was forgotten. I didn't even take time to put it back in the box, for the incident suggested—and correctly so, as it turned out—that if I let the bug rest quietly on the surface for longer periods, or only moved it slowly, the bass would hit it. They did, and as a result I discovered one of the first principles of bass bugging: let your bug rest quietly on the surface for about a minute after each cast and then move or twitch it very gently. It generally ruins your chances to retrieve or move a fly-rod bass bug as quickly as you would a spinner or plug. When I left the lake that night I had six nice largemouths...."

No one can make the stalking or capture of a fish more suspenseful. At times you feel you must cheat by letting your eyes drop down the page to see how the encounter came out.

"Then, in a tiny baylike spot between two huge boulders, I tangled with a dandy. When I cast the spoon struck the shore and bounced back into the water. At the same instant there came a tremendous swirl, and when I struck I felt a solid and thrilling weight. For several minutes it was touch and go. The fish thrashed around so furiously in the rockbound hole that I was sure either the lure would be thrown or the line cut or broken...." P.S. He caught the fish.

Numerous other examples illustrative of Ray's knowledge, thoroughness and enthusiasm could be quoted, but these will suffice to limn the character of this dedicated angler who declared, "In my opinion fishing should not be competitive or comparative. Rather, it should be contemplative—a sport to build up the soul and refresh the mind, so that after a day or more on lake or stream a person goes back to the job of making a living with renewed vigor and new ideas."

In a day before airplanes had made remote wilderness areas accessible to sportsmen Ray fished widely throughout the United States and Canada. Drawing upon the rich fund of experience gained from these travels and from earlier studies nearer home, besides his well-known books, Ray Bergman contributed a fishing department to *Outdoor Life* Magazine each month for twenty-six years. It is from this vast store of angling lore that the chapters in this book have been assembled. Much of it is material never before published in book form.

In compiling and editing this volume, it has been my attempt not only to carry out Ray's avowed purpose in his writings of helping his readers to improve their angling knowledge and techniques, but also to capture something of the spirit of the outdoors—the woods and lakes and streams—which Ray Bergman loved and knew so well.

To achieve both these goals, I have chosen what I consider to be the best article on each subject—not always an easy choice—and have then combined with it outstanding sections from other articles on the same subject. The result, I am hopeful, has been a useful and also entertaining book for both the beginning and advanced angler, a reference book to consult during the season as well as a friendly volume to enjoy on winter nights. Although I have fished rather widely for upwards of half a century, I know that editing this book has made me a better fisherman and I feel sure that reading it will do the same for you.

INTRODUCTION

This will be the last time any of us can have the advantage of Ray Bergman's knowledge, gained through a lifetime of fishing experience, the last time he can take us by the hand, so to speak, as Izaak Walton took his disciple, Venator, and show us his methods of fishing on lake and stream. For a new generation coming along, it is an opportunity to learn about angling from a master craftsman. For an older generation it is an opportunity to have one last visit with a friend.

E. C. JANES
Westfield, Massachusetts

FISHING WITH
RAY BERGMAN

CHAPTER I

Tips for Early Trout

Early spring may provide exceptionally good fishing or no fishing at all. It all depends on the weather and water conditions in the particular area you fish. The angler's early spring starts just as soon as winter releases its hold on the waters. This may be in February in southern states, or as late as June in northern regions. It's the weather, not the calendar, that sets the date for spring fishing.

Worms have my vote as the best natural bait for trout at the start of the season. They probably account for more highwater trout across the country than any other bait or artificial lure. The various earthworm baits are so well known that I want to devote most of this piece to another subject—the handling of artificial lures to take trout under spring fishing conditions.

High and discolored water need not prevent the successful use of artificials unless the stream is so muddy the fish can't see the lure. In my opinion, the water must be clear enough for a fish to see an artificial at least three feet away—often more than that—before artificials are consistently effective. Trout take lures such as you would use in early spring (spinners, wobblers) with a rush. I believe they strike at them because they look like something good to eat that's trying to escape. At times they will take lures made of metal, plastic, wood, or feathers more readily than real food.

There's a lesson in early spring fishing in an experience I had on a stream in southern New York, a stream that runs south into New Jersey. This stream is on the sluggish side and isn't at all like the general idea of how a trout brook should look. It runs smoothly through a flat valley of meadow and farm country. In some places the stream bottom is sand, in others clay, and there are some sections which are just soft mud. However, the water is good and the fish of fair size. The stream was sometimes fished with artificials of some kind on opening day. I wanted to try out a new spinning outfit, one especially designed for casting artificial lures of less than an eighth ounce, so I left my natural baits at home.

When I saw the height of the water and its very dingy color I fervently wished I'd brought along a can of worms. Since I hadn't, it was necessary to fish with what I had. As I knew the stream quite well I picked out a section which had produced some good catches under more favorable conditions, and started fishing it downstream.

The current was so swift wading was tough. The small lures were carried downstream so fast that they rarely got more than a foot or two below the surface before it was necessary to retrieve and cast again. I fished the entire stretch of five hundred feet without getting a single strike or even an investigating touch.

After I'd reached the end of the stretch I felt like quitting. I sat down on the bank a while to rest before starting home. Once rested, I decided to fish back upstream to where I'd started. I felt quite sure that the light spinning lures I was using had not got deep enough to be effective when fishing downstream. Fishing them upstream should remedy the trouble.

The light spinning outfit cast the small lures easily for a good distance. I soon learned that the cast distance had to conform to the speed of the current and depth of the water, with slack line taken in just fast enough to keep a lure from snagging, but not so fast that it didn't touch bottom once in a while. It was the real secret of success for the time.

The trout were feeding on bottom; there wasn't any doubt about that. I'd feel the bait bumping along the bottom, then I'd have a solid strike from a fish. I missed many more than I hooked, but I hooked enough to make the catch a good one. The secret was in making the lure bump the bottom frequently.

Another time, when fishing a different stream at the same time of year and under approximately the same conditions, I fished with a regular spinning outfit, using lures from an eighth to a quarter ounce. The quarter-ounce lures were heavy enough to fish downstream satisfactorily. They reached bottom when fished slowly, and they also had action enough to look like something alive. Again the trout were bottom-feeding, and when the lures got deep enough I caught fish. As the water became clearer and lower, the lures didn't need to be fished as they touched bottom. They did quite well when fished just reasonably deep.

On many early spring fishing trips I've had good fishing using flies—wet flies, streamers, and bucktails. In northern trout ponds and lakes these flies often prove to be great fish-takers for a short period after the ice goes out. Let me tell you of a typical experience.

It was a shallow northern pond, approximately a mile long and half a mile wide. The trout in it averaged on the small side, but there were some twelve- to fourteen-inchers that hit often enough to make it interesting. Worms usually did a good job here, but conditions were such that I wondered if flies wouldn't do as well. The water was very clear and lower than normal for the season. It was early May, just after the ice went out. When I arrived I could see scattered rises all over the pond, so I couldn't resist starting to fish with dry flies, though I rarely use them on ponds and lakes except in late summer or early fall.

First I checked the flies that were floating on the surface. They ranged in color from light to dark blue-grays and from light ginger to ginger. They were so small that a size-18 dry artificial looked big alongside them. I tried dry flies in size 18 of patterns Blue Quill, Ginger Quill, Dark Coty, and light Cahill. They only interested the small fry.

Next I tried some very tiny 18, 20, and 22 wet flies that I'd purchased in England in hopes they might sometimes help me out of a tight spot. (They had done this several times during the low waters of summer.) These hooked fish, but none larger than 8 inches. Disgusted with the small fish, I'd almost decided to quit when I thought of the many good trout I'd caught in this pond in the past when using big wet flies fished with the old-time method. I decided to give it a try.

I changed to a heavier leader than the very fine one I'd been using with the tiny dry flies and tied on two wet flies. On the end I put a size-8 Alexandria—a fancy fly that also looks like a morsel worth eating. For the dropper I used a size-10 Blue Quill. Before starting to use them I got them thoroughly wet and soaked the leader in wet mud so that it would help them sink readily. The first cast was made toward a very small and weedy bay. I'd chosen the spot because I knew that a tiny but ever-active spring brook ran into this bay and that trout frequented the place.

The end or tail fly dropped at the very edge of the weeds and I let the entire cast sink, watching it carefully for any sign of action. As the leader completely disappeared and the line itself began sinking, I noted a slight twitch. My quick responding strike hooked a fish that felt like a good one. About half a minute after the fight started there was a change in the feel. In fact there was no pull at all. For a moment I thought I'd lost the fish, but a second later the pull became so heavy I believed I'd really hooked a dandy and it had just started to fight. However, the feeling wasn't exactly like that of a good fish.

About five minutes later I knew the answer: I had on two good fish of about the same weight. I figured that the odd feeling of the fight was caused by the two fish fighting each other at times. I had quite a time landing them both but finally succeeded. They were a nice pair, each weighing in excess of 1¼ pounds.

I thought this must indeed be a hot spot, so I worked it again with the same flies and tactics. I took two more keeper trout, besides missing several. After that I fished hard for about two hours, working the shoreline and out in the pond. I took quite a number of eight-inchers and kept some because that's the size I best like to eat.

By this time I'd come to the outlet, another weedy and small bay. Again I cast to the edge of the weed growth and let the flies sink. They'd probably sunk about five feet when I saw the line twitch. I struck. It felt like a good one, but I was either too fast or too slow. I didn't hook the fish. I cast again, watching the line on the surface intently as the flies and leader sank under the surface. I'd decided nothing was going to happen (the flies must have been near the bottom) when the line twitched and I struck. This time the fish was hooked and landed. It was a plump fourteen-incher.

This location provided reasonably good action for about forty-five minutes, then went dead. All of these fish were either taken while the flies were sinking or when they were being fished back with the hand-twist retrieve. After that I worked slowly along the shoreline again, fishing all the places that looked good. I never got a touch until I got around to the spring-brook bay where I'd taken the double. Here I got some more trout, all of them taken deep and while using the hand-twist retrieve.

Now where these fish were caught in the pond isn't too important. In another pond or lake and at the same season they might have been taken in entirely different types of water. The important part of this experience is to point out that "luck" is a matter of finding out where the fish are and then fishing for them so that they respond. This takes work and thought, not some magic, sure-killer lure.

Often the best method to use for fishing regular wet flies for trout in early spring is to sink them and use the hand-twist retrieve. However, that isn't always the best way. Often making a fast retrieve with the flies close to the surface may be better. Never let yourself become a one-method angler. When your favorite method and flies fail, try other ways to fish them and change both patterns and sizes. The use of the natural drift—letting the fly or flies sink and drift with the current—is often more effective than giving them any rod or line action.

Here are two suggestions for using wet flies or nymphs in streams. You may weight a leader with small split-shot and cast upstream. When the flies get close to the bottom, give them upward movements with pauses in between. This is the action of live nymphs rising from the bottom to hatch. If the water is high and dirty and you wish to use flies, try wets in sizes 6 and 8 tied on heavy wire hooks. In my opinion, a fly that looks like a piece of meat does best under such conditions. For myself, I make a fly I call Bloody Mary on size-4 heavy wire hooks for fly fishing under such conditions. I fish the fly very deep, using a sinker if necessary. It has done well by me, though I must say that natural bait is generally better for high and muddy water.

Sometimes I have found streamers and bucktails very good for early spring fishing. This is especially so in waters where the trout feed on a lot of small fish. Streamers and bucktails were originally tied to imitate minnows, so they usually do best when they're fished to simulate the jerky, darting motions of small fish. The trolling of streamers and bucktails in lakes and ponds is often effective during early spring as well as it is later. However, in the early spring one need not fish as deep as is sometimes necessary during late spring and early summer months.

At the same time, I suggest that you always go prepared with equipment that can get deep. Otherwise you may travel many miles expecting wonderful fishing and then catch nothing. It would have been this way had I gone unprepared on one trip I'll tell you about.

The weather was raw and the water mildly rough. The lake was on the large side, which would make it tough if conditions got really bad. It looked as if deep trolling would be the right method, but I'm a light-tackle fan, so I started fishing with a fly rod, casting for a short time with flies. I soon quit this because it didn't catch any fish. Then I started trolling a weighted streamer —no luck.

After that I changed to a spinning outfit, using lures as heavy as three-eighths ounce, trying many of the popular numbers. These didn't get any response either, even though I was fishing the locations about which it was said: "If you don't catch any fish there, then you might as well not fish at all, because they just ain't bitin'!" I didn't get a bite but I didn't quit.

Fortunately, I'd brought along a light bait-casting outfit. It was one that could efficiently handle lures as heavy as five eighths of an ounce. I rigged it up with ten-pound test monofilament line. To the line I attached a nickel wobbling spoon weighing five eighths of an ounce. Then I started trolling again over the very water I'd fished unsuccessfully with the flies and the lighter lures. This heavy spoon sank considerably deeper than the others and it wasn't long before I hooked a fish. The combination of bait-casting rod and reel with the heavier lure seemed to be the answer. It took fish consistently until it was too dark to fish any longer.

Early spring isn't always the most pleasant time to fish, but often it is the most productive. It also relieves the tension built up during the winter. At this time of year most northern anglers are chafing at the bit, fretting to use a rod and reel. Just be sure you go prepared. Take varied tackle and clothing so that you will be ready for anything.

CHAPTER II

Early Trout Like Worms

I WAS fishing a strange stream, the most promising trout water I have ever seen. Selecting two lively night crawlers from my bait can, I threaded them on a No. 4 hook and dropped the worms into a deep enticing pool. I knew for sure that I was going to connect with a big trout. Sure enough, I hooked a whopper instantly. The great fish rushed downstream, then leaped so high I had time to study every phase of its brilliant coloration as it rose and fell through the rays of rising sun.

I first noticed that something was wrong when I tried to recover some of the line I'd lost. Not a foot of line would come in, though I tried both reeling and stripping. While I struggled with this peculiar line trouble the trout surfaced lazily about thirty feet below me. Then the fish actually spit at me, making a loud insulting sound.

I sat up in bed at that point, gradually coming awake. The spitting sound was made by a gust of rain and sleet against the east window near my bed. It was four a.m., still pitch dark, but I decided to get up and make breakfast. My alarm clock had been set for four thirty anyway.

It was still dark as I drove my car to the trout stream I planned to fish that early spring day. The rain and sleet turned to snow as daylight came, wet snow that melted as it touched bare ground but whitened the grass and brush. The only thing that brightened my gloomy outlook was the large can of night crawlers I'd gathered two nights before. They'd be the right bait for these conditions.

I didn't like the thought of fishing in the brush or beneath the trees in this weather, so I went to a bog meadow, a stretch of stream that had produced good catches for me in previous years. By the time I reached a pet hole I was warm from hiking and full of pep.

The dream was still in my mind as I put two large night crawlers on the bait hook and flipped them into a current that led into a deep hole under an overhanging bank. I let out line and guided the bait so that it drifted and sank into the hole. I felt a fish take the worms and immediately forgot the snow and cold.

I let the fish mouth the bait for about forty-five seconds and then struck. My dream had come true, with two differences: the trout wasn't big, weighing only a pound and a half, and I had no special difficulty landing it. However, it was a good fish for the location and I was happy to get it safely in my creel.

As the day advanced, the snow turned into a steady downpour of rain. By ten a.m. I'd picked up six more trout, running from half a pound to a pound each. By that time the stream had risen several more inches and the water had become very muddy. The fish quit taking the night crawlers then, even though the rain stopped and the sky cleared. I fished from ten till noon without getting a nibble. But I was satisfied. The seven trout in my creel made a pretty catch.

Spring trout fishing with a worm is usually very rewarding if you know how to use such bait. A good job of worm fishing requires some know-how. The two general problems are finding the fish at this season and presenting the bait so that it attracts rather than repels the trout.

As the season changes from winter to spring, trout will either be concentrated in the deepest holes or just starting to scatter to smaller, more shallow holes. If it's a late cold spring the fish will be a bit sluggish. As the air and water warm, the trout begin prowling hungrily, and nothing suits an early spring trout better than a worm that's drifting slowly along the bottom.

To fish a worm in the early season it's rarely necessary actually to cast it. Just use an easy flip of the rod to drop the bait in a suitable current and let the water carry it along to the hungry fish. Either a fly or spinning outfit will do a good job. Because I've used the fly outfit for bait fishing so many years I still like to use it. But the spinning reel and monofilament line is a dandy worm-fishing combination, and an increasingly popular one.

It's easy to understand why worms are such a good natural bait. Heavy rains wash earthworms into the streams and lakes containing fish. The fish eat the worms. This has been going on ever since fish and worms were created.

However, this does not mean that you can simply put a worm on a hook, drop it willy-nilly into the water, and immediately catch a trout from that location. That can happen now and then, but only when conditions are just right for the haphazard offering. In the long run, it's intelligence and a knowledge of the fish being fished for that brings consistent success.

Stop and think about how a worm acts when it gets into the water. In quiet pools it simply wriggles and squirms as it sinks to the bottom. After getting there it keeps on struggling until exhausted, dead, or eaten. In waters where there is a current, the action is the same, except that the worm will drift downstream or be whirled around in an eddy. Once it sinks to the bottom, it keeps rolling along. In any case, a worm that is washed into the water does nothing more than wriggle; all other movement is imparted by the water.

Thus it seems clear the best way to fish with a worm is to let it be as natural as possible—to let it drift as if unattached to a fishing outfit. This seems easy enough, but the fact that the worm isn't free causes complications. Rod and line will give the worm unnatural action unless you compensate by manipulation of your tackle.

One sound strategy, when fishing in moving water, is to flip or cast the worm across and upstream into a current tongue that leads into a hole or pool which regularly serves as a "safety home" for trout. "Safety home" is my name for the kind of hiding place fish seek when threatened from above. This can be a deep hole or pool, a cluster of sunken rocks, a jam of logs, or an overhanging bank. It will be close to a shallow feeding or sunning area, so the trout can reach it quickly in case of danger. It is rare indeed to find game fish in shallow water that isn't reasonably close to such havens.

As soon as the bait sinks under the surface, follow its progress with the fishing rod by pointing the tip of the rod at the worm as it travels with the current. At the same time take in any slack line that occurs. Some slack is needed to allow a natural drift. Too much slack may let the bait get too deep and snag, or you may miss a strike because you neither feel nor see it on the loosely slack line. Ideally, the line should be kept just short of being taut. Then the bait drifts naturally and you can tell when you get a strike, either by feel or by seeing the line twitch at the point where it enters the water.

This same principle applies when the bait drifts downstream below you, but here it will be necessary to release slack line instead of recovering it, in order to keep it just short of getting taut. Without sufficient slack the pull of the current will bring the worm to the surface. Once you feel the worm touching bottom (without having had a strike before that) gently urge it along by manipulating your rod and line. Keep it from settling permanently. If it isn't taken by a fish by the time you have rolled it to the limit, retrieve it and start over again.

Remember that it's better to get snagged frequently, even if it means losing both hook and bait, than to fish too high. You'll lose tackle flirting with the bottom, but you will also catch fish. This also applies to fishing a worm into log jams, under bushes, and drifting it into other places where the hook is likely to get snagged. If you keep the bait away from the hazard for fear of losing tackle you probably won't hook any fish either.

You should also learn the difference between the feel of a strike in deep water and getting snagged. Often they feel very similar. When you think you're snagged, handle the line cautiously. It may be a big fish. If you sense a slight throbbing, just keep the line gently taut for several seconds and then lightly but steadily increase the pressure. If the throbs become more pronounced as you do this, it's quite sure that a fish is working at your worm. Let things remain static for several more seconds and then strike as hard as your terminal tackle allows.

The secret is to allow enough time for a hesitant trout to get the worm and hook in its mouth, without allowing so much time that an eager trout gets wise and spits the whole thing out before you attempt to set the hook. Small fish will usually swallow both bait and hook if allowed too much time. To avoid catching illegal or very small fish that can't be returned to the water in good condition, it's best not to wait too long before striking. If you hook a small fish deeply, I suggest you cut the leader and leave the hook in the fish rather than extracting it. Do this without mishandling the little fellow and he will most likely survive. The extraction of a deep hook will nearly always kill a small brook trout.

Sometimes a trout will pick up the worm and run off with it quickly and viciously. In this case, strike back fast and hard. You may not hook the fish, but you'll have a better chance than if you try to feed out line until the run is completed.

Some trout will take a worm and bring it upstream to swallow it, instead of staying put or easing downstream to an "eating bunk." You feel the throbs, but when you strike you realize too late that you are striking at a belly in the line rather than at the mouth of the trout. To avoid missing such fish, always make sure that the tugs or throbs are absolutely solid before you strike. Do this by slowly tightening the line, with your eyes on the line where it enters the water. If the fish has taken the bait upstream the tugs will not increase in strength and you can see that the line or leader is pointed upstream. You must take in that slack before you can make a successful strike.

Sometimes it's best to fish the water directly below you instead of making a cast out into the stream. This downstream drift requires a different technique, but it isn't difficult. Let the worm drift downstream from you as you feed out line. If the water is fast enough, it soon brings the bait to the top where it splashes or wallows. Then, using the pull of the current as an aid, haul back on the rod. This causes the worm to leave the water and arc toward you. When given just the right impetus, the bait will drop into the water almost at your feet. This automatically provides the needed slack line to allow the worm to drift and sink naturally with the current. I call this move a "back-flip." It's very useful.

The methods I've just described are for fishing a worm without using a sinker. I say a sinker should rarely be used, because the bait acts more natural without it. However, where the worm does not get deep enough without a sinker, you must use one if the fish are hanging close to the bottom. The weight of the sinker will depend on the depth of the water and the speed of the current. A single split-shot may be sufficient, but you may need up to half an ounce or even more. You can determine this only by trial and error until you get to know the water you are fishing.

Worms can be productive in still waters and ponds. Pick out deep holes near the banks in the quiet stream waters and then drop the worm in without any sinker. Let it sink to the bottom and wait. If you don't get any response within fifteen minutes, change your location. In some places the bottom may be so rough that you can't fish the bait without a float to keep it from getting hung. In this case, rig up the line so that your worm is held just above the bottom. Ponds are usually more difficult to fish from shore than are streams. Often the shorelines are so shallow that the fish come in only for surface feeding, and then you scare them when attempting to cast to them.

To reach out for trout, nothing is better than the spinning outfit. With it you can cast an unweighted worm a good distance.

Once the worm touches bottom, let it lie there a few minutes and then start retrieving it ever so slowly, easing it over the bad spots so that you don't get snagged. If one location doesn't produce, try another, but give each place a thorough test before racing to another. Trout are often slow and sluggish in early spring.

Very slow drifting with a boat, dragging the worm along the bottom is often very productive. The slower the craft drifts the better. With reasonable water depth and a very slow drift, you won't need a sinker to keep the worm on bottom behind a boat. But use a weight if you must to get the worm down deep. One thing certain: when the trout are deep you must get to the bottom to catch them. In such fishing you must expect and accept some snagging, but that's a necessary evil.

Often it's best to use a gang-hook rig for trolling a worm. This is two or more hooks tied together one after the other. The worm is strung along these hooks so that it slides through the water easily and often catches trout that would otherwise not get hooked. A spinner placed ahead of a worm gang is frequently very effective. This makes a sort of combination natural-artificial bait that causes trout to strike when they may be refusing to take a worm that is being fished naturally. Of course, the speed of the troll must be fast enough to make the spinner revolve. This same combination is also good for use in streams where trout won't take a worm on a single hook fished with the natural drift. Cast it out and reel it in just fast enough to make the spoon spin. For this work nothing is better than a spinning rig.

There are a number of different worms. Some choose one, some another. When I can get a pint of large night crawlers, I'll forsake all smaller worms and use them. But when I need a worm, I consider any worm I can dig up a prize.

Worms are nearly always a good choice for small trout streams, not only because trout like them but because you can fish them in quarters too cramped for fly or lure casting. Once you locate a likely hole in such a stream approach it very cautiously. Either the tremor of heavy footsteps or the sight of so much as your shadow will alarm wild trout in little brooks. But if you can get a worm to them without first scaring them they'll usually strike with abandon.

A short fly rod is good for such places. A seven- to seven-and-a-half-foot rod is long enough to let you stay back out of sight without being too unwieldy to work through holes in the brush. I like monofilament line testing three to six pounds and a worm bait heavy enough to pull it out through the guides. With the bait held up near the tip of the short rod, you can poke it through holes in the brush and let the weight of the worm pull out the fine line to reach the pool. Odds are that any unalarmed trout in that hole will smack it.

I remember one shallow, brush-screeened hole that well demmonstrates this system. It was in a tiny brook, but there were some good trout in it. I'd seen them run several times after I frightened them with clumsy approaches. So one day I spent twenty minutes easing up to the one opening beside this pool. The light was just right for me to see the bottom, and there with spots and fins showing clearly was a good-size brook trout. In slow motion I worked the rod tip through the brush and slipped the worm down to the water three feet from the fish. The brookie had it in a flash. After a bit of a tussle with fish and foliage, I had the trout—a plump fourteen-incher.

I'd scared the appetite out of the rest of the fish in the hole for the time being, but I could work on another such hole until they calmed down. The system will work again and again, and the clues to success are always the same: locate the fish or promising pools first, make a quiet stalk out of sight, and put the worm where the fish can reach it. It really produces.

Perhaps the toughest waters to fish with worms are those clear, shallow mountain streams. Except for times when they're clouded by storms or spring run-offs, they're the acid test for worm fishermen. I must confess my own worm fishing in such streams is often discouraging. (I prefer to work them with flies or spinners.) But I have wormed them often enough to understand the game, and some of my companions are expert at it.

Again, it's largely a matter of knowing where the fish lie and presenting a natural-acting worm without alarming the trout. Normally, rainbows and brooks will be in holes, either deep, clearly defined pools or sheltered pockets of water in the shallows. Brown trout favor these places too, but they're more apt to range the shallows for flies, nymphs, and minnows. It's hard to intercept them there with worms.

Once you've located the best pools—and erosion or other factors will change them from year to year—study them from a distance to plan the most concealing approach. Some crystal-clear streams have fish-filled holes so unapproachable that expert worm fishermen just pass them up. There's plenty to strive for in worm fishing, but I'd start with the biggest, deepest holes. There's some cover in the water depth itself, and you can drift a worm into them without much trouble.

Big-river worm fishing is about the same proposition except that longer casts are the rule unless the water is high or discolored. An experience on the White River below the Bull Shoals Dam in Arkansas one summer showed me that trout there go for a well-managed worm as fast as those in Eastern brooks or high Western meadows. The water below the dam there became quite cold after the impoundment filled up, and trout stocked there grew mightily. In 1953 anglers really went to town catching them with worms and a variety of other natural and artificial baits and lures.

But, in the sad pattern of touring anglers, we got there a few days too late. The big biting spree was over. Still, our outfitter, G. O. Tilley, wanted us to have a try at the rainbows, even though fishing was generally conceded to be rotten. So we made a three-day float trip for trout on what is left of the White River.

Worms were our bait, but the only kind we could get were tiny red ones from a nearby wormery. Even two of them on a No. 8 hook looked insignificant, but Tilley's method of rigging them to fish the big stream saved the day. He tied a barrel-shaped, swiveled sinker—one that would roll along the bottom easily—on the end of the line and dangled the hook from a leader tied to the line about three feet above the sinker. The leader was about four inches shorter than the line between it and the sinker and was tied on with a small, smooth knot. This way the leader and the sinker line would both run up into the guides side by side after each cast. That let us reel them in just inches from the rod tip, so they were balanced just right for long casts with either bait-casting or spinning tackle. At the end of the cast they would separate, the sinker rolling along the bottom and the bait drifting just above it.

With this system and Tilley's excellent judgment of where the trout lay, we made out very well. That tackle arrangement is one worth trying on any large trout stream. It gives a little trouble with the leader wrapping around the line leading down to the sinker, but that doesn't happen often enough to be exasperating. You can shake it loose in a second. And that combination of long casts and bottom-holding bait and sinker is a prize.

Just be careful to get a smooth knot where your leader attaches to the line with this long-casting hookup. Size of leader used should vary according to the clearness of the water you're fishing and the weight of the fish you're after. In very clear water you can use one of the new synthetic leaders as fine as .007. A size heavier is more sensible for big fish, however, and in dirty water size .009 or heavier works very well.

As with all angling systems, worm fishing is about what you make it. Handled properly it's a splendid sport, worth the attention of anyone who likes to fish.

CHAPTER III

The Real Trout Bugs

A FISHERMAN using artificial flies will find it very difficult to duplicate the action and appearance of many of the natural nymphs and larvae in trout waters. Since trout depend on these underwater bugs and worms for much of their food, the angler who knows how to collect and fish live nymphs and larvae always has an ace in the hole for those days when the fish shun artificial flies and lures.

Let me tell you of just one experience. Although conditions seemed ideal that day, fishing had been deplorable. Only small fish would take my dry flies. Wet flies and bucktails were ignored. So was an assortment of nymphs, including imitation hellgrammites.

After fishing from daybreak until about eleven a.m. without taking a trout larger than eight inches, I decided to try live hellgrammites. It was lunchtime anyway, so I went to a nearby village to see if I could buy live hellgrammites. The only two bait dealers I found were out of this bait, however, so I went to the general store and bought a piece of screen, determined to capture my own hellgrammites.

Back at the stream, I looked for likely places to operate. I picked out a fast, shallow stretch that was loaded with small to medium-size rocks. Starting near shore, I anchored the screen a few feet downstream from me and overturned a dozen rocks. The larvae were there, all right. I picked one from a rock and held it in my hand. Then I went to the screen and found two other dislodged hellgrammites clinging to it. Now I suddenly realized that I had stupidly neglected to prepare a container for the critters. All I had that might work was a deep dry-fly box that was filled with choice dry flies of mayfly design.

Wincing at the damage to them, I stuffed these expensive dry flies in a spare pocket and buttoned it up. Then I punched a number of holes in the top of the new dry-fly box and filled it with lush moss. My hellgrammites were lively as crickets, and I had trouble keeping them in the container.

They worked like a charm on the trout, however. I'd catch a few fish, gather some more bait, catch some more trout. I knew I'd have a big job steaming out and reviving the abused mayflies when I got home, but I had promised some friends a mess of trout, and the hellgrammites were filling the order.

At sunset a big batch of mayflies appeared, and the surface of the stream was soon alive with rising fish. But I already had my legal limit. Besides, I was so tired I could hardly wade out of the stream. I'd had a great day, yet I wondered at the time if it had been worthwhile losing out on that mayfly rise, for I like to take trout on artificial flies when I can. Later I learned that four good fly fishermen who worked the mayfly hatch took only seven fish among them. As so often happens with big rises, the fish glutted themselves on the naturals but weren't much interested in artificials.

It's a simple matter to fish hellgrammites. Grip the live bug below the head, which helps you avoid pincers that can give you a sharp nip, and slip the hook under the tough "collar" just below the bug's head. If your hellgrammites run about 1½ inches long, a size-6 hook should be a good choice. A smaller hook, say a

No. 8 or 10, may work better. Use your judgment. Hooks that are too big will kill a small bug quickly and give it an unnatural action and appearance in the water. Smallness is generally a virtue in hooks, as long as the hook isn't so tiny it's hopelessly smothered in the bait or too delicate to hold a fish played with reasonable pressure. I suggest sneck-shaped hooks for hellgrammites. They have a rather square bend which keeps the bug from sliding along the bend of the hook to the barb.

Unless the water is extremely fast, no sinker is needed. Cast up and across the stream into a likely current and let the bait drift on a slack line. Just be sure the line isn't so slack that you don't know where the bait is. You won't always feel a tug when you get a strike. Watch the line where it enters the water. If it gives a jerk or twitch, you've got a customer. If the hellgrammite is a small one, strike back rather quickly, waiting just a few seconds. With a large bait, give the fish more time to gulp it. Different types of water and the mood of the fish all enter into this matter of timing strikes. Either you yank back instantly or wait much longer if such action seems to hook the fish better.

Often the hellgrammite will grab bottom with its tail, where it has claw-like pincers similar to those on its head. When this happens you may think you have snagged, but you can usually pull the live bug loose with gentle pressure. (A jerk will break the collar and cost you a bait.) Some anglers remove the little claw-like appendages at the tail to lessen the hazard of getting hung. If the unweighted hellgrammite doesn't sink, add a sinker, using a split BB shot to start with and always avoiding overweight.

Another good natural bait is the fish-fly larvae, which is similar in appearance to the hellgrammite. It's usually found in the more sluggish stretches of trout waters and favors mixed bottoms of mud and stones. In shallow water it's possible to gather them by scooping up a netful of muck and searching through it. If you find larvae in it that look and act like hellgrammites, you will most likely have fish-fly larvae. Fish them like hellgrammites. They are a bit more hardy than hellgrammites. Like many anglers, trout seem to confuse fish-fly larvae with hellgrammites. Trout in waters where there are no native fish-flies will usually gobble up fish-fly larvae that an angler has bought or collected in some other stream.

The best way to carry either hellgrammites or fish-fly larvae while fishing is to pack a suitable container with moist moss. Lacking moss, I've done very well using soaked newspaper, paper towels, or toilet tissue. Paper works best when it's crumpled tight, well soaked, and then squeezed free of excess water. Damp moss or paper in a large container will keep a supply of hellgrammites or fish-fly larvae for days. Put the container in a shaded place. A cool cellar is ideal.

Caddis worms are another staple trout food that the angler can collect and use with excellent results in most trout streams. They live in twiglike cases made of sand or bits of wood glued together. For many years imitations of caddis worms have been used with a moderate degree of success. But these artificials often fail at times when the real thing will be taken with enthusiasm.

Caddis-worm cases, held together by secreted adhesive supplied by the worm itself, vary in shape. Most are cylindrical, about the size and shape of a one-inch length pipe cleaner. Often what you may think is a curled leaf, a twig, or a small patch of pebbles will be a caddis worm in its case—just the bait you need to catch the trout you want. The majority of caddis worms live in portable cases. That is, they crawl with them along the bottom, or allow themselves to be carried with the current.

As they move, the head and legs protrude from the case to provide propulsion when crawling and a degree of direction when being carried along by the current. In my opinion this is why naturals are more effective than artificials, no matter how cleverly the imitation may be tied. The natural shows life in a way that the artificial can't quite duplicate. An artificial fly with a fluffy head and feather feelers does simulate life quite well, however—far better than a stamped plastic imitation, even though the feather-fashioned creation may not be as exact an imitation.

Some caddis worms attach themselves to rocks and debris in running water and cover themselves with a netlike substance. I've often seen a trout run along the edge of a log, picking off these luscious morsels, often at times when I'd given up in despair trying to catch them on the regular run of artificials. Unfortunately, I've never been able to find an effective way to use this type of caddis either naturally or artificially.

If you prefer, you can break open caddis-worm cases and put the bare worms on a hook. I'd rather bait with case and all, running my hook through the edge of the case near the center. If you penetrate the body of the worm while doing this, you'll kill it. But with care you can insert the hook so it will anchor the worm in its case and yet not penetrate the body deep enough to cause quick death. Even if the worm is hooked badly it will live through a couple of casts.

I think caddis worms left in their cases are easier to cast and fish than the naked worms. If you hook the case carefully, it will stay on the hook better than a bare worm. Also, because the case adds extra weight, the worm will sink faster, getting down toward bottom where it will do the most good. At times I have found it necessary to use a weight to reach the bottom. A caddis worm bait resting on the bottom of a still pool can be very effective if you have the patience this sort of fishing requires.

Caddis worms in their cases can be picked one at a time by hand, but using a fine-mesh dip net will allow you to collect in minutes a supply that would otherwise take an hour or more. If you plan to do a lot of this sort of bait fishing you should carry suitable equipment in your car to gather it. There's a book, *Collecting Insects for Bait Use*, by Alvah Peterson of the Entomology Division, Ohio State University, Columbus, Ohio, that gives detailed advice and diagrams on this subject.

Crane-fly larvae, which run from an inch to an inch and a half long, are top-notch trout baits in many waters. They should be hooked near the head, which is often hard to find because they can withdraw it. Hooking this larva directly in the body may cause the juices to run out and leave you with merely the shell of a bait.

Crane-fly larvae are found in concentrations of leaves and other soft debris in the quiet backwaters of eddies and pools. Usually you'll find some of these larvae by grabbing up a few big handfuls of leaves mixed with muck and debris and searching through it carefully. If you find one or two larvae, you can be sure there are more there. If you make a dozen tries without getting any results you might as well give up; either the larvae aren't there or your eyes aren't trained to spot them. They blend perfectly with the muck-soaked leaves and debris. This crane-fly larvae isn't used by many anglers, but I have made good catches with it when other things failed.

Mayflies are widely distributed and occur seasonally on most waters. The nymphs of mayflies make excellent bait. The small sizes can be fairly well imitated with artificials, but when it comes to the large ones, those one and a quarter inch or more in length, I've yet to find an artificial that will do even one quarter as well as a natural.

These larger mayfly nymphs are the ones that burrow in mud or clay. Look closely for small holes in any smooth, soft bottom of a clear-water stream. Such holes indicate the presence of these nymphs. Many times I have grubbed for them with my hands. It's an exhausting and often exasperating job, but I have always been rewarded by catching some trout with the mayfly larvae I've captured. A strong dip net, one you can push into the bottom, makes easier work of this kind of nymph hunt. Bring up a netful of muck, place it on a wire screen, and then wash away the soil, watching carefully for the nymphs as you do so. The nymphs should lodge on the screen.

While fishing, I keep my mayfly larvae in a container with about one inch of mud. They will remain alive if the mud is kept wet and cool. Don't cover the mud with water. Soaked and shredded absorbent paper will serve in place of mud if you object to getting your fingers dirty.

The smaller mayfly nymphs that live on or under stones in fast water may be gathered like hellgrammites. However, these small ones are fragile things. It's almost impossible to cast without throwing them off, and they die quickly after being captured unless given exacting care. At the times I've used them I've gathered only a few at first. If they worked, I've caught a few more. This is tough fishing, though, and if you can take trout with an artificial it's far more satisfactory.

There are days, however, when the real thing will take fish while the angler who insists on using artificials goes home with an empty creel. One day I was fishing a good stream without success. It was water that usually produced for me splendidly, and I'd never fished it with anything but artificial dry and wet flies. This time, fishing it at a time of the year I'd never fished it before, I cast and cast, getting more discouraged every minute. I kept seeing the shells of large nymphs on rocks and other resting places in the stream and along the shore. I gathered a few of these and saw that they were the shells of stone-fly nymphs. I soon found some of the live nymphs in the stream and began using them with great success.

Stone-fly nymphs may be found almost anywhere in waters having a high oxygen content. They may be found under stones as small as six inches in diameter or under big rocks. They also live in sunken masses of dead leaves and debris or in rotted wood. When mature they crawl out of the water to the surface of rocks, logs, or anything else available and then hatch into adult stone flies. I like them best for bait when they are nearing maturity. I catch them by hand, overturning rocks, digging into debris, and looking carefully over sunken limbs. Again, a screen placed strategically below the water you are working will catch many nymphs that you'd otherwise lose.

Only the large ones, those from one and a half to two inches long, stay on a hook well. I prefer using a dry-fly hook made of very fine wire for this work. Insert the hook in the hard part of the shell at the head, being careful not to injure the soft body. With care, you can insert the hook between the shell segment and the flesh, much the same as hooking a hellgrammite through the collar. But it takes a very light wire hook, such as a No. 12. A bait hook as large as those you can use with hellgrammites usually kills a stone-fly nymph quickly.

If you have your bait can filled with well-soaked leaves (those taken from a stream bottom are ideal), stone-fly nymphs will live in it without any trouble through a day. Just don't crowd the container. An ordinary bait carrier will take care of a dozen or more. If the fish are taking fast, you can start out with two dozen bugs because you will be using them up. If you want to gather and keep these nymphs for future use, the treatment is the same as keeping them for a day, but it takes a large container and repeated dampening of the leaves or paper in it.

In addition to the stream-dwelling larvae I must mention that various worms and caterpillars found on trees or bushes make excellent bait. For instance, there's the oak worm. These worms often drop into the water while birds are feeding on them. The trout like them as much as the birds do, and if you can gather a mess of them you'll do well using them as bait.

Among the low streamside bushes you'll often find cocoons. I've used these at times with great success, fishing them on the surface. Caterpillars of many varieties can be found here and there. If you put them on hooks and fish them on the surface they will take fish. You can also find grubs in rotted stumps and on the ground. Present these to trout and they'll be taken—unless you mess up the works by scaring the fish by carelessness in approach and fishing.

I've used various water beetles or water bugs with some success when I could find them. This refers to any rather flat, wide, hard-shelled insect you may find in the water, not to the land beetles. Once while fishing a sluggish Adirondack stream for brook trout, and having abominable luck, I noticed a lot of black beetles coming to the top of the water and then going back to the bottom. I gathered a mess of them for bait, getting some painful bites in the process. I used them to take eight trout that ran from half a pound to two pounds.

On the rocks of many trout streams you'll find a rather hard-boiled worm ranging in color from green and olive green to a greenish-gray. As far as I can tell these worms are the larvae of a small water beetle. They often make an excellent bait. I first became acquainted with these greenish worms while fishing a Catskill Mountain stream in New York. When I found that fishing with artificials was poor, I started looking for some natural bait that might work. By chance I picked up a rock in the creek that had a greenish worm on it. This gave me the clue.

I laboriously captured thirty of these worms. A small hook was needed. I had no loose hooks with me except regular size-4 and -6 bait hooks for worms and minnows, so I had to cut the feathers from a size-16 dry fly to get what I needed. The worms took fish, so I was soon cutting up another expensive dry fly to replace the first one, which was lost on a snag. Since then I've made a practice of carrying a few plain hooks in very small sizes, as small as 18 and 22.

On my last day of trout fishing in 1957 our party had abominable luck. Only one trout was taken, by Ezra Cole. It was only a thirteen-incher but was very fat and heavy. We opened it up and found it full of very flat, wide beetles or waterbugs about an inch long and half an inch wide. They were almost black. While this trout was caught in fast water leading into a big pool, the pool itself was very weedy. I imagine this fish had taken its fill of beetles from the weeds and then run up into the fast water, where my friend hooked it on a small spoon.

Considering my experiences of the past, I believe we could have used those beetles to make a nice catch in that pool, if there had been time enough to try it. Trout could be seen moving in this water, but they wouldn't take spinners, wet flies, bucktails, or dry flies. They also refused worms, which were used by two anglers in the party.

I keep thinking, even now, that beetles might have done the job that day. We still have much to learn about fishing with natural aquatic baits. We also have much to gain by learning to use them properly when other baits and artificials won't produce.

CHAPTER IV

How to Fish Wet Flies

I THINK wet flies are being sadly neglected these days. Most beginning anglers are attracted by the easy effectiveness of spinning or the glamor of dry-fly casting. Wet-fly fishing has been left in a middle state of disregard. That is unfortunate, because sunken-fly fishing is often the most successful strategy of all. The lack of recruits is also puzzling, for any average pupil can learn to do a good job with wet flies.

Simply stated, wet-fly fishing is just a matter of offering the fish combinations of feathers, hair, or other such materials that are arranged on the hook so they look like something good to eat—or perhaps resemble something the fish would strike out of anger or curiosity. Unlike dry flies which are designed and handled to ride the surface like floating insects, wet flies are fished under water. You sink wets down where the fish are, which may be a few inches under or right on the bottom. Except that the offering is fake rather than real fish food, the approach of the wet-fly fisherman is about as basic as that of a boy dunking a worm in a trout hole. In fact, a ten-foot cane pole with a few feet of line tied to the end is a dandy outfit for a certain kind of wet-fly fishing. More about that later.

I have many times used wet flies to catch trout in pools where I never had much success with dry flies, spinning lures, or natural baits. One Eastern trout stream I fished often had such a pool—a long run of water with a swampy cow pasture on one bank and heavy brush along the other. There were plenty of trout in this run. I could see them. Catching them was something else. A dry fly presented just right would take a fish now and then. Sometimes worms got a few. Spinning lures tossed into the rather shallow water seemed to frighten the fish, and didn't pay off at all. It was a troublesome, intriguing pool.

Most of my fishing at this meadow run took place at a time when I had become rather neglectful of wet-fly fishing. Spinning tackle was a new thing then, and I was testing it. I always spend a lot of time experimenting with dry flies. Wet flies? I had used them off and on for years, but somehow I hadn't yet given them a thorough test on this problem pool.

I ordinarily use two wet flies at a time, one on the end of the leader, the other on a short dropper leader tied in a couple of feet above the end fly. My two flies for the first meadow-pool test were a No. 12 Blue Gill as an end fly and a No. 14 Ginger Quill on the dropper. I'd previously tested both these patterns on trout streams from coast to coast. They're consistent trout-takers. Though neither one is a particularly close copy of any existing insect, both appeal to trout.

I began fishing at the upper end of the pool, making a number of flip casts upstream into a hole that often produced when I fished with worms. I persisted in this until the flies got wet enough to sink readily, but not a hit did I get.

Then I made a fifteen-foot cast downstream, dropping the flies at the edge of the brushy right bank. As they went under I released a foot or so of slack line to let them get deeper. When the line got almost taut I gave the flies a twitch and then released about six inches more of line. Just as the current took up this extra slack I felt a tug and hooked a trout. Then another trout took the second fly (I don't know whether the end fly or the dropper was taken first) and I had the pleasure of getting a double from water that had been treating me most shabbily.

I tried the same technique in the same patch of water a couple more times, but got no action. Then I lengthened the cast about five feet to reach new water. This time I didn't need to release the second bit of slack line, because I got a hard strike just when I started to do this. Soon after, I landed the best fish I'd ever taken from this stream.

Then I lengthened my cast another five or six feet—and took a fish the instant the tail fly touched the water. I tried this cast a second time. No response came at once, but on releasing some slack and then giving the flies some action I took another good trout.

After that I didn't get another response from lengthening casts until I reached the deep hole at the bend. Here I released extra slack the instant the cast was completed, then waited a few seconds watching the leader where it entered the water. When it had straightened out with nothing happening, I retrieved a foot or two and then released still more slack. As the fly sank deeper I saw the leader give a jerk. I struck back and had another trout. I tried this again and took a second trout out from under the bushes.

That seemed to end all action. I started all over again from the head of the pool, but never got another strike throughout the entire stretch. I was quite happy about the results, however. I'd never taken seven trout—or anything else—from this piece of water, not even when fishing under ideal conditions with worms.

From then on I could always use wet flies to take at least three trout from that long run. I found that casting upstream from the lower end, letting the wet flies drift and sink with the current, got more strikes than downstream drift. But fewer trout were actually hooked on upstream casts, because it was difficult to control the slack caused by the drift, which often made my striking reaction just a bit late.

No matter how many times I tried, I could never get any more fish for many hours after I'd covered it once. For instance, if I'd fished it in the morning, I couldn't do anything there again until late afternoon. The pool needed at least six hours' rest between fishing times. The time of day didn't seem to matter. I had good fishing there at daybreak, at noon, and at varied hours in between until sunset.

Often you will fish fast-water streams with boulder-strewn stretches that form many small pocket holes in which trout lie. These places may often be fished with great success with natural bait, but on the whole I prefer a cast of rather large wet flies for such streams.

This is always short-line fishing. Casting a long line will usually get you into difficulties and will rarely bring you any worthwhile results. Since the water is fast and broken, you can get close to these pocket trout without scaring them. I like to fish the pockets with a cast of three wet flies. For the end fly I like a rather large and meaty looking job, say a No. 6 Montreal. A minnow-like fly such as a Wickham's Fancy or a Silver Doctor is also a good end fly. This end fly should be tied on a heavy wire hook so it will sink readily.

For the middle dropper I like a size 10 or 12, using one of the following patterns according to the stream being fished and my thoughts and whims at the time: Gold-Ribbed Hare's Ear, Lead-wing Coachman, Blue Dun or Blue Quill, Quill Gordon, Cahill, Light Cahill, Ginger Quill, March Brown, and either Coach-man or Royal Coachman.

The flies just mentioned are all acceptable for the top dropper also, but here I usually use one of the Coachman patterns because a gaudy Coachman is more visible to me, thus aiding me in fishing the cast properly. Without some guide of this sort you may lose track of your sunken flies, letting them drift into a snag or missing strikes because you don't see the line twitch.

The feeding range of a trout in a pocket hole is very small. Trout often locate close to a boulder, either in the bulge of water above it, on each side, or in the actual hole below the rock. If you can get into position directly across the stream from such a boulder and not more than twenty feet away, you can direct the cast so that the tail fly drops several feet upstream from the rock. As the cast drops into the water, be prepared for a strike. If there's a willing fish above the rock the reaction will be quick, and it takes a quick response to set the hook.

If the fly gets past this first spot without being taken, let it drift close to the side of the boulder and then wash into the small eddy hole behind it. Often a trout takes as the flies drift along the side or swing into the eddy hole. Strike back instantly at any twitch of the leader or a visible fly. There are lots of strikes that you won't feel on a somewhat slack drifting line.

The side of the stream you fish from may be very important. That is, casts made from one side may produce much better than casts from the other shore. I remember vividly a stretch in a turbulent Wyoming stream where choosing the right approach was a must. There were dozens of good-looking boulder pocket holes to cast to from the smooth and level side of the stream, but I couldn't get any fish from them. I took a fish now and then, but never made a good showing.

It was a tough job to reach the other side of this deep river. I had to walk about a half mile upstream to reach a place that could be waded, and the other side was rough and steep all the way down to the fishing territory and all through it. But the effort paid off. Each pocket yielded from one to three scrappy rainbows, none under two pounds and some of them over three pounds. Of course, I didn't land them all, because I couldn't follow them. I fell in several times because of the footing, and casting was tough because of the background. But by the end of the day I had hooked, landed, and released fourteen nice fish and kept four—eighteen trout landed and none under one and a quarter pounds.

All these fish were taken on a cast that had a size-10 Royal Coachman as the tail fly and a size-12 Gray Hackle with a yellow body for the dropper. The Royal took about sixty percent of the trout caught, but this might have been reversed if the end fly had been a Gray Hackle and the dropper a Royal Coachman.

Lest you get the idea that this was the complete answer to

catching the fish in this water, let me add that on other trips to this stream wet flies didn't do too well; dry flies did, and from the easy-fishing side of the stream. But having a knowledge of wet-fly fishing was responsible for that one wonderful day—and successful fishing is a matter of solving your problems a day at a time. Conditions can change quickly.

It is often best to give wet flies action rather than fish them with a natural drift. For instance, here's an experience I had on another swift Western stream. I'd been fishing it with dry flies without success and then switched to wet flies, using the natural drift method. I tried casts of wet flies from all angles, up and across stream, directly across stream, and down and across stream. The down-and-across drift was the only one that produced, and this worked only after the flies had started dragging across to my side of the stream at the end of the drift.

I took a couple of trout this way. Then I thought, "Why not make the same casts as before but deliberately bring the flies back fast and with jerks?" So I cast up and across, letting the flies get under a bit, and then hauled them back fast and jerkily. This way I took trout consistently from all angles.

Another time, while having no luck at all in fast water with anything, including wet flies, I made a wet-fly cast. Then, just as the flies settled on the water, I began to sneeze. Whatever had irritated my nose caused me to sneeze about five times in rapid order. Meanwhile the flies did just what they wanted to. On recovering from the sneezing fit, I saw that the flies were deep in the current near the opposite shore. I started stripping them in fast. At the third strip I hooked a brown trout that weighed just over two pounds.

I knew that the reason for the success was the way the flies had acted in the water while I was sneezing. So I tried to duplicate that action. The flies needed time to sink deeper than I had been working them before the sneezing fit. Then they needed to be retrieved rapidly with long jerks. That action caught fish the rest of the day.

Through the years I've had many successes that came from

such accidental happenings, including stumbling, making a bad cast, getting hung and pulling loose, coughing, and falling. In ponds and other still waters, giving some movement to wet flies is good practice and in most cases necessary. Sometimes it's best to start the retrieve with fast jerks the moment the cast has been completed. When this near-surface fishing doesn't produce, the flies should be allowed to sink, often right to the bottom, before starting the retrieve. You are likely to get a strike while the flies are sinking, too, so be constantly alert for it. It will usually be indicated by a movement of the line or leader at the place it enters the water.

At the beginning of this piece I mentioned cane poles and promised to tell of an experience I had wet-fly fishing with them. It happened years ago at an Eastern brook of ordinary size. In this stream there are several long and shallow meadow stretches, all difficult to fish except when the water is high and discolored. One run in particular intrigued me, because it contained a lot of trout, including a fair number weighing nearly two pounds.

The difficulty in fishing this place with a regular fly rod was that I couldn't get closer to the fish than thirteen feet without spooking them, and I had to crawl to get that close. This left a strip of boggy meadow between me and the stream. At that distance and position the water couldn't be seen, as I'd cast far enough to be sure the fly got into the water and then wait for action. I'd have several feet of line draped over the bank, and the only way to detect a strike was by noticing a twitch of the line or by hearing a faint splash in the stream.

I took a few trout fishing this way, but in order to land a good one I had to get to my feet in sight of the other fish, which ruined all chances of taking another fish for considerable time after. I often had my line or leader snagged on the edge of the bank or on rank grass. This often happened when I missed a strike or tried to retrieve a cast that had been ignored. My eight-foot rod was just too short.

One day, while complaining to myself about snagging a fly at this meadow pool, I muttered, "Here's where a long cane pole would be helpful. Then I could stay back far enough not to scare the fish and still reach the water without having any line or leader lying on the meadow."

Well, I found an old gentleman living near this stream who had such a pole, a fifteen-footer. It was long enough to drop a fly directly into the water with room to spare and with no casting necessary. I tied a short piece of line to this pole and to that tied a six-foot leader tapered to 1X. The total length of line and leader was about ten feet. For a fly I used a No.-10 Alder, a wet-fly pattern I've often found good.

I experimented with this outfit enough to get the feel and then crawled into fishing position. I eased the tip of the long pole out over the water and lowered the fly slowly until the fly and some leader seemed to be in the water. Then I gave the rod a slight twitch to flip the fly downstream.

After that I waited for perhaps fifteen seconds and then started to jerk the fly. Before the first jerk was completed I connected with a trout about eleven inches long. I played the fish a moment and then flipped it out on the bank without moving from my crouch.

I got five more trout this way, none less than eleven inches long. Then I hooked one that was too heavy to flip out. I had to get to my feet and follow this trout to have any chance of landing him, and I was two bends downstream before I finally got him up on a small beach. This bank-running tussle spooked all the remaining fish. In the weeks that followed I often borrowed that long cane pole and made good catches with it. There was no better rig for that stretch of stream.

The gentleman who loaned me the pole died the next year and his possessions, including the cane pole, were scattered. I guess it was false pride that kept me from buying and hauling on my car a cane pole of my own. I did a bit of experimenting with long poles that were jointed, but I never got the right combination. They were easy to handle in a car, and they looked a good deal more professional than a one-piece cane, but those with the necessary strong joints were too heavy and had poor action.

If I've talked you into trying the sport of wet-fly fishing, that long rod is one of the things you might work on some time. The routine tackle should be mastered first, of course, but there are a lot of wary, angler-shy trout across the country that could be fooled by a careful approach with a fifteen-foot rod. It would add to our sport if some craftsman could use the strong, light materials now available to work up a wet-fly rod of cane-pole length.

CHAPTER V

How to Use Nymphs

FISHING with imitation nymphs and larvae definitely produces. The catch comes in getting an artificial that's acceptable to the fish and in knowing how to present it so they'll take it. In my experience, knowing how to fish a lure is more important than how closely it resembles some particular form of animal life.

The subject of imitations is too involved to be covered adequately here. Besides, all the average fly fisherman wants is a lure that will catch fish. However, you need to know something about the underwater life of streams and lakes, and if you are inclined to delve more deeply into the subject, here are some books I recommend: *How to Fish From Top to Bottom*, by Sid Gordon; *Matching the Hatch*, by E. G. Schwiebert, Jr.; *Fishing Flies and Fly Tying*, by Bill Blades; *Streamside Guide*, by Art Flick; and *Fishing with Natural Insects*, by Alvah Peterson.

It will pay you to take the time and trouble to gather some of the nymphs and larvae in the water and examine them. Release them while alive and see how they act in different types of water.

Observe the stream bottom carefully and patiently—you may discover things that will increase your angling knowledge. The more you know about the bottom and the insect life of any water the better your chances of fishing success. To fish with underwater lures you must know something of what the fish in any particular waters feed on, what to use in order to interest them, and, above all, how deep to fish the lure.

On the whole, nymphs and larvae may be successfully fished with the natural-drift method in any water where the current is strong enough to carry them along. Natural drift is letting the lure be carried along as it sinks, like a natural, without being pulled contrariwise by your line.

Probably the best cast for this is across and upstream a little. As the lure drifts downstream, take in enough line to keep pace with the current, but don't bring the line taut unless it is necessary to give some action to the lure. Unfortunately this is not as simple as it reads, for you must make allowance for your line and leader. But often a change in position and where you drop the lure will make a good drift out of a poor one.

You have to watch the drift of your lure to know when you have a strike. If the lure is out of sight below the surface, you must watch the place where your line or leader enters the water. Should it suddenly twitch, pause, or otherwise change its natural course, then strike at once because you may have a fish on. Unless you respond quickly, chances are your artificial will be dropped before you can set the hook.

Watching the line as you follow the course of your lure, you may think you see something moving in the water. If you do, strike! It may be just your imagination, but on the other hand it may be a fish. This underwater artificial-fly fishing is tricky and elusive. Unless you take it seriously and try to cultivate the partly intuitive reactions necessary, it isn't likely that you'll be too successful. Sometimes it has taken me five years to learn how to take fish consistently from one particular stretch of water with sunken lures. You must know the water, the bottom, and your lure to get results.

If a fish takes your artificial and you don't know it, or you react too slowly to set the hook, that fish probably won't take that particular lure again until it's been forgotten. That may be within half an hour, or it may be several hours. But as other fish in the same stretch will likely be interested in your lure, keep using it as long as you feel or see strikes or get an occasional fish.

Two men fishing the same water with equal skill, and using the same nymphs, will get different results. One takes a good number of fish, the other takes almost none. Why? The more successful angler recognizes strikes, where the other angler doesn't. If you find yourself on the losing side, make up your mind to learn how the other fellow does it.

At times the fish may be feeding on nymphs that are moving or darting quickly from place to place. So, if you get no response fishing with a natural drift, combine it with some rod-tip action. Let the lure work deep at the start, then give a twitch of the rod every twenty seconds or so. A split BB shot, or its equivalent in lead wire wrapping placed a foot or two above the fly, may help. This weight may prevent you from twitching the nymph upward above the range of the feeding fish.

A large lure here, say one tied on a No.-4 or No.-6 heavy wire hook, may do the trick better than the shot. But for a very small lure, the added weight will be necessary. Actually, there isn't any cut-and-dried formula for success. Of course there's a limit to working any one spot without having the fish get wise. With too much noise and carelessness in casting, wading, handling of a boat the fish may suddenly quit feeding for anywhere from half an hour to several hours.

In very swift water you can't give the nymphs much extra action when fishing up and across stream. It's hard enough to keep the line taut, so your artificial will drift about the same as a natural. However, whether the fish are feeding deep or near the surface, you must get to them. I start near the surface and then go down, either by using lures tied on heavier wire hooks or by using shot, lead wire, or a sinker. When needing a weight a flyrod can't handle, spin tackle will do a good job.

For up-and-across-stream nymph fishing, the use of a dry fly as a dropper, or a bit of cork painted a color you can readily see, will signal when a fish has taken the sunken lure. If you're using a dry fly, be sure it's a good floater and of a size and color you can follow.

Place either the dry fly or the cork two or three feet above the nymph, so you can watch for any sign that a fish is taking. If it stops or twitches, respond with a strike on the instant. Watching it in broken water is far easier than trying to keep your eye on the spot where a line or leader enters the water. Also, you may take a fish on the dry fly, and this may indicate that a surface rise has started, in which case you should change to dry flies.

Using two nymphs or larvae or a combination of each may bring better results than fishing with only one. For instance, you can tie on an imitation crane-fly larva for the bottom lure, and a mayfly nymph for the dropper. Use a 6½- to 7½-foot leader, and have the lures about twenty-four inches apart. Place the shot or other sinker, if needed, about six inches above the dropper. The casting problem here is harder than when casting only a single lure, and the addition of a shot or sinker will make it still more so, unless you use a spinning outfit.

Across and downstream fishing with nymphs is good, too. To do this effectively, use a modified roll cast to keep the lure from slashing across the current. The roll cast also mends or corrects the course of the drift. If you cast out and let the lure go along on a taut line, it will stay near the top until it comes over to the quieter water on your side. Now sometimes this produces—especially if you realize what has happened. Give a bit of slack line to let the lure sink and then retrieve slowly. But to reach fish that may be lurking in the main current to grab food drifting down, you must handle rod and line so the lure drifts this main water in a natural manner.

The cast must be made loosely to start. Overcast, in actual line thrown out, but fail to complete the cast, so that while the nymph drops about where it should, the line lies slack and in curves instead of straight. This gives you a certain footage of drift without drag. As soon as the slack has been taken up, then you must mend by making a roll cast.

To do so, retrieve a few feet slowly and raise the rod tip until it's almost vertical. Then switch it downward rather fast, but direct the tip upstream. If you have calculated correctly, the nymph will roll out across the stream, the few feet of line you've retrieved will shoot out at the completion of the cast, and the lure—dropping above where you took it out of the main current —will be ready for several feet more of natural drift.

Continue this procedure until the main current stem has been covered, wading a few feet downstream after you've made one or two roll casts and mends. Of course if you take a fish, keep on casting and mending until you get no more response.

It may be that the only immediate fishable area is so small that it can be covered with one cast, or with one cast and one mend. If so, after you've worked it thoroughly without getting trout, or have taken some and they've quit biting, you should seek other pastures. Alternatively, you can wait an hour or two and then start fishing the same spot again.

Sometimes wading fishermen will so stir up the insect life on the bottom that limited periods of feeding will start a few minutes after they've passed by. I've had this happen many times—and after half an hour without further traffic, upon renewing my offerings I've had fair to good response.

Frequently, after fishing a deep pool or deep run without success, I've gone into the shallow rapids upstream and purposely waded roughly, to dislodge all the underwater life possible from the muck, rocks, and sand. Then, back at the pool or run below, I've taken fish on the same lures that had been refused only minutes before.

Proficiency in nymph fishing usually requires a lot of dry-fly techniques. Up to a point there is little difference in the handling of the two types of lures. Once they hit the water, though, the similarity ends. It's easy enough to see what—if anything—happens to the floating fly. Not so with the nymph. It disappears from sight, and thereafter you must depend on the signs and portents discussed earlier to tell you what is going on beneath the surface.

Before using a nymph you must prepare it so that it will submerge immediately and start for the bottom. To accomplish this, you can apply a wetting compound—there are a number of excellent commercial preparations on the market—or you can smear the nymph and leader copiously with mud. As I've said, I always have nymphs and leaders in my soak box, in case I want to make a quick change from a fly.

If the nymph reaches bottom without a strike, let it rest a while and then start it *gently* toward the surface. (This is in fishing quieter waters.) An abrupt jerk may snag the hook or scare the fish that are lurking in the vicinity. But if you lift the nymph unhurriedly, it may simulate the rise of a hatching larva. If that doesn't produce, you may try variations on your next cast. Bring the nymph slowly away from the bottom, give it a twitch, and resume the slow rise. Or lift it for a while, then let it drop back. And watch that line! When you are using a long line, start your lift cautiously, as usual, then bring it to the surface in a series of short, mild jerks. The hand-twist retrieve is very effective here.

Unless you're fishing very deep water, use unweighted nymphs. I could never see any virtue in a weighted nymph in quiet or slow-moving water. It drops to the bottom much too quickly— more like a rock than anything alive. In anything but fast and rather deep water, you'll find ample sinking power in well-soaked lures and leaders. Nymphs call for a heavier hook than dry flies— I like the "regular" weight for slow-moving glides and quiet pools, and the "extra stout" for fishing in fast or deep water.

When fishing glides you'll want to get the lure down a few feet below the surface but still keep it away from snagging bottom. That is not hard to achieve: measure off the depth you want to reach on your leader, then grease the rest of it so it will stay on the surface. However, I don't advise the use of greased leaders except on broken or discolored water. Do not use one in strong sunlight, either; like anything floating on the surface it will throw an alarming shadow. Line that goes below the surface, on the other hand, throws practically no shadow. That's something to remember when you're fishing water that has a smooth, unbroken surface.

For nymph fishing in most waters, I prefer my line to float well, as it would in dry-fly angling. I get the depth I want by varying the length of the leader. It may be as short as seven and a half feet for some faster waters, or fifteen feet and longer on exceptionally clear pools, where the fish may be wary. Sometimes when fishing ponds, it's a good idea to treat the extreme end of the line so that it will sink and put the leader completely under water.

Nymphs may come in very handy in spots where a dry fly simply won't produce. I've had that experience many times, but I'll cite just one instance. I was fishing a Wyoming stream, a very difficult one. Picture the scene: I was on a bank, amidst tall grass, with the swift current running just below my feet. The opposite side of the stream consisted of a deep hole flanked on two sides by log jams and backed by tangled, impenetrable forest. Downstream from me, and on my side, the grass dwindled away to a barren spot. And it was just off this spot that I'd seen a big trout rising for several days. I had cast fly after fly to him from the grassy bank. But all I did was put him down.

Finally, I decided to use a nymph. I cast across and downstream into the pool, and let the current swing my sinking nymph across the stream in front of the trout's hideout. I planned the cast carefully, so that it would come within a foot of where I'd seen him rise.

I followed the line with my eyes as it cut across the stream. There was a sudden twitch. I struck—and was fast to plenty of action. The trout seemed chagrined at having fallen for my trick, and he showed it by fighting savagely. I had all I could do to keep him out of the log jam, and it was a touch-and-go affair, since my leader was a little too delicate for that sort of work. Once, twice, three times he made a surging dash for the logs and I just managed to stop him. After the third attempt, though, he gave up and came in without much fuss. I reached down, with considerable satisfaction, and lifted him from the water. Then I removed the hook and, with even greater satisfaction, put him back.

Well, that was only one of the many times that nymphs proved their utility. That's why I believe they have a place in every fly fisherman's kit. If you don't have one when you need it, you can always make shift by trimming down a wet fly of the right size. Better yet, put some nymphs in your soak box and try them next time out.

CHAPTER VI

How to Fish with Streamers

FLIES of the streamer type are somewhat neglected in many regions where they'd pay off if given a chance. On the West Coast, for example, you rarely see an angler using this type of fly, despite the large following that the smaller, conventional wet flies have there.

Because of the current spinning tackle trend, metal and plastic lures are getting a bigger play than feathers. There's no question about the effectiveness of the metal and plastic devices, but I believe that anglers who fish only with hardware or natural baits miss the chance of catching more fish, on occasion, and also the extra enjoyment of using a fly and fly rod.

Of course, it is essential to select the right streamer for the water, and to know how to handle it efficiently. That is perhaps why these big wet flies are less popular than spoons and plastic lures, which have a built-in action that does most of the work for the angler. With streamers, it's your choice of size, design, and color, and your manipulation of the fly in the water that makes it either effective or useless.

Learning how to fish streamers is probably the toughest part of your education. So often the most trifling error in your handling of the fly will make your effort fruitless. Unless you have a natural knack, it takes a lot of study and application to become a consistently good streamer fisherman. If another angler and you are fishing the same water with the same streamer fly and he is getting fish and you aren't, don't blame it all on luck. The fellow catching them knows how to work the fly and at what depth and you don't. And believe me I've often been on the "don't" side.

My first experience with a streamer fly was as far back as 1920. My fishing buddy and I had gathered a nice mess of night crawlers and were well prepared, so we thought, for plenty of easy trout. The early-season weather had been bad, but we knew what worms could do in the stream we were headed for.

We got up three hours before daylight, and it was still pitch dark when we reached the stream. As we parked, snowflakes were assailing the lights of the Model-T. We sat and shivered until it was light enough to assemble our rods. It was sleeting quite hard by this time. Then we looked in the back seat of the car for the worms so we could fill our personal wading cans. But they were not there. We searched the car frantically, but it wasn't any use—we had left the worms at home.

There was nothing to do but get out our fly boxes and tie on some wet flies. We started fishing and four hours later had five trout between us, though they hadn't been caught on wet flies alone. We'd managed to dig three worms from a sheltered bank and these had been partly responsible for our small measure of success. Now, lacking a fork or spade to dig more worms, we were about ready to quit.

But the sleet had stopped and the sun was doing its best to disperse the clouds. In one of my fly boxes I found a collection of feather streamers called at the time Rooster's Regrets. I also had some deer-hair streamer flies, bulky and crudely tied things I'd carried for some time but never used.

We each selected a bucktail, a brown-and-white creation with a silver body and a dash of bright red. We went to the head of a good pool and took turns fishing it. We'd cast downstream and work the fly back with jerks, trying this both at the surface and as deep as we could fish when working against the current. But nothing happened.

My pal thought it was useless and quit to go looking for more worms. I was about to do the same thing when I got the urge to go to the foot of the pool and fish the fly from that position. But the water was too high and the current too swift for me to get depth.

This was clearly a time to use a sinker with a fly. All I had were some split buckshot, so I put one on close to the fly, cast, and let it sink. This time the fly got to the bottom. I could feel it touch the rocks. I kept it just moving and scraping the bottom, and after it had traveled ten feet I felt a solid pull and had the great satisfaction of landing a big brookie. The rest of the day was a success. Before sunset we both caught our limit of fish with the same fly and the same strategy.

The best material for a streamer fly to be fished slowly on bottom is something soft, something that looks juicy and meaty when wet, and which reacts to the slightest motion of the water. A heavy hook will often get you down without a sinker, but if it doesn't you can add the necessary weight to the leader near the fly. Sometimes a light wire hook alone will do the trick, and heavy wire would spoil your chances. But the soft material is a must.

One fine pattern is the Bloody Annie. Another killer is the Crayfish Fly. I've found it particularly useful on black bass, as illustrated by the following experience. The location was the Delaware River bordering New York and Pennsylvania. Usually, live hellgrammites are a good bait there, as are small stonecats and lamprey eels. But none of the bait dealers had any.

I had been using a black-and-orange feather streamer named Conger's Lassie and getting good results, but this time it didn't get a tumble. I had one freak in my box that I'd tied to resemble a crayfish. I fished it upstream, letting it sink before starting the retrieve. When I thought it was deep enough I started giving it short, sharp jerks. Suddenly a vicious strike almost tore the rod from my hands and I was fast to a mite of fury. As fast-water small-mouths go, it was a nice fish—3¼ pounds.

I've used that same fly many times since, where water currents were suitable, and have had some fine fishing with it. Here's a description of this outlandish-looking fly: Body, soft yellowish-orange material, tied thick and heavy. Tail, a pair of soft, red-brown feathers from a ringneck pheasant or a chicken on the red or ginger side. They should be tied down so that they curve outward instead of sticking out straight. Wings, fiber of the same type of feathers used for the tail. Tie in flat—they actually serve as both wings and hackle. Of course the original idea for streamers was to have a fly that would simulate a natural minnow. The idea is good because all game fish eat other fish.

Some of the early streamer-fly advocates made very intriguing and provocative patterns, and improvements on these gave rise to many new designs. The improved originals are still doing business, the Optic Bucktail, for instance. You often see eyes on flies today and that actually was the idea of W. H. Hobbs of Connecticut. Around 1928 he gave me several dozen to experiment with. They were excellent fish-getters and had a lot to do with my becoming interested in other streamer patterns. One large Eastern fly-maker also got interested and made some special polar-bear-hair streamers.

About this time Jesse Wood, a close friend of mine and an excellent fisherman, got an idea for a fly that soon became known as the Jesse Wood streamer. Its minnow-like appearance was effected by the use of bali-duck feathers (also known as yanosh feathers). This fly was and still is a killer in many waters, but it's not easy to get the feathers to make it.

I've had great fun fishing with various feather and bucktail streamers. For instance, there was a time in Michigan when dry flies and spinners hadn't done any good, so I dug out a badger-hair streamer. It was a simple fly, tied by a Michigan friend. The streamer feathers were whitish badger, with hackle of the same color. It didn't have a tail. A dash of red at the head, on the underside, imitated gills. The body was silver tinsel.

When wet, this fly was extremely minnow-like in appearance. On this day it surely did make the trout hit, and I had a wonderful time. Of course it has been copied and changed, and variations for special conditions may be necessary. But I believe that the badger-hair, either in the whitish or creamish color, will serve a need here and there along your fishing trail. Fish it to simulate a minnow in action, giving it jerks, letting it pause a second or two and giving it slack, then starting the retrieve action again.

The original marabou feather streamer is a reliable old-timer. It was named Ballou's Special, and made especially for Maine waters. Mr. Ballou sent me several samples, and from the start, with both these and with the many variations that have been produced since, I've had good luck. One of my satisfactory experiences with this pattern follows:

It happened in Wyoming, on a most entrancing trout stream. The fellows fishing with me were dry-fly purists, and when the trout refused to rise to the floaters they got disgusted with me for first trying standard wet flies and then going still lower, in their estimation, with streamers.

Getting the right streamer wasn't easy. I tried a squirreltail, a bucktail, and regular feather streamers without getting any response from these fussy fish. I decided to try a marabou, tied on a No. 4 long-shank hook, and made a tentative cast to the far side of the stream. I started the retrieve almost as soon as the fly hit the water, then brought it back with a fast and jerky action. Before I'd made six jerks I was fast to a good trout. The following cast netted a two-and-a-half-pounder. For about an hour I had some rare sport.

The particular marabou I used was an improved copy of the original Ballou's Special. Here's the description: two matched and generously fluffy marabou feathers tied as close as possible to the shank of the hook; this is topped by six or seven strands of heavy peacock herl tied in so that it hugs the top of the marabou. When wet this gives the effect of the dark backs and light bellies of some forage fish. The body is of heavier silver tinsel. For gill imitation a bunch of bearded crimson hackle is tied in at the head and on the underside of the hook. It has jungle-cock eyes.

For average streamer fishing I've done well with Nos. 8, 10, and 12 squirreltail flies. Sometimes these work best when tied in combination with badger, barred rock, and furnace or cochy-bondhu streamer feathers. Generally the patterns can be made as follows: badger streamer feathers with white bucktail, barred-rock streamer feather with gray squirrel; furnace or cochy-bondhu streamer feather with red or fox squirrel.

An experience of mine in Quebec shows the usefulness of streamer patterns. It was bitterly cold and windy. We'd tried all the regular brook-trout flies without getting any response. Finally my guide placed me close to a fast spillway and from my box selected a colorful but nameless three-inch-long bucktail streamer. I tied it on and started working.

I cast and then started the retrieve with snappy jerks. At the third jerk I was fast to a fish. From this same spot, using the same fly, I took about fifteen nice fish. I believe the fly's size and weight had something to do with its success, because the other anglers didn't do any good with smaller ones. It was mostly red, white, and yellow, and was tied on a No. 4 long-shank hook. The body was silver tinsel.

Any fish that will take a minnow is a sucker for the right streamer fished in the right way. I've used them successfully on trout, salmon, panfish, pickerel, pike, and muskies, as well as lake trout and white bass. Here are some patterns which should be reasonably easy to find in tackle shops: Badger Streamer, Black Ghost, Dark Tiger, Gray Ghost, Gray Squirrel Silver, Gray Squirrel Gold, Royal Coachman Streamer, Mickey Finn, White and Black Bucktail, White and Brown Bucktail, White Marabou, Yellow Marabou. The most popular sizes range from 12 through 6, though I often find that the larger ones are the killers.

It's uncertain who made the first streamers. Theodore Gordon probably had a big finger in the pie, although he didn't call his flies streamers. Emerson Hough is often credited with having introduced them to anglers in the United States. Anyway, it's sure that both men would look with pride at the beautiful array of streamer patterns available today. Streamer, loosely, means any long-shanked or regular hook tied with comparatively long feathers or lengths of animal hair.

There's some puzzling evidence when we dig into the reasons why streamers are good medicine for trout. In general, you'll be right in studying the coloration of the minnows in the streams you fish and trying to copy them with your streamer patterns. You should make an attempt, too, for a minnow-like movement of your fly in the water. Yet trout will often smash a streamer that neither looks nor acts like any fish in this country. I believe that's because trout, like bass, are simply pugnacious at times. They fight the streamer.

I've never seen a really good imitation of some of the rather dull-colored minnows found in so many streams, but there are many streamers that come close enough to suit the trout you're after. Try combinations of brown and white; blue-gray and dark green; dark green and cream-white—or blue-gray with a purple cast. The latter is especially good for waters with chubs or red-nosed minnows. When wet, streamer materials of different colors tend to blend together. So remember, as you plan them, it's a lot like mixing paint.

And don't forget that trout take some really gaudy patterns. I can't believe, though, that such bizarre imitations of minnows as the Mickey Finn, Spencer Bay, Anson Special, and Marabou fool the fish. Trout hit such flies as if to "kill that thing." I've often teased fish into such strikes when they were not feeding at all; I've seen a trout strike a streamer, miss it, then swirl around to hit it again.

So when should you use streamers? Well, they'll work 'most anytime, if in the right size and pattern and properly fished. But they have their strong suits. One of them is high water, a stream condition where you'd ordinarily put your faith in natural bait. Big streamers in gaudy colors are your ticket to trout in such streams—sizes 2 and 4 won't be too big—and the more glitter and sheen they have the better.

A commotion in the water or other evidence of trout taking minnows is a signal to try streamers. Decrease the hook size as the water becomes clearer, perhaps to as small as a 10 or 12 in a very slow, clear stream. Start with your somber minnow imitations, but keep your gaudy patterns handy. The trout may get sore about missing the elusive minnows and welcome a chance to poke at anything.

Streamers are also good to back up wet and dry flies and nymphs on fast runs. Flip a streamer into such places after the other methods have failed. This has paid off for me on many occasions, even after the trout had refused a spinner. Always keep in mind that trout, like all other fish, are curious. There's something about a streamer that excites them, so play on that trait, as well as on their appetite for real food. If one pattern fails, try another. I've done that as many as four or five times before I got a fish to strike, perhaps just because I pestered it until it got mad.

There's one exception to the rule of changing the streamer pattern—when a fish strikes late, just as you are lifting the fly from the water for another cast. Then the fish will patrol that area for a moment, alert for either food or trouble. The faster you can get your streamer back to such a spot, the better.

As for handling streamers, the many anglers I've watched make me think the most common fault is fishing them too slowly, as you would a wet fly or nymph. The rod-jerk system is generally more productive. I usually cast across or slightly upstream and work the streamer through the current with long, positive jerks. The idea, of course, is to copy the action of a frightened minnow, and quick movements have the added advantage of preventing the fish from seeing your fake minnow clearly.

Try both up- and downstream quartering casts before you leave a hole, using a fast retrieve for the upstream cast and a slow one for the downstream, since it gains action as it moves against the current. As a general rule, start your retrieve immediately after each cast (only deep, discolored water or especially whimsical trout should cause you to vary that system), then let your streamer sink much deeper than usual.

I use three more or less standard systems for retrieving streamers. The first is the rod-jerk method already mentioned, accomplished entirely by the rod and casting arm without stripping or holding line in the retrieve hand. It's for short casts only. You make this retrieve by lifting your rod from about horizontal with a series of sharp jerks that gradually lift the tip to an almost vertical position at the end of the retrieve. As I said, it's a system to use at close quarters.

The second method, the combination hand and rod retrieve, allows longer casts, which you can retrieve at once, as in the rod-jerk system, or let sink to the desired depth first. The system is a combination of jerking in line with the retrieve hand and lifting the rod tip. Vary or combine the two to suit the conditions.

Deep waters are best for the third system. Cast the fly and let it sink—to the bottom if necessary (and it often is), then pass the line loosely through the grip of the fingers holding your rod. With your other hand jerk the line through the guides and the fingers holding the rod. Use long, vigorous jerks, tightening the grip of the hand that holds your rod as you finish stripping in each length of line. That prevents your being caught with a slack line if you get a strike during the pause between jerks.

Those are the three systems I find satisfactory for casting and retrieving streamers with a fly rod. Some may say there should be a fourth—for handling weighted streamers with a sinker. Well, you can cast these on a fly rod, but I don't like the action of weighted-body streamers in the water, and casting a sinker with a fly is a miserable job with a fly rod. That's when a spinning reel made to fit a fly rod comes in handy. Filled with proper spinning line, it's a good thing to have in your pocket for such use. Just change from fly fishing to spinning with a weighted fly. Spinning tackle does a good job with streamers.

Some anglers may need to be warned that these systems for casting and maneuvering streamers can be darned hard work, but they do get results, and we all go fishing to catch fish—whether we keep them or not. Add streamers to your bag of tricks.

CHAPTER VII

Dry-Fly Strategy

Amid all the discussion of *how* to fish dry flies, I think many anglers lose sight of the importance of knowing *where* to fish them. I'm talking about the ability to scan a trout stream and spot all the places where a dry fly can be used to good advantage.

Shallow, rock-studded rapids found at intervals along a typical trout stream are perhaps the most neglected type of dry-fly water. Anglers using wet flies commonly work such stretches, and so do the bait and hardware-lure fishermen. Dry-fly men? They're inclined to hurry past these broken runs to get to water they consider more suitable for their type of fishing. In doing so they often pass up some good fish that would take the floating fly eagerly.

At a glance, the shallow rapids are all rocks and white water, but the angler who reads them with a keen and understanding eye can usually locate patches where the water is comparatively deep and calm. These pockets—places where the foaming rush of the main current is slowed by a sunken rock or a deep hole in the stream bed—will appear smoother and darker than the rest of the flow.

Any natural fish foods adrift in the stream are likely to wash into such pockets, so they become natural feeding stations for trout. And any stretch of shallow rapids that has a fair number of small, dark eddies is worth working with dry flies.

The dry-fly fisherman is usually better off if he starts at the lower end of these broken runs and wades and casts upstream. The angler is fairly well concealed from the trout by foaming water and rocks studding the stream bed. The main hazard, so far as alarming the fish goes, is in overlooking a small hole that holds a lone fish. The angler who wades through such a one-fish pool while getting into position to cast takes a double loss: he misses his chance to catch the lone fish, and he sends the frightened trout zipping up to another hole with a commotion that will spook other fish along the way.

Another hazard is approaching the selected fishing pockets with the sun slanting too much against your back so that it throws your shadow in front of you. Even shadows showing at your sides can cause trouble, scaring fish to your right or left, which in turn frighten fish above you. Plan an approach that will keep your shadow off the water as much as possible. This applies to trout fishing in any type of water.

Otherwise, fishing in fast water is comparatively easy. Short casts are the rule, casts from twelve to twenty feet from your body often being the most productive. I've often taken a nice fish from a small pocket with a cast of not more than nine feet, a case of dapping the fly rather than casting it. Remember that the closer you can get to the fish the more naturally you can make the fly float. Get as close as you can without scaring the trout as you advance.

I believe that to fish this type of water most effectively with a dry fly you should fish all of it, even places where you can't see the fly. After fishing all the water ahead and to the side with a short cast, rest the water for ten or fifteen minutes before advancing. This allows any fish you've scared to quiet down and start feeding again. In this broken water a trout won't stay frightened long.

I prefer rather large flies for shallow rapids, from sizes 8 through 12, and I choose the color according to light reflections and backgrounds. On the whole, a fly with large white wings will show best on the smooth dark spots, but for the more broken places I find a ginger or brown fly more visible. Gray flies are most difficult to see, but there are times when only this color will catch fish.

Personally, I think your best chance of taking fish in such water is to use a fly big and bright enough so that you can keep track of it. Trout in broken water are not nearly as selective to pattern and size as they are in still pools. My favorite dry flies for the broken shallows are large fan-wings, bivisibles, spiders, and variants. Small, hard-to-see flies may get more attention from trout at times, but you'll miss a lot of strikes because the little flies are so hard to follow. In rapids, I use the small, drab flies as a last resort.

The second type of water you'll find on the typical trout stream is the still-water pool, the sort of basin where the current slows and collects before spilling downhill again. These pools are obvious hotspots for any kind of trout fishing, and it would be a rare dry-fly angler who passed one up. However, there are tricks to fishing still pools. Lots of fly fishermen neglect the tail of the pool, that part where the quiet water pauses for a moment before slipping over the brink of the low waterfall that heads the rapids.

Advancing upstream after fishing the pocket below a pool, I make it a point to sneak up on the patch of smooth water just above the spill-over. If the drop of the stream bed is slight at this point, I crouch as low as possible, wading on my knees if necessary. The reason for this is to avoid scaring any trout that may be rising just above the drop-off. That's a good feeding place for trout, but a very difficult location to fish. The trout frighten easily. It's hard to get even a few inches of float for your fly and difficult to set the hook when you get a rise.

One of my experiences, a rather typical one, illustrates how I fish such spots. Coming upstream to a still-water pool, I crouched low some twenty-five feet below the drop (after first fishing all the water between me and the low natural dam) and moved forward very slowly. About fifteen feet from the overflow I straightened up until I could see the smooth water at the very end of the pool. There were trout rising, some so close to the break-over that the circles of their rises were broken by the start of the falls.

It was still too far to make a cast. If I did, part of the line and leader would fall into the fast water below and pull the fly back with a rush, perhaps even causing a disturbance that would put the fish down. I got to my knees and waded on them until I was within six feet of the rising trout. From this distance I figured that I could make a flip cast with just a part of the leader and the fly alighting on the smooth-topped water.

On the first flip a trout came for the fly but refused it. Before the current took full control, a matter of about two seconds, I lifted the fly and immediately flipped it back for a second try. I could just barely see it when it settled on the water, and I was about to pick it up again when I sensed rather than saw a rise. I struck—and was fast to a good trout. The fish dashed upstream, and because it was a good one I got to my feet so I could better handle the situation, finally landing the fish on shore close to the tail of the still water. Of course this disturbance put down all the rest of the trout that had been rising near the lip, but I was satisfied. The fish I'd taken was a 1½-pound brown, a good size for that stream.

Many times when fishing such spots I've taken trout which could be pulled over the lip and played out in the fast water below. If I could keep low while doing this, I could usually take several trout from the lip.

These places are always good for at least one fish, more if you are skillful. Yet many anglers either pass up the pool lips or approach them as if it were impossible to frighten trout. In recent years I've found many trout that don't seem to mind the appearance of an angler, but these are legal-size hatchery fish recently stocked in the stream. Wild trout spook easily.

Once you've fished the tail of a pool, rest it a while and study the water ahead before starting to fish again. It may be that you haven't frightened the fish in the lower part of the pool too much. If this is so, they'll start rising again, provided a hatch is on. You can also spot rising fish upstream and plan a way to cast to them without putting them down.

You may need to tie on a longer, finer leader when you move from shallow rapids to a smooth, clear pool. A 7½-foot leader is long enough for broken water, and I wouldn't use one finer than 3X. But trout can see the leader much better when it's cast to a smooth pool, and suspicious still-water fish may require a leader as long as twelve feet tapered to 4X or 5X. The "X" designation of various makes of leaders isn't very well standardized, by the way. The "3X" rough-water leader should be .008 of an inch thick; the smooth-water leader I recommend would calibrate about .006.

From a position at the extreme lower end, start working the still pool with short upstream casts. (Never start by shooting a long cast to a fish rising at the head of a pool; such a cast will likely drape the frightening line over half a dozen fish closer to you, fish that could have been taken with shorter casts.) Lengthen your casts gradually until you're throwing as far as you can without strain. It doesn't pay to try to cast more line than you can handle confidently. That leads to botched casts that frighten fish. Wade closer when you've reached your distance limit.

After the fly is floating on the surface, keep line and leader under control, letting them be slack but only slightly so. If the leader sinks it will be to your advantage, though you may do all right if it floats. If the fly floats unnoticed for some time, cautiously bring the line taut and give the fly a gentle twitch. Keep twitching this way until you either get a strike or retrieve enough line to make a clean and quiet pickup of the fly from the water. Making a disturbance when taking the fly from the water can scare fish just as much as a splashy delivery. I have taken hundreds of trout by twitching a dry fly on still waters where a motionless fly was ignored.

I prefer small flies for still-water pools, say size 14 as the largest and as small as 22. The quiet surface makes it comparatively easy to see small flies. However, it will sometimes be necessary to choose a color different from the one you wish to use or think right for the hatch because of light reflections and backgrounds. You will be able to see some colors easily, others you won't be able to see at all.

Small flies are also easier to handle on the long, fine leaders that suit smooth pools of clear water. It is difficult to cast a large, air-catching fly when using a long, thin leader. It is almost impossible to straighten out the cast or to make the fly light just where and how it should. Yet I have sometimes had great success with a large fanwing fly on such waters for the very reason that it twisted the long leader and lighted where I didn't expect it to. As the leader untwisted it gave the fly a lifelike action that interested a trout I'd failed to fool with a perfect cast.

There's something to be learned from this: even if you make a poor cast, let the fly float with the current until you can pick it up from the water without any fuss. It may have fallen by accident in a better place than the one you had in mind. And if you take it from the water prematurely, you'll frighten the trout nearby so that they'll temporarily stop feeding.

The third kind of water on the typical trout stream—and perhaps the hardest to fish with dry flies—is the smooth, deep run that's broken into swirls by strong and conflicting currents. The surface will be smooth enough to give trout a good look at you and your tackle, and those colliding currents will make it difficult to cast a dry fly so it will float far without being dragged by the pull of the current on your line or leader. Many times such water will be spotted with many dimples denoting surface-feeding trout, fish rising to adult insects. You think, "Well, here it is. I'm going to make a killing." But it's seldom that easy.

In this sort of water you must make the right approach and plan casts to avoid drag. Frequently you will also find the trout most selective about the natural fly they're feeding on—which requires the selection of an artificial that's a close imitation of the real insect. In making the selection from your supply, remember that size is about as important as shape and color. On the whole the most needed sizes will be 12, 14, 16, and 18. Sometimes you'll need flies as small as 22.

Trout will be scattered all through these deep, smooth-topped runs of strong current. The main thing to remember, whether you approach them from the shore or by wading, is to be slow and quiet in your movements. As with most dry-fly fishing, I prefer to ease up on these deep runs from downstream. I keep in mind that my legs are visible to the fish as I wade, and I walk softly to avoid causing vibrations in the bank stream bed.

Since the trout will be facing upstream in the current, you will be less visible to them when you approach by wading upstream. A trout's eyes are positioned so that it can see ahead and to either side clearly, but it has limited vision to the rear.

You can get in trouble with casts made from a position directly below a trout, however, for the leader is likely to fall over the top of the fish as you drop the fly above him. Unless you have the skill to consistently toss a curve with your leader, you're better off to make your casts from one side or the other, angling them up and across the run to drop the fly above the fish. This keeps the line and leader farther away from the trout.

A very important thing to remember, again, is to cast to the nearest rising fish. If you can't hook this closeby fish, though it and others near it keep rising, this is the time and place to try different fly patterns and sizes. First try to imitate the natural flies on the water. Catch some, examine them, and look through your fly book to see if you have something that is close to the natural in color and size.

If close imitations fail, try a rather exotic fly. Sometimes a fly quite different from the natural both in size and color will interest the trout more than one that's imitative. This is most likely to happen when the trout are rising to a big hatch.

Should you hook a fish close by, don't let it rush upstream to frighten other trout unless it happens to be a big one that you don't want to lose and it wants to go that way. When fishing with a cast of two or more *wet* flies, letting a hooked fish run and fight where others are located will frequently bring a double or even a treble catch. But the fight of a trout that has taken a single dry fly usually frightens other trout in the immediate area. If you can control the hooked fish, bring it down near you to do its fighting.

If you can't take the trout rising close by, lengthen your cast gradually until you have reached the limits of your skill. If you need to move, either upstream or to one side, do so slowly and be sure to take only a few steps at a time.

Some fish in these runs of deep water may respond better to slack-line casts made from a position upstream from them. The slack-line cast (a forward cast that is halted abruptly with rod tip high) will drop the line to the water in snakelike curves. These unwind gradually as the current takes the fly downstream, giving the fly a good stretch of natural, drag-free float. At times this cast will do better than upstream tosses.

These are the basic approaches for the three types of water that are the most common on trout streams. But if you run into an unusual situation, don't hesitate to try an unusual approach. I have crawled to the edge of pools on my belly to lower a fly to a wary trout. In broken rapids, I often inch forward on the knees of my waders to reach a pocket beyond the low rock that conceals me from the fish.

There are endless opportunities for experiments in dry-fly fishing. That explains in part why I can often be found fishing with dry flies on a stream where I know some other method would likely catch more fish. A trout is a little more important to me if I take it on a dry fly.

Trout are rising on the far side of the current, an easy cast distant. Being a reasonably skillful caster you put your dry fly over that spot with the utmost confidence that you'll raise a fish. The fly alights so delicately and seems to float so naturally that you mentally congratulate yourself. An experienced angler, crouched behind you and thus watching from your angle, says, "That's swell—perfect!" and you glow from the compliment.

But nothing happens. You think surely you'll get a rise with the next cast, and the old-timer who is watching thinks the same. But still nothing happens. Failure follows each of succeeding casts. It is very depressing. Half an hour later perhaps you still are trying, if you haven't put the fish down. The experienced fisherman who was watching you has left to try his luck elsewhere, doubtless in some location where "selective" trout have never bothered him.

Meanwhile, no doubt, you have changed flies many times. It is natural to blame the fly or lure for failure. You also may blame your leader if it is a bit heavy. But if, after you have put on the lightest leader that is practical, you still fail to get a rise, then probably you turn again to the wrong-fly supposition. You are convinced that those particular fish are so selective to some special natural fly that no artificial possibly could interest them.

Perhaps your diagnosis is correct. Everyone has had experiences of this sort for which no other explanation seems to suffice. But there might be another reason—drag, that troublesome bugbear of fly fishing. Perhaps the drag has been too slight to detect, especially if the water glistens in such a way that it hides telltale wrinkles that would show your fly to be floating differently than it would if it were unattached to a leader and line.

Such undetected drags cause many a disappointment; for, not being detected, nothing is done to remedy the situation. If you knew there was a drag, and could correct it, you might find out that the fly you had on at the start is perfectly satisfactory to the fish.

For many years I always had blamed my lack of success under such conditions on not having the right fly. But one day, while watching a friend fish such a place after I had given it up in despair, I started to cross the stream to look at the fly from a different angle. I didn't get to the other side. On the way over I paused to look and saw clearly that my friend's fly was dragging—only slightly, it is true, but quite enough to tell the fish that it was a fraud.

The fault was corrected by casting a loose line and by making a slight change in the casting position. Just as soon as the fly began to float as a natural insect, the trout at once rose to it. It didn't make much difference what pattern we used, provided it somewhat resembled the natural hatch. These fish, then, were not at all choosy about patterns, but they were *extremely fussy about the way the fly floated.*

That experience was an eye-opener to me, and it had a sur-prising effect upon my fly fishing, especially for trout that were supposedly selective. Instead of always blaming failures on the pat-terns used, I now began to question the way I presented the fly. True, in some instances there could be no doubt that a particular fly was required—where size, color, shape, or all three were wrong —but in most cases I discovered that the fly itself was not at fault.

For instance, on one occasion I had been trying to take some very good fish which were rising steadily in a patch of swirling current. Because drag was most troublesome I had tried fishing the water from all angles and had used both slack and curved casts. Finally I hit upon a spot and a method which seemed good, and so far as I could tell the fly performed perfectly. How-ever, results still were lacking, though I kept changing patterns until my patience was exhausted.

Suddenly it occurred to me to find out whether they'd take an artificial unattached to a line. So, going above the fish, I began to drop upon the water the same patterns I'd been fishing with. I sacrificed six different flies to the experiment—and to my surprise the fish took them all!

However, I never was able to take any of those fish on a dry fly when they were feeding in that particular current, though I had some success with bucktails and wet flies. Evidently my casting and delivery failed to overcome the drag there, though I couldn't see just what was wrong. One thing is sure: had I left those fish without trying them with the unattached flies, I'd still be thinking that their refusal to take was due to my not having used the right pattern.

Drag is most noticeable when fly, leader, and line fall on water of different speeds. When they all fall on water of the same speed there isn't any drag to combat. Also, if the line only falls on water of a different speed from fly and leader, then you'll get a little natural float before the drag takes effect. It is when you're fishing to the far side of the current that you have the most trouble.

Let us assume that you have just made a cast among some trout that are rising on the far side of a riffle, where the speed of the current is slight. You make a perfectly straight cast; the fly alights just where it should. Since leader and line fall on much faster water the fly is at once pulled along in a very strange manner compared with that of a natural floating fly. The performance of fly, line, and leader is subject to considerable variation, being determined by the ratio between the speed of the current and the speed of the water upon which the fly lands. If the difference in speed is not too great it may be overcome by throwing a slack line—the very cast a beginner strives to overcome, in his efforts to master a straight-line delivery which he knows is preferred.

Now the perfect cast is unsuited to many fishing conditions, and in particular to a cross-current cast when you are trying to avoid drag. This probably will make you throw your hands up in despair. You're likely to say, if you're fairly new at the sport, "Here I've just got so I can make a perfect cast, and now this fellow tells me I'm all wrong."

It's nothing to be upset about. It is necessary to master the straight-line cast so that you'll learn to feel instinctively the rhythm necessary in all fly casting. Only then can you make *controlled* imperfect casts. Only then can you ignore with impunity the rules for making a perfect cast. I assure you that those rules are often scandalously violated, of necessity in actual fishing practice.

A slack-line cast causes the line to fall on the water in a wavering rather than a straight line. While there are several ways to accomplish this, two are perhaps the easiest to master. In the first you cast as when making a straight-line cast, but aiming high at a point some distance in the air above your objective. If such a cast is made with vigor, so that the power directed forward is expended while in the air, this will cause the line to recoil and fall to the water in curves.

The other way to get this effect is to check the line as it is falling during the forward stroke of the cast. This check is made by drawing the rod back toward the body. In either of these casts you must use enough extra line to allow for the necessary curves or slack between you and the spot on which you wish the fly to fall.

My experience has led me to consider one rule very important:

whenever you have trouble in getting a fish to rise consider drag as a possible cause of failure, and do what you can to eliminate it. Do this even though you feel certain that drag is not the trouble. Do it whether you are casting over rising fish or over water where you feel fish should be, even though you can't see any moving.

An experience I had on the Gallatin River in Montana is a case in point. The pool was a fair-size one, starting at a right-angle bend of the stream into which the water rushed, turned, and then straightened out. In general the tongue of the main current ran close to the right bank as you looked upstream, sometimes almost touching it, and at other times swerving out a foot or so. The left bank was a sandy sloping shore extending out into the water, and deepening at the edge of the current.

There were numerous indications that all fishermen fished the pool from that side. This was a natural thing to do, for it was an easy place to fish from. It made possible a perfect float for the fly out as far as mid-current, without need of slack line, and there was nothing to bother you on the backcast. When first I fished that pool a few trout were rising along the left side of the current tongue. Fishing just as all the other fishermen had done I took four trout. These fish were all keepers, though rather small.

However, between the current tongue and the right bank, which was several feet high and undermined, was a strip of slow-moving water, just the sort of place which harbors good trout. I fished that strip, but found I could never obtain more than a couple of inches of natural float before visible drag set in, and I couldn't get a rise. Neither did I see a fish rise to a natural on that particular water, so I assumed that either there were no fish, or else they were not feeding.

But I kept thinking about that pool after I'd left it. It was the best-looking hole along that entire stretch of river, and I couldn't feel satisfied with what I'd accomplished there. So I went back and tried again, fishing as before from the easy left side. This time, however, only one small fish rose in the eddy at the left of the bend. As before, I couldn't get a rise in that alluring space between the current and the far bank. Being confident that there were fish on that side, and also being reasonably certain that the vexatious drag was making it impossible to raise the fish, I decided to try fishing from the right bank.

It was a mean place to cast from, brushy and rough, and I had to get down on my knees and keep away from the edge so that the fish below couldn't see me. But only a very short cast was needed, and the fly floated perfectly, with no line and only part of the leader touching the water. The fly floated so cockily and naturally I was sure something would happen. It did. I took five fish, all good, average-size trout for the stream, much larger than those I had taken from the opposite side of the current.

There was no fancy fishing involved in this. Anyone could have done the same. All I did was to fish from a position where it was possible to cast a short line and get a perfect float. Whenever you can achieve this combination, and the fish are there, you're sure to get a rise if the fish will rise at all. Of course, you musn't scare the fish. That is a basic rule which must always be followed.

As I look back over the years, I can recall hundreds of experiences where elimination of drag in one way or another has brought me success. So get drag-conscious, and your score will improve.

CHAPTER VIII

Landlocks and Lakers

COLD and blustery March weather may not suggest much in the way of fishing to people accustomed to opening the season in late May or June, but it starts a kind of spring fever among another group of anglers. Just shout, "The ice is out!" within hearing of a man who knows lake trout and landlock salmon. That's warm enough weather for him.

Maine, for example, uses "ice out" rather than a date to start its legal season on landlocks. Dates set in other regions, May 1, say, are usually guesses at when the ice will go. In Canada, that may be as late as May 15.

Both of these fish actually prefer icy water. They lie deep during most of the open fishing season, ranging the shallows only in the opening weeks of spring and again when fall weather chills the water to their liking. But the legal fishing season closes in many areas before the landlocks and lake trout come up from the depths in the fall, so it's mainly a spring sport. You have to get into action fast, for the cream of this fishing sours quickly.

Hope for a cold and miserable spring this year. That's perfect, if you can get to the northern border of the United States or into Canada while it lasts. The most efficient way, if you're an outsider, is to write or telegraph ahead for advice on last-minute conditions and to arrange accommodations. Hiring a guide is a great help, too. Once the rush is under way, there's a big advantage in having someone direct you to the hot spots where you can use your limited time to best advantage. If you lack the funds or inclination to hire a guide, go anyway. You'll have lots of company, and I'll try to tell you how to make a good catch.

The landlock salmon is really the star of this spring show. If that's the one you want, look over your waters as soon as you get there and try to locate a windswept shore. One strewn with rocks and with a stretch of shallows bordering deep water is ideal. The more the shore is battered by wind and waves the better. That draws landlocks, apparently because it piles up food there—aquatic life driven onto the rocks, tidbits washed off the shore.

This is difficult fishing, so you won't be crowded by other anglers. Dress for biting cold and flying spray. You'll need a trustworthy boat to get into position, and at least one anchor—two are better—to hold it there. And don't go armed with extremely light tackle. Take an outfit that will cast in a stiff wind and hold a hooked landlock where the odds are on his side. Add to these requirements a good store of patience. Those blood-warming strikes may not come frequently, which often causes anglers to give up just when they're working into the edge of a landlock bonanza. I've so often seen other boats move in and clean up behind anglers who've quit too soon.

Of course you get calm days, too, but the rocky shallows are still good then. Landlocks will simply move out to the depths bordering your beach, bar, or rocky point. Sneak near enough for good casting and gradually work from the shallows out to the depths. If this fails, try trolling. That gives you greater coverage in locating the fish, which is the big problem, and you can tie up and cast when you've found them. That area where shallows break off into depths is also a fine place to start trolling.

Landlocks may be scattered all over a lake, even in spring, and that again calls for trolling at different depths. Only when you hit a fair concentration of fish is it worth stopping to cast. When trolling slowly, as I do with natural baits, I like to team up with a partner and work so that one of us is trolling behind the boat while the other keeps casting toward the shallows. When one of us scores, we have a hint on where the fish are lying, deep or shallow. With artificial lures, fast trolling ordinarily does better. By fast I mean top speed with oars, faster than that if you have a motor.

Cold-weather strikes may come at depths anywhere from three to fifteen feet, so that leaves the door open to a lot of lures. A fly fished near the surface may get them; so may a spoon that goes down a bit deeper, or a lure that dives for the bottom. Experiment. Add a sinker and go deeper if there's no response in the shallows.

A natural minnow will often take landlocks when nothing else will, a fact that's often demonstrated when anglers hook a minnow on a fly or spoon that was useless before and start catching fish. Smelt are probably a landlock's favorite natural food, and spoons or flies should be chosen with that in mind. Lots of good landlock flies don't actually look like a smelt, but the consistently good flies and lures do have the general appearance and action of minnows. Landlocks often trail artificials without hitting, whereas it's a good bet they'd whack a piece of real meat. That's why fast trolling helps with artificials—there's less time for the fish to examine the fake and make up his mind.

To be well armed for landlocks you need natural minnows, lures that imitate them, and an assortment of flies. Gray Ghost, Green Ghost, Black Ghost, Supervisor, 9-3, and Family Secret are all famous patterns for minnowlike bucktails and streamers. Landlocks will even take a dry fly, sometimes very readily. Dry flies in regular trout sizes and patterns may do the trick. At other times they go for big ones and become very fussy about pattern.

Among the good dry-fly patterns are White Wulff, Gray Wulff, Irresistible, Coachman, Cahill, Green May, Black Gnat Quill, Grizzly King, and Ginger Quill. I'd carry an assortment in sizes 6 through 14 and fish them on nine-foot leaders. Leaders should be somewhat heavier than for the usual run of trout, say tapered from .018 to .009, .010, or .011.

If you fish with a spinning outfit and monofilament line, there's really no need for a leader. Just use a line of a size suitable for the conditions and fish a bait, streamer, or lure on the end of it. Remember that heavy spinners naturally require stronger line than streamers.

If more sportsmen knew how to locate lake trout and how to rig to take them consistently, I believe the fish would have a surge of popularity among sport fishermen. At present, a large share of the lake trout taken each year are hooked by accident—boated by anglers fishing at random or trolling for some other fish.

Few fishermen concentrate on the lake trout, which is also known by the local names togue, lunge, salmon trout, namay-cush, forktail trout, and great lake trout. The limited range of the lakers—the deep, cold lakes of the northern states and Canada —partly explains the shortage of lake-trout anglers. But a good many fishermen in easy reach of those cold northern lakes shy away from lake trout simply because they don't know the answers to two complicated questions: how do you find the schools of fish? What kind of lures and tackle will take them? I have managed to pick up some tricks that should help answer those last two questions.

My first laker was boated years ago in a deep, clear lake in the Adirondack Mountains of New York. It was mid-summer, and I had brought along an outfit calculated to catch lakers in deep water—a stiff 5½-foot bait-casting rod and a light salt-water reel filled with braided copper line. At the end of this line was a string of large spoons about 3½ feet long, a trolling device that at the time was new and highly recommended. When trolling this rig, it felt as if you were fighting a fair fish all the time.

I knew the lakers were on bottom this time of year, but on which part of the vast lake bottom? No one I talked to had more than a vague idea which area might produce. So I had to start out blind, planning to troll systematically until I found fish.

This was before outboard motors were common in the Adiron-

[71]

dacks, and my trolling plan called for a lot of tough rowing, but a friend who was fishing the same lake volunteered to help me. This pal, who was big and strong as an ox, gripped the oars and said, "I don't know anything about fishing or lake trout. I'll row; you catch us a laker."

We trolled for three hours without getting a strike. It was steady trolling, too, and that big string of spinners was probing the lake bottom all the way. Another thirty minutes passed before I felt a hard pull on my line. Since the lure had been flirting with the bottom constantly, I at first thought I was snagged. Then a powerful throbbing was added to the pull. I had a fish on—a big fish. It took a lot of pumping to get the fish up off the bottom. As it neared the surface, it made several powerful runs. Then it gave up. I reeled in a twelve-pound lake trout.

The people who watched us unload this laker at the dock considered it a sensational catch. Personally, I was rather disappointed. I had expected a more dramatic fight from a fish that size. As I thought more about it, however, I realized that the lake trout had no chance to put up the kind of leaping, slashing battle you expect from other species of trout. The twelve-pound fish was from the beginning fighting the weight of a heavy and cumbersome chain of spinners, not to mention the drag of that wire line. In addition, the fish undoubtedly had physical trouble with the abrupt change in water pressure as I hauled it up from the depths to the surface. Some ocean fish brought to the surface from great depths almost explode from the pressure change.

It's no wonder that the lake trout has a poor reputation as a fighting fish. Most of the fishing for lakers is done in summer, when the fish are deep, as far down as two hundred feet. The angler commonly uses a heavy lure, and he may have as much as 150 yards of wire line slanting back from the boat to the lake bottom when the strike comes. Let's assume that our typical angler weighs 160 pounds and is braced on his boat seat to crank in his lake trout with a salt-water reel and stiff rod. Would you expect a ten- or twelve-pound fish to put up a dramatic, tail-walking fight against such odds?

Unfortunately, you have to scrape the bottom of deep waters

to get lake trout in summer, and it takes wire line and heavy trolling tackle to do that. At other seasons, as I'll explain in a minute, there are several ways to catch lakers with tackle that evens the contest.

Lake trout seldom range all over a large body of water the way many other fish do. Instead, they'll school up in a few comparatively small areas. If you find one of these hot spots, a little experimenting with different lures will usually turn up at least one that the lakers will take readily.

Locating them—that's the toughest chore with lakers. It brings to mind the time my wife and I went with a guide on a wilderness canoe trip. Because our route involved a great many portages, we had a light load of grub. We figured on fish to furnish the bulk of our meat. This plan worked fine as long as we were on waters where northern pike, bass, and walleyes were plentiful. Then, on the fifth day out, we reached a beautiful camp by a lake that was supposed to supply us with lake trout.

Our guide paddled us here and there about this lake, with my wife and me trolling different lures along the bottom. We went from lake center to deep cove, from cove to channel. We snagged bottom and lost lures. The guide paddled and paddled. Hours passed. We kept trying. Then we hit a spot where the lakers were —a part of the vast lake bottom no more than three hundred feet square. With my lure a hundred feet deep and bumping bottom, I hooked a laker on the first pass through this hot spot. Another pass got me another fish. And so on.

But finding these lakers wasn't the only chore: they had another lesson to teach us. Grace, trolling at the same depth from the same boat, didn't get a strike until she changed to a lure exactly like mine. The fish were particular about what they hit. We fished that lake for several days, and that same small portion of it was productive all the time we were there, as long as we used the right lure.

I was further impressed with the need for locating the right spot and using the right lure on another trip soon after that. This time my wife and I were fishing the Lake of the Woods area of Ontario. It was September, but the lake trout were still down deep.

We trolled a full day at depths ranging from thirty to two hundred feet without catching a single lake trout. The second day I went down to 250 feet with my fifteen-pound test wire line and hooked a laker that weighed about fifteen pounds.

When Grace got down to the same depth in the same area, she also hooked a good fish. Each of us took several that ran from twelve to sixteen pounds apiece. (Lakers are said to grow as large as a hundred pounds, but a fifteen-pounder is a good one most places.) There were two lures that suited the lake trout this time—a wobbling spoon about four inches long, and a trolling rig made of a string of spoons.

These trips I've just described are typical of my experience with summer fishing for lake trout. You must troll deep and patiently, perhaps putting in a day or more before you locate the fish. When you find a hot spot, mark it well with a buoy or landmarks ashore to help you find it again. Start out with a standard lure or a local favorite, but don't hesitate to change it if it fails to produce. Strings of spinners or spoons are often good. A single wobbling spoon about four inches long is a reliable lure. Bass-type plugs are sometimes excellent.

Once, after all my routine lake-trout lures had failed, I saved the day with a floating bass plug that I held in the depths with a heavy sinker. This was rigged by tying a swivel to the end of my wire line and trailing the sinker and the buoyant plug behind the swivel on short lengths of strong leader material. The heavy sinker was on a two-foot leader, the plug on one about three feet long. So the sinker bounced along the bottom some distance ahead of the plug and below it. I use a lighter leader for the sinker so if it snags I can break it loose without losing my plug. This rig has become one of my favorites for summer lake trouting.

The best tackle for this deep trolling? I vote for a solid metal line, called monofilament metal in today's parlance. Lines made of fine strands of metal braided or twisted together hold too much air to sink quickly. Lines made of silk, nylon, or other such fiber have two weaknesses for deep trolling: they sink slowly and they stretch too much. It's difficult to feel a strike and respond quickly when you have out several hundred feet of line that forms a great belly with a lot of give in it.

A light salt-water reel with star drag and level-wind device is fine for dredging the depths for lakers. These reels have spools that are as much as five inches in diameter, so that a single turn of the spool brings in quite a length of line. A heavy-duty casting reel of freshwater size will handle most lake trout trolling. A rod 5½ feet long is a good average choice for this trolling. It should be a sturdy trolling rod or a particularly stiff and powerful bait-casting rod.

As for trolling strategy, a slow and steady pace with the lure or sinker practically bumping bottom is the best bet as a rule. You should experiment with other speeds, however, if slow trolling isn't taking fish. A change in speed requires a change in the length of line being trolled. Otherwise the lure will either snag on bottom or ride too high in the water.

There isn't much you can do about varying the action of a lure that's being pulled at the end of two hundred feet of line. The one stunt I know that may help is to haul in a few feet of line with your hand and then release it quickly. This makes your lure dart a bit.

Sad to say, the very best sport with lake trout is available at a time when many states have the season closed on all kinds of trout. I mean early spring, right after the ice goes out, and late fall, just before winter closes the waters. That's when the lakers are in the shallows where you can hook them with a bait rig, spinning tackle, or a fly outfit.

You can judge your chances of finding lakers in shallow water by taking the water temperature. Lakers love frigid water, and there's little hope of finding them near the surface if the shallows are warmer than 45°. Best surface temperature for lake trout is 35° to 45°, and water that cold is seldom found except in late fall and early spring. The place to look for lakers when they're ranging the icy shallows is along rocky shores or over bars that slant out into deep water. They like to school up over a bottom that's studded with large rocks.

Look for lakers around shoals away from shore, too. The color of the water is a good guide to those offshore shallows. Shoal water will appear to be light tan as the result of light reflected off sunken rocks, while the depths will be dark blue. You can see the difference for some distance.

Perhaps the most reliable lure for these shallow-ranging lakers is a large spoon, one weighing from ½ to ¾ of an ounce. They will also take big wet flies that resemble minnows and minnow-like plugs. Fresh minnows or small eels are good natural baits. Prepare for miserable weather when you go after lakers in the shallows. Spring or fall, you can expect rain, sleet, snow, high winds, and wild combinations of those.

But what fun I've had with lakers on such outings! As with duck hunting, storms over lake-trout water merely add to the promise of a good day's sport. Perhaps you'll take several fish weighing from twelve to twenty pounds. Say you hook them in water less than twenty feet deep and play them with ten-pound test monofilament or with even lighter fly tackle. They'll make runs too powerful to stop, churn up the surface, pull their typical stunt of rolling their thick bodies up your line. A day of that kind of action, I submit, is a day you'll remember.

Usually the larger fish lie on the outside of the reefs, or off the rocky stretches jutting out from a point. That is not always the case, however. One day while fishing at Crow Lake, Ontario, my wife and I came to an island with many large broken rocks hugging one shore. On the outer borders of this island reef, and well in toward shore, we took several fish up to four pounds. But when we began to cast our spoons into rock pockets close to shore we had some real excitement. My wife caught a ten-pounder and I one of eight pounds. Then, in a tiny baylike spot between two huge boulders, I tangled with a dandy.

When I cast, the spoon struck the shore and bounced back into the water. At the same instant there was a tremendous swirl, and when I struck I felt a solid and thrilling weight. For several minutes it was touch and go. The fish got rattled and thrashed around so furiously in the rockbound hole that I was sure either the lure would be thrown or the line cut or broken. But everything held.

Finally the fish got smart, saw its way out, and shot into lake where it headed for deep water. From then on it was just a question of tiring him out, a matter of from 10 to 15 minutes. The fight probably would have lasted longer if the trout hadn't wasted so much of its strength in the frantic struggle in the small pocket. As lakers go, it wasn't so very large, but it weighed 19 pounds, and I'd taken it on a lightweight rod with a 12-pound test line.

It is in such places, and the shallower parts of outside reefs, that I've always had my best fly fishing. The only productive flies have been enormous things, at least 4 or 5 inches long. A combination of white and blue or white and green, each with a dash of red to simulate gills, and with silver or gold-tinsel bodies, works about as well as anything. White feathers or hair predominate in these flies, with green or blue used as topping. This dressing makes the fly resemble a minnow. Orange instead of the white makes an effective pattern on occasion, while a good dark-center badger without any topping also resembles a minnow. Dr. Edgar Burke's Family Secret, the latest laker pattern I've tried, seems more effective than any of the others.

The Family Secret is tied as follows: body—flat silver tinsel ribbed with oval tinsel; cheek—jungle-cock eye; tail—heavily bunched peacock sword; hackles—guinea fowl feathers ti rather long; wing—white gamecock hackle feathers tied strean style.

When fishing for lakers, I've found a long rod—9½ to 10 feet—the most satisfactory. Powerful rods of this length are required not so much for playing the fish as for making distance casts and working the fly properly in the water. Unless the fly action is well emphasized, I never have good results, no matter what fly pattern I use. As action is given with jerks of the rod as well as with the hand, and the flies must be sunken to be effective, the length and power of a ten-foot rod help a lot.

True, there are days and places when the lakers lie close to the surface, ready to grab anything that comes along. In such cases, it matters little what tackle you have, for the moment the lure touches the water it is taken. But even at such times the long and powerful rod is best. Lakers are rightly called stormy-weather fish, and the stiffer the wind and the rougher the water, the more likely you are to have good fishing. Under such conditions the most powerful rod works best. You can't get real power in a short rod without also getting excessive stiffness, and that I don't like.

As yet I haven't tried a spinning outfit on these fish. A streamer fly with a spinner attractor can get good results, and casts well with the spinning outfit. But for all waters and under all conditions nothing can beat the bait-casting rod and large lake-trout spoons.

After you finish casting over the shallow waters of a reef, you should troll near bottom along the outer borders. Not all lakers will be in really shallow water, either in spring or fall, and often the larger fish will be in the deep water. I've found the practice effective. Cast over waters up to twenty-five feet deep. As the water deepens, allow extra time for the lure to reach bottom before starting your retrieve. While doing this, watch your line carefully, just as you do when letting a wet fly sink, for a laker may hit while the spoon is sinking. If this happens you must strike hard and fast.

When fishing waters where there are muskies or northern pike, you're quite likely to get one of them instead of a laker. Once, when fishing an Ontario lake in the fall, I was casting a large lake-trout spoon around some huge boulders rising out of the water from thirty to forty feet deep, letting the spoon sink to the bottom before retrieving. On one cast, while the spoon was sinking the line suddenly cut the water with a pronounced hiss. I struck and at once lost my lure, although I was using a six-inch wire casting trace. Doubtless it was a muskie. It had taken the spoon in such a way that the line was cut above the trace. This same thing has happened to me a number of times when casting for lakers on the shoals, usually when the lure was sinking.

CHAPTER IX

Know Your Bass

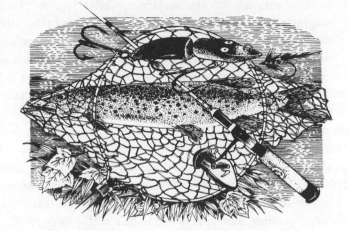

SPANISH explorers wrote of finding black bass in Florida in 1515, but it took Dr. James A. Henshall to focus the attention of American sportsmen on them. Henshall's vivid magazine articles and his famous *Book of the Black Bass*, published in 1881, brought these great game fish the recognition they deserved. To-day there are probably more persons fishing for the different varieties of black bass than for any other freshwater game fish.

Ichthyologists recognize several varieties of black bass, including the fairly common Kentucky or spotted bass, but the bulk of bass fishing is for the largemouth (*Micropterus salmoides*) and the smallmouth (*Micropterus dolomieu*) bass.

The largemouth prefers quiet waters with plenty of weeds, stumps, or other underwater cover. He'll often be found in very shallow water and is at times seen feeding on mucky, muddy bottoms. He'll also range over hard, clean stream bottoms, some-times seeking out such an area and sticking to it for days, but you seldom find the largemouth out in the fast water that the small-mouth favors.

The largemouth has a well-earned reputation for hitting surface lures. In fairly shallow water, artificial bugs or lures that pop, splash, or otherwise disturb the surface are effective. As the bass go to progressively deeper water, it's sound practice to follow them down with bait and lures. For example, largemouths schooled up on the bottom in fairly deep water are often taken with baits or lures that actually bounce along the bottom. Once in a while an unpredictable largemouth may shoot up from the depths to hit a surface lure, but there aren't enough such individualists to provide much action.

As for the size of lures for largemouths, there are days when tiny panfish bugs are best. Other times the bass will be gobbling up hardware lures the size of a hen's egg. *Micropterus salmoides* has a big mouth and pugnacious, inquisitive attitude. He'll often attack things moving near him whether he's really hungry or not, and a hungry largemouth is fairly easy to hook on most any standard bait or lure.

The smallmouth usually prefers clear water with a rocky or gravel bottom. These fish seem to delight in the fast waters of streams, as well as the deeper waters of lakes. Sometimes they will be found side by side with largemouths, though rarely so in my experience.

The smallmouth is not consistently as ready a biter as the largemouths, nor is it as likely to take artificial lures. Many times one would not catch smallmouths at all without resorting to natural bait, whereas some sort of artificial will usually take the largemouth. On occasion I've had great smallmouth fishing with both surface and underwater artificials—with bugs and spinners in Northern lakes and rivers, and with plugs and spoons in Southern rivers. In the South I have also found deep-running, lead-headed feather rigs deadly at times. On the whole, however, I have caught far more smallmouths on minnows, hellgrammites, and worms.

In my opinion the smallmouth is the best of the black bass in appearance and fight. Anyone who'd never caught anything but largemouths before would readily notice the difference when he hooked a smallmouth of comparable size. There's tremendous power and vitality in the well-formed body of the smallmouth.

My experience with the Kentucky or spotted bass is limited. Those I've taken seemed to combine the characteristics of the smallmouth and largemouth. They looked more like the largemouth but are as active as smallmouths when hooked. The Kentucky bass responds to the same lures and strategies as the other two black bass.

Largemouth black bass are found almost everywhere in the United States, with the exception of cold trout waters and some waters that have been taken over by carp and catfish. Many areas that had no native population of largemouths now have excellent bass fishing as the result of stocking programs. This is true of many Western lakes and reservoirs.

The original range of the smallmouth roughly included the territory from Norfolk, Virginia, north to Winnipeg, Canada, and east to Augusta, Maine. Of course, there were waters inside those rough boundaries that had no smallmouths and some outside them that did. Alabama, for instance, had smallmouths in the Tennessee River, which still produces whoppers. The range of the smallmouth has been expanded a good deal by stocking, but not so much as the largemouth, which is not so finicky about the water it lives in.

Once bass are stocked in suitable water, they take hold so tenaciously that they may clean up most of the food in the water. For this reason it was once common practice to stock carp along with the black bass, with the thought that the bass would feed on the carp fry. Trouble was that the bass seldom ate enough of the carp, and many such waters have been taken over by the rough fish as a result. Large carp (they grow to thirty pounds or more) have been known to shove spawning bass aside to eat the eggs.

Yet bass are very hardy. In some places largemouths have held on in stagnant ponds which ordinarily support only the lower orders of aquatic life. As an example of black bass durability, there's a government report that tells how workers put some adult bass in a rearing pond that was allowed to go dry in the fall. It remained a muddy depression until early spring, when it gradually filled with rain and seepage water. Shad fry were put in the pond then and it was soon noticed that some kind of large fish were feeding on the young shad. They turned out to be bass. When the pond went dry in the fall, the bass had burrowed in the mud and remained dormant until the combination of seepage water and warmer weather brought them up to feed.

In very cold climates bass ordinarily spend part of the winter in a dormant state akin to hibernation. Once in a while someone catches a bass through winter ice, but this happens so rarely that it must be attributed to some unusual condition. Winter after winter ice fishermen catch perch and bluegills steadily without getting a single bass—and this in lakes that in summer teem with bass. The reason is that the bass are holed up in underwater crevices, brush, or in the mud. They have actually been found in such places in drained ponds.

Bass living in warmer waters never hibernate, which is one of the reasons why those from Southern waters run larger. They have more time to feed. In years of bass fishing, I've never had really good luck with largemouths in water colder than 65° Fahrenheit. My better catches have been made in water ranging from 68° to 75°. The hot summer months usually produce the best surface lure fishing.

The largemouth bass has a big appetite and one that's satisfied with a great variety of natural foods. Minnows, worms, and crawfish are always good bets as largemouth baits. Largemouths will hit frogs, grubs, bugs, mice—most any small creature that lives in the water or falls into it. That's why artificial lures, some of them large, splashing chunks of hardware, take so many largemouth bass.

Most authorities say the best times to catch bass are early morning and late evening. This hasn't been true in my experience. I've caught a good many bass at those times, but I've consistently had better luck in the hours between eight a.m. and two p.m. There will be times, of course, when bass go on feeding sprees early or late in the day. The evening hours especially will produce marvelous action at times. Night fishing with surface plugs can also be most rewarding. But all in all, give me the sunshine hours. They've brought me more fish through the years.

Smallmouths are not nearly as active in surface feeding as largemouths. Though they hit surface lures from time to time, smallmouths have a preference for deeper water, so bait and lures fished deep pay off better in the long run. The idea in fishing for either kind of black bass is to find out where the fish are and adjust your fishing depth and tactics accordingly.

Black bass begin building nests for spawning in the spring when the water warms to sixty degrees. They start depositing eggs when the water temperature gets to sixty-two degrees. Thus bass may begin spawning as early as March in the South, or as late as May in cold Canadian-border states. The eggs are usually dropped on gravel bottoms in water eighteen to thirty-six inches deep. The fish will vary the depth somewhat in order to get a suitable location. A bottom pebbled with blueberry-size stones seems to be the most satisfactory for spawning bass, but coarse sand is also acceptable. So is a clay bottom in some waters, and a sunken tree or the top of a submerged weed bed is sometimes used as a spawning place.

Silt stirred up by boats, the feeding of carp, or other such disturbances is the main menace to bass eggs. Few eggs hatch if silt settles over them. Owners of muddy ponds have improved their bass fishing by installing sand boxes on stilts that hold the sand a couple of feet beneath the surface. Bass spawn on these elevated beds, safe from attack or disturbance by the rooting bottom-feeding carp.

The size of black bass depends on water, food supply, and other factors. In general, the bigger bass are apt to be found in the large bodies of water, especially those waters in the South where food is plentiful and the weather warm enough for year-round feeding. The world-record largemouth is a twenty-two-pound, four-ounce, whopper taken in Montgomery Lake in Georgia. The top smallmouth, taken in Dale Hollow Lake in Kentucky, weighed eleven pounds, fifteen ounces. The average

FISHING WITH RAY BERGMAN

angler, however, can figure he has a nice largemouth if it weighs around two pounds. Smallmouths run a little smaller, 1½-pounders being good keepers.

There has never been any valid criticism of the gameness of black bass, either largemouths or smallmouths. Both have plenty of spirit. I rate the smallmouth the better battler of the two. Some will disagree with that, I know, but the hundreds of smallmouths I've hooked have fought harder than a comparable number of largemouths.

As food fish, bass are considered tops by some persons. Others don't like them at all. It's a matter of taste. Just let me suggest that the best bass for eating are the smaller ones from clear water, and I believe the flavor is best if the fish is skinned and soaked in salted water for twelve hours before cooking.

Perhaps "white bass" isn't the correct name for the game fish which I recently caught in the South for the first time. But I believe it is—even though authorities say that the geographical range for white bass doesn't include the waters in which I caught my best specimens—and in that belief I'll continue to call them white bass until I'm proved to be wrong.

Both white and yellow bass are described by David Starr Jordan in his book *Fishes*. Of the white bass he says, "White bass—*roccus chrysops*: Similar to striped bass or rockfish—*roccus lineatus*—of the Atlantic coast but shorter and more compressed and reaching a smaller size. Abundant in Great Lakes and upper Mississippi as far south as Arkansas." And of the yellow bass, "Yellow bass—*morone interrupta*. A coarser and more brassy fish. Replaces white bass farther south. Seldom seen above Cincinnati and St. Louis."

In James A. Henshall's book *Bass, Pike, Perch and Others*, I find the following: "*Roccus chrysops*—also known as white lake bass and freshwater striped bass. Fly fishing best in spring. In summer and fall the fish are in the lakes or deeper water. Abundant in Lake Erie, Lake Michigan, and the Upper Mississippi, and Lake Winnebago, Wisconsin. Essentially a lake fish except in spring when it undergoes a semi-migration. Usual size a pound or less but occasionally grows to three pounds. Has six or more narrow, dusky lines along the body, most conspicuous above the lateral line. Those below broken or not continuous." Then he describes the yellow: "*Morone interrupta*—yellow bass. Named *interrupta* because of the interrupted lines along its sides. Also known as brassy bass. Found only in lower Mississippi River and its tributaries, sometimes extending the range a short distance up the Ohio River. General color brassy or yellowish, the lower stripes being broken or 'interrupted' similar to a fault in a stratum of rocks. It is fonder of the deeper pools and clear water bayous, and of the foot of rapids and ripples. Grows to a pound or two in weight. Sometimes reaches three pounds."

Now the fish I caught were taken a considerable distance south of Arkansas, and not in a tributary of the Mississippi River. They were very silvery in color and did not have an interrupted stripe as described by Henshall. In one of my specimens there is a clearly defined steady succession of five stripes above the lateral line, three of which are very distinct. Below the lateral line there are no distinct stripes. In the other specimen there is a regular succession of stripes running well down to the belly, but no sharply defined stripes such as are shown in the first fish.

The two fish are otherwise about the same. Where they differ is in the darkness of some stripes in the first specimen, and the fact that this fish shows distinct interruptions in the two plainly visible upper stripes. The other fish does not show such interruptions in the straight line but it does show separations. It is probable that the differences represent a sport in one fish or the other.

I also made a tracing of a *morone interrupta* which I caught in a bayou near Moss Point, Mississippi. This tracing was carefully made from a specimen which was typical of all fish of the kind caught there. There isn't any doubt about its being a *morone interrupta*—a yellow bass. It was caught in the right territory so far as latitude goes, though I can find no mention of the fish being found outside the Mississippi River and its tributaries. However, it is quite possible that they have found their way into the Mississippi bayous from the lower reaches of the Mississippi River, working out through Lake Pontchartrain, and so along the coast of the Gulf of Mexico to the streams running into the Gulf. The specimen I describe came from the Pascagoula River. At the time it was caught, and in that particular location, the water was slightly brackish with the tide running out.

But how did those white bass get into the South where only *morone interrupta* is supposed to be found? Was the white bass stocked in this territory? The fish looked to be the same as those we caught in Arkansas, supposed to be the southern boundary of their range. Another possibility suggested itself: were white bass really native to Texas? I could get no information on this while down there. Possibly the fish I identify as white bass were really yellow bass. Whatever they were, I'm for them now.

The best specimens I ever caught were taken about a hundred miles north of San Antonio, Texas, on that short stretch of the Colorado River between Buchanan and Inks Lakes. At the time we were stopping at a cabin near Everett Badger's office, and Everett was anxious that we become acquainted with the fishing in that section. We had spent two hard days on the big lake without getting a bass of keeping size.

"We're going below the dam in the morning," said Everett. "They're getting some good fish there now. But you've got to get up early. We should be there by daybreak."

He woke us by shining a bright flashlight in our cabin window in the inky darkness of early morning. He'd allowed plenty of time to get ready and down to the dam before daylight, but I'm not so quick on the morning start as I was when younger, so by the time we had breakfast and got started it was plenty light, though still some time before sunup.

We arrived at the dam to find at least half a dozen others ahead of us. It was an interesting sight. On the left was the enormous dam, white and impressive in the early morning light, stretching away across the river and disappearing in the distance. There was the exciting roar of rushing water, and close to the dam it was white and turbulent. This swift and agitated water continued for about three hundred feet to the beginning of the shallow rapids below. Those anglers who had preceded us were scattered from a point directly under the dam to a spot probably two hundred feet below.

I didn't begin fishing at once, but waited until I could get into position without disturbing any other fishermen. It looked like fly water to me, so I rigged up my fly rod although everyone else was using a bait-casting rod. Everett had said nothing about the kind of fish we might catch. I had expected largemouth bass, but this didn't look like largemouth water to me. Rather it seemed to be smallmouth water, reminding me of the Delaware River between New York and Pennsylvania.

As I watched, several fish were caught. Each seemed to give quite a tussle, and I was puzzled when I saw the fish as they were landed. Being more than a hundred feet away, I couldn't see them clearly, but their shape and color were certainly not those of either largemouth or smallmouth bass. They looked more like overgrown crappies or calico bass.

I had no idea of what might be a good fly-rod lure in that water. On a chance I attached a propeller-spinner fly, the pattern a Professor, in size No. 2. Casting it across the current and retrieving did not produce, nor did several other casts; so I stopped fishing, moved nearer to the man who was casting above me, and closely watched what he did. You could see that he knew his business. Every movement was rhythmic and sure, and soon after landing one fish he would take another.

He was fishing with a plug. It was pearl-colored, and of a different style from that ordinarily used for black bass. It looked like the sort used in salt water for the spotted weakfish, otherwise known as the spotted trout. The fisherman, after making his cast, did not start retrieving at once. Instead he cast the lure into the current, and then fed out line grudgingly while the water carried the lure downstream. The bait was of the sinking variety, descending at moderate speed. Thus, as the current carried the plug downstream and the line was fed out at the proper pace, the lure sank, followed the current's natural drift, yet at the same time against enough resistance to bring out all the action which the plug possessed. So the bait drifted naturally and looked as if it were alive.

Suddenly the fisherman's rod arched and the line ripped the water. Some minutes later he landed a fish of about 2½ pounds. It was a silvery, shining fish, quite deep and sunfishy in shape, making me think of a Hudson River shad. What it really was I had no idea, nor did I ask questions. I was too anxious to start fishing and put into effect the angling technique I'd just observed. It was really the same kind of fishing I'd often done for smallmouth bass and trout in similar waters, but I hadn't realized it until I'd watched somebody else.

So I returned to my original position. It wasn't in the white water, but the current was strong there and made me think of a swift glide in a trout stream. Just below me a man was fishing with a surf outfit. It looked out of place but wasn't, as I realized when I took the time to see what he was doing. He was fishing with bait, a large float, and a sinker having plenty of weight. With this rig he could get a lot of distance, and he did, putting the bait to the far side of the stream—a distance which even the good casters present failed to equal with their bait-casting rods. He didn't catch white bass while I was there, but he did get some fine catfish.

I now fished my propeller-spinner fly in the natural-drift manner, making the initial cast up and across the stream, and letting the fly fall on the far side of the current. This let it sink a bit before the water pulled against the line. As soon as I felt the pull I released the line slowly, just enough to feel the pull and make the spinner revolve without spoiling the natural drift. It was quite deep when it passed me and I could just get a glimmer from the spinner.

I had let out about thirty feet of line and was considering a retrieve when something hit with a smash comparable to that of a grilse or a steelhead trout. The fight which followed was as pleasurable as that given by a scrappy rainbow trout of about 1½ pounds. The only thing missing was the aerial display. I thought I had at least a five-pounder, and was surprised when I beached the fish to find it weighed exactly 2½ pounds, was 15¾ inches long, and had a girth of twelve inches. He'd certainly acted like a lot more fish than that!

An experience like that is thrilling even to an old-timer. My prize was good-looking and well formed. I wished I'd found out about these fish long before. A neighboring angler came by and stopped, beaming with a friendly smile.

"What do you call these fish?" I asked.

"White or striped bass," was the reply. "They hit pretty well about this time of year, but this run is pretty well cleaned out. No doubt there'll be another along any time."

That was in November. No data that I had on hand or found at home showed a white bass migration of any sort at that time of year.

My spinner fly did not continue to produce, and half an hour passed without a touch. In the meantime my wife took one fish and Everett took two, using a regular, small-size water bass plug, colored something like a minnow. The most successful anglers that morning were all using that pearl-colored saltwater type of plug, so I ransacked my kit in hopes of finding a fly-rod counterpart. The nearest to it that I had was a surface minnow made of balsa wood. I'd made it myself, giving it a bluish-black and white belly. At first I tried it as it was, but it didn't work. Then I put on a sinker heavy enough to sink it, but that was no improvement, for while the lure had action on the surface, the sinker destroyed it. So I took off the lead and attached a spinner. This gave the lure the proper sinking quality and apparently the right action, for the fish responded generously. The lure was a bit clumsy for fly-rod work, especially with the steep bank behind me, but I could handle it well enough to get by, and once in the water it had an enticing appearance to the fish.

Those white bass have intrigued me. Unfortunately, we only had one more day at Buchanan Lake, and as I needed some photographs I spent that day taking pictures instead of fishing. However, I found that pork-rind lures are good for white bass, as are some wobbling spoons and small plugs. Certainly we'll be going back for another try at those fish. I've got myself a new outfit which I believe will be ideal for use on these bass as it will make it easy for me to use more suitable lures—lures too heavy for a fly rod, yet too light for the average bait-casting rod. The rod is seven feet long and limber enough to afford plenty of action. The reel is the true spinning type. With it, lures less than ¼ of an ounce in weight cast with incredible ease. I'm just hoping that the white bass will be in the river when I get there. If they are, there'll be something to tell.

CHAPTER X

A Sure Way to Catch Bass

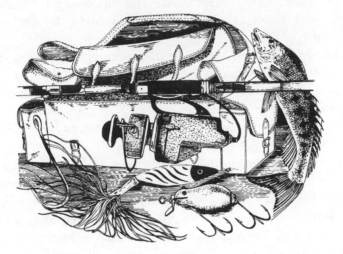

A FEW months ago I would have said anyone who claims he can always catch bass was either crazy or just bragging, but I'll listen politely now. It may be true.

My new faith in infallible bass fishing is the result of an invitation to fish with George Hary at a lake in central Florida. His letter reached me just when I was planning a fishing trip to Arkansas, Alabama and points south, but the mere convenience of the trip didn't influence me. Neither did George's technicolor description of the place. I was used to the glowing terms of resort advertising. The thing that sold me was the blunt statement that George absolutely guaranteed me bass each and every day I fished. If I didn't catch them, my stay there was free.

I finally arrived at the lake along with a nor'easter that had plagued us for a hundred miles or more. The wind was even worse the following two days. It kept us off the lake altogether. There was still only a slight lull on the third day, but George was impatient to put his boast on the board, so we went fishing.

My bass tackle, he claimed, was all wrong for the method he was going to show me. He insisted I use a rod that made me feel like Tom Thumb. It was a glass job cut down to about three feet in length, fitted with a bait-casting reel that held monofilament line of about twenty-pounds test. The lure was an odd-shaped nickel spoon about 2½ inches long, fastened to the line with a tiny snap.

With our poles ready in the boat, George opened up the motor as if to make a fast run to some distant hot spot, but I was surprised to see that he was letting out his line as he steered. He motioned for me to let mine out, too.

"Feel your spoon wiggle?" he yelled. I nodded. "Good," he came back. "Jerk your rod hard if you get a weed."

Before we had gone another fifty feet, George gave his rod a terrific jerk. At the same time I struck weeds. "Jerk it loose," he commanded. Not knowing what else to do, I heaved back on the rod with all my might. The spoon jerked free and wobbled perfectly again. Then George suddenly cut the motor. I glanced at his throbbing rod and reeled in to watch him land a good bass.

We fished about two miles of water like this; speeding along, jerking at weeds, feeling the spoon recover its vibrant wobble, only to hang up again. But we caught nine fair bass. And we continued to take them after we left the lake and trolled down the middle of the river that forms its outlet. I tried my fly rod on some sheltered coves in the river, but I couldn't even interest a panfish.

Then the wind strengthened until we decided to get back to camp. It was a wild ride, traveling at high speed through high, white-capped waves, but we trolled the spoons anyway, and darned if they didn't get several bass. Drenched by flying spray during the run back to camp, I climbed out of the boat and thought it all over. I wasn't sure I liked this kind of fishing. I'd never been wild about trolling, and this wasn't even like any trolling system I'd known.

My top speed for trolling previously was about the pace a man would set rowing a boat. Imagine running a five-horse motor near top speed on a small boat and catching bass behind it. Still I couldn't deny that the method worked. In fact we made our catch while other anglers on the lake were failing with orthodox systems. I suppose I resented this new strategy just because it seemed such a rough, coarse way to fish—almost like snagging them.

That was before I met Buck Perry, the fisherman who originated this method. Buck blew into camp just after I had returned from fishing. I had only a few words with him at the moment, but it was enough to make me conscious that I'd met a scholar as well as a fisherman. I wanted to hear more about his system then, but a friend of his from Wisconsin was waiting to go fishing. The wind was blowing a gale now, yet they hurried to get ready and were soon out on the lake. A few hours later they came in with two limits—and they'd released a lot of keepers.

I was just finishing supper that night when Buck stopped by. "Can you go out with me tomorrow?" he asked.

"I've been wishing you'd invite me," I replied. "You sure seem to have something. George gave me a taste of it this morning, and I guess he's safe in offering his 'No bass, no charge' challenge. But there must be more to it than what he showed me."

"Well, you're responsible for the system," Buck answered surprisingly. "Your books and articles, in which you pointed out the need for controlled depth, speed, and action in fishing different lures, gave me the idea. I had to make my own lure—in different weights and sizes—to get what I wanted. The result is the spoon and the system you saw. I call it spoon-plugging. Let me show you tomorrow."

The weather was still in a black mood the next morning. The same northeast wind was making Florida positively chilly. We stalled until about ten o'clock, hoping the wind would die. It got worse instead, but the air warmed a little, so we went out anyway. To dodge the soaking we'd get on open water, Buck headed for the east side of the lake where the wind was partly blocked by the swamp forest. We started trolling near the weeds, in comparatively shallow water, moving out some twenty feet farther when we got no response. There we picked up four bass in two trips across the same small area, so we anchored at that spot to try

casting. Buck tied on a larger version of the spoon he'd been trolling with, while I got out my spinning outfit and a spoon.

Buck's spoon took two bass to my one at the start. Then, since
the fish that struck seemed to be coming in from deeper water,
we moved out another hundred feet. Buck's lure, which hugged
the bottom throughout his retrieve, also performed better than
mine out there—until I started bringing mine in by alternately
reeling and letting it sink. Then we both hooked them fast. We
spent the rest of the day that way; trolling to locate fish, then
working the productive area by casting. But the casting was just
to liven the sport. It was more fun. But trolling—Buck's spoon-
plugging—was the deadly system. It seemed infallible.

The following day the weather got worse. There was no place
you could fish where the waves weren't rearing up and throwing
water with both hands. So we spoon-plugged, bouncing the little
flat-bottomed boat through the nor'easter with our spoons ripping
through the weeds. We caught our bass that way. Everybody on
the lake who used Buck's method took their limit. Those who
didn't came in talking about poor fishing.

I was already convinced, but Buck continued to sell his system during the next two days. The foul weather kept me on the
shore casting. I took quite a few small fish, but only one worth
mentioning. Buck always came in drenched to the hide and lug-
ging his limit. It was spoon-plugging that made the difference.
As Buck pointed out, it works because it gives you a chance to
control more factors that make fish strike. Those are the depth
fished, speed of lure, action of lure, and size and color of lure.
Buck claims the right combination of those things will take bass
every time, regardless of weather, barometer, or anything else.
"Bass never stop striking," he keeps repeating. "They just change
their locations and moods."

Buck's system is not intended to replace casting as a means of
taking bass. It's just a way to fill your stringer when casting won't
work. You can make systematic experiments with spoon-plugging
that will hit on the right combination sooner or later. Just follow
these general rules: start by casting in the shallow water—the
zone ranging from the shoreline out to a depth of about eight

feet. Small lures work best here as a rule, and this is also the place to try your surface lures. If they fail, move out past the eight-foot zone and start trolling along the shore. (Generally you'll want to use a bright lure for a bright day, a dark one for a dark day.) With your lure at moderate depth, experiment with fast and slow trolling. Still no fish? Get your lure down deeper, bouncing off the bottom if need be, and vary your trolling speeds again. You'll soon find a combination of speed, depth, action, and lure that works. When you do, stick to it—but only while it works. Don't get so sold on one combination that you won't junk it when it fails you. Find still another combination when conditions change. It's easy to do that with spoon-plugging. That's the beauty of the system.

Spoon-plugging has a way of digging the fish out, whether you have to scrape them off the bottom in deep water or gouge them out of the weeds in the shallows. This Florida trip offered a good illustration of what it will do with fish that are holed up in the weeds in shallow water. We cast over such a stretch with surface plugs and bugs without getting a touch. So we spoon-plugged at high speed. Our lures tore through so many weeds we were fouled seventy percent of the time, but we took four bass on our first pass.

Sure, spoon-plugging sounds cockeyed. I hardly think I'd believe it myself if someone told me about it. But, dammit, this really happened. I had hold of one of the rods.

CHAPTER XI

Times and Places for Bait Casting

WHEN I speak of bait casting, I mean fishing with a short and comparatively stiff rod fitted with a multiplying, revolving-spool reel. This reel—ordinarily filled with line of about fifteen-pound test—is seated on top of the rod, and the outfit is used to cast heavy baits or artificial lures. So the term bait casting denotes the use of specific tackle combination, in the sense that a spinning outfit or a fly rig combines a particular kind of rod, reel, and line.

Bait-casting outfits were originated in this country and have remained substantially the same in design through about half a century of widespread use. They've acquired a lot of fans who are all for this delicate but aggressive style of fishing—and a few enemies who have trouble developing the skilled touch bait-casting outfits require. Fly-rod addicts have tried to do all their fishing with fly tackle; and spinning gear, which so deftly casts light lures, has in recent years won over a lot of anglers. But there's still no substitute for a bait-casting outfit in a lot of fishing situations.

Let's go fishing, as I have, and see how it works out in actual practice. And keep in mind that I'm a devoted fly fisherman and a willing wielder of spinning tackle when conditions suggest that either of those rigs would do a better job than bait-casting gear.

The first time I fished the waters impounded behind an Ozark dam I felt sure that the bass there could be handled with my favorite fly rod. So I set out in a boat with companions who had bait-casting tackle and began whipping out an assortment of fly-rod surface bugs. The result: two hours without a strike—and all the while my boatmates were taking fish regularly.

Next I tried a spinning outfit, mainly because I hoped to show these skeptical friends what spinning gear could do. The light surface-working lures I flipped out with this new tackle didn't interest the bass, though the lures I used were a smaller version of the surface plugs my partners were using with success.

Then I tried on an underwater spoon that had paid off big on other lakes. The spoon hooked bass all right, but the light spinning line simply wouldn't hold them. They weren't monster fish. It was the flooded brush that made them tough. At the sting of the hook they'd dive for these underwater jungles, and my six-pound test spinning line was too frail to stop them. When I put on a spool of eight-pound test line and one of the heavy top-water lures my friends were using, the springy spinning pole and the stretch of the line cost me a big bass because my outfit lacked the beef to sink heavy hooks past the barb.

I ended my troubles that day by turning at last to bait-casting tackle. Using it, I could give a heavy plug just the action the bass wanted, which took a kind of control my spinning tackle wouldn't give me. Gone, too, was the discouraging business of losing fish and lures in the sunken brush. The sturdy bait-casting rig would turn and hold them.

On another trip I actually planned the outing as a demonstration of the good work ultra-light tackle would do. We were on a weedy bay on the Canadian side of Lake Erie, a stretch that was obviously better suited to bait-casting tackle, but I started fishing for bass with a fly outfit just to try to prove my point.

In short, I failed. Fly tackle wouldn't handle the kind of lures needed to power through those weeds, nor would it hold a frantic bass once you hooked him. Okay, fly tackle's too fragile, I realized, but how about spinning gear which is just a little sturdier? My test casts quickly answered that question. Spinning gear was even more troublesome than the fly outfit. Weary of my experiments, I fitted a casting reel full of twelve-pound line on a sturdy 5½-foot bait rod and started muscling weed-shedding plugs through and over the tops of weeds. This was the rig that caught bass.

There's an idea prevalent these days that small lures, the sort that spinning outfits cast so well, catch more fish than large ones. I think it's decidedly true, if you count all the small fish that small lures take. But I believe big fish more often go for a large mouthful—the kind of lure a bait-casting outfit throws so well.

I recall one trip that dramatically supports the idea that big fish go for large lures. A friend and I were on a lake in the far West that has some really big largemouth bass. This fishing pal knew the water well and started me off with some good advice: "Big lures for the big ones," he urged.

"I agree with the rule," I said, "but I want to make a test case of this outing. I'm going to try some fly-rod and spinning lures, little ones."

What happened was that I caught about ten fish to my friend's one—but my larger ones were under two pounds, while his ranged from two to five pounds. My big chance of the day came at dusk, after my partner had quit fishing to handle the boat for my experiments with spinning gear and a huge bass bug. The bulky bug was light and had too much air resistance to handle well, but I finally got out a good cast that hooked a breath-taking bass.

Knowing that the limber rod and elastic line required quite a jolt to set hooks in a tough-mouthed fish, I gave the bass an extra sock to make sure the barb went home. Then I settled down for a long tussle. As the exhausted bass neared the boat we got a good look at him—at least eight pounds and all but whipped, coasting in so we could see the artificial bug far back in his open mouth. Then, almost in reach, the bass seemingly spit the bug out. No yank or quick pressure. He just blew it into my face. Obviously I hadn't been able to sink the hook past the barb with two hard strikes. One would have been enough with bait-casting tackle.

About the same thing—either losing fish or netting them and having the hook shake out of their mouths a second later—has happened to me often when I'm using fairly coarse hooks on delicate tackle. Often enough that I'm convinced the hook never drives in past the barb.

If you've ever tried to release a fish by giving it slack line, you'll know that a well-hooked fish is hard to lose in that way. The one exception is a fish that's jumping and shaking a heavy lure that's swinging outside of his mouth. I like to keep a tight line when a jumper comes up with a lure swinging. Tension on the line keeps the lure from flopping about so much and reduces the chance of it being flung out entirely. Bait-casting tackle does this in fine style, while the lighter rigs are a little short on the power and line strength needed.

Bait-casting tackle is also my choice for fishing that requires a deep-running lure. The weight you need to get down there and maneuver a lure requires power in your tackle, and bait-casting gear, for all the delicacy it takes to use it artfully, is at home on rough, tough waters.

It's not super tackle. Don't get me wrong. Used where it doesn't belong, bait-casting gear will fail you completely. But nothing works better when fish, water, and other conditions call for big lures, strong lines, and quick, positive control.

Bait-casting tackle has improved considerably in recent years. Perhaps this is due to the surge of interest in spinning tackle. Competition often brings about improvements in older equipment that has been riding along nonchalantly. Anyway, there has been a great advancement in the quality of bait-casting rods, reels, and lines.

The old-time bait tackle was heavy and unresponsive. The rods were rigid and clublike to handle, most of them only 4 to 4½ feet long, with some as short as three feet. The lures obtainable ran from ¾ of an ounce or heavier down to ⅝ of an ounce. These could be cast right well with the short stiff rods and the sluggish reels, but it took considerable skill to handle the outfit. Many never could master it. In expert hands, however, the combination caught plenty of fish, including many big ones. It didn't pick up so many small fish such as are often caught with the present spinning tackle and its small lures. Today the average rods made for bait-casting have a pleasant degree of limberness and lightness that makes them really sporting to fish with. At the same time they have the additional backbone that the average spinning rod lacks.

Some of the bait-casting reels made today are as easy to use as the "fool-proof" spinning reels. Any reel does better work in the hands of a skillful operator, of course, but modern bait-casting reels have such fixtures as anti-backlash devices and adjustable drags that allow a beginner to do creditable casting with them. There was a time when I had almost abandoned my bait-casting tackle in favor of spinning equipment. New developments in bait-casting rods and reels have won me back. The bait-casting gear has positive advantages for several kinds of fishing.

I consider at least thirty days of fishing necessary for a good field test of a new item of fishing tackle. The following evaluations concern only the bait-casting rods, reels, and lines that I have used that long or longer.

My choice for an all-around bait-casting rod is a hollow-glass job 5½ feet long. It should be fairly stiff in the butt and limber in the tip. It handles lures of ⅝ to ⅜ of an ounce perfectly. With a free-spool reel it will also cast lures as light as ¼ of an ounce nicely.

If you're a light-lure enthusiast, you may be more satisfied with a six-foot bait-casting rod. Many fishermen claim that the longer rod will cast light lures better and also give more pleasure when playing a fish. Personally, I haven't found this so. I've used a six-footer a lot, but finally chose the 5½-footer as my all-around choice. Some of the fellows I fish with use and prefer 4½- or 5-foot bait rods made of solid glass instead of the lighter hollow glass. Some still use metal rods. They do great casting with them, too.

A split-bamboo bait rod is one of the finest instruments in the fishing tackle field, but a good one costs a great deal more money than a glass rod. And bamboo rods need far more care than glass, which needs very little. The best bamboo rods may take sets (permanent bends) in time. That doesn't happen with glass.

However, there's one company that makes split-bamboo rods that are impregnated with a plastic resin, and these rods resist set admirably. The impregnated rods are also waterproof and do not need varnishing, the finish being through the bamboo itself and not merely on the surface. While these rods are expensive, they are a delight to use and are showpieces of fine workmanship.

I suggest the offset style of handle for all bait-casting rods. In my opinion, and that of the majority of bait-casters, the offset reel is far more efficient than the straight-handle model that seats the reel several inches above the line of the rod. The reel is badly balanced and awkward to reach with the thumb when mounted on a straight-handle rod. Most manufacturers fit offset handles on their bait-casting rods these days.

My favorite bait-casting reel is a free-spool model with a level-wind device. It does a good job with both the light and heavy lures. There are still some old-style and rather sluggish bait-casting reels on the market. These are OK for weighty lures but rather trying with light ones.

One high-priced bait reel has a free spool that's made ready for casting by simply pushing in a convenient lever. At the end of the cast, gears are engaged again the instant you start turning the handle for the retrieve. The spool can be regulated for casting lures of different weights by adjusting one of the hubcaps, which is appropriately marked. The spool can be further adjusted by changing the brake blocks to conform to the lure weight and your personal casting technique. Extra blocks are provided with each reel. The reel originally comes set up with brake blocks that are suitable for lures that weigh as little as ⅜ up to ¾ of an ounce.

When I started bait casting there were no reels with level-wind devices. You used your fingers to keep the line level on the spool. If you didn't do a good job of this, a bunch of line would build up on one side or the other. This made for poor casts and many backlashes. It wasn't too hard keeping the line even when re-trieving the lure; the trouble came when you hooked a fish, especially on a long cast. It was almost impossible to fight a fish without getting ridges of line on the spool. After the fish was landed, the line was in poor condition for the next cast. Nearly all modern reels have level-wind devices.

There's a good medium-priced reel on the market that's made with an anti-inertia spool. The spool starts fast with no drag and stops when the lure strikes the water. You won't have any back-lash with it if you adjust the spool cap properly for the lure weight. I've used it with lures from ¼ to ¾ of an ounce in weight and found it a pleasure to fish with.

There are some very sturdy, long-lasting bait reels which are extra good for casting lures of the heavier weights, for fishing fast water, and for trolling deep. If you're an excellent caster, you can also use these reels to cast lures as light as ¼ of an ounce.

A more modern type of bait-casting reel is made with a fixed spool and a closed face. It works like a spinning reel but sits on top of the reel seat the same as a standard bait-casting reel. With these reels you thumb a device on the reel to stop the cast, instead of putting the thumb on the line or against one edge of the spool as you do with a revolving-spool reel. Many folks prefer these new reels to any other, and so far as casting goes they are very good.

You really need two reels, the extra one filled with line and ready for immediate use if something goes wrong with your other reel. The extra reel can save the entire trip if your first reel breaks down in some out-of-the-way area where you'd planned to fish for several days. Bait-casting reels are rather intricate machines, and the best of them can be put out of order by hard knocks.

Before leaving bait-casting reels, let me say that I think a built-in drag on the reel is of great aid when playing large fish. You can set it to the strength of your line, making the drag a bit less than the line's breaking strength. Then you can play a heavy fish with-out worrying about breaking the line, because the set drag will feed out line when the pressure becomes too great. One company makes a "handle drag" to fit some of its reels. It's easily attached and very efficient, almost as good as a star drag. The handle drag is very low in cost.

Lines for bait casting may be either braided or monofilament. I prefer monofilament, unless I need a test heavier than ten pounds or a calibration greater than .014. Some reels are not built right for monofilament line, however. The thin line gets behind the spools and causes a devil of a mess. In order to handle light monofilament properly the spool ends of the bait reel must be very carefully fitted into the frame, so that the gap is too narrow to let the line work into the reel gears.

For me, 9½ to 12-pound test monfilament that calibrates about .014 in diameter serves very well for lures of from ⅜ to ¾ of an ounce. I use this size line more than any other. I can even use it to cast lures as light as ¼ of an ounce, if they are compact enough to offer little wind resistance. To cast wind-resisting lures or compact types lighter than ¼ of an ounce, I need a smaller line, say eight- to ten-pound test. When I want to use extremely light and hard-to-cast lures, I quit bait casting and turn to spinning tackle, which was originated to handle featherweight lures.

Some anglers prefer braided line for bait casting because it clings close to the spool instead of coiling outward, something that monofilament is very likely to do if given a little bit of slack. The latest monofilament is easy to handle in calibrations up to .014. Heavier monofilament may be difficult. For anything over 9½ to 12-pound test, I prefer braided lines. There's one exception: for deep fishing with a very heavy sinker or lure I much prefer the monofilament, often using as heavy as twenty-pound test.

Braided lines are best in those sizes ranging from twelve- to twenty-pound test and for casting lures in the ½ to ¾ of an ounce bracket. For casting with the heavier lures, especially for large muskies, pike, and lake trout, I usually use a braided line testing fifteen to eighteen pounds. In the case of lake trout. This is only when casting for them. When it's necessary to troll deep I prefer a wire line.

The extra strength of the braided line isn't needed to play a large fish in open water. But if you're fishing where weeds or snags are present you'll need this extra strength to keep a big fish away from such hazards. There's a need for both light, low-test mono-filament lines and for stronger, thicker braided lines. When choosing a bait-casting line, get the most suitable test and material for the conditions and the average size of the fish you expect to catch.

CHAPTER XII

Surface Lures for Black Bass

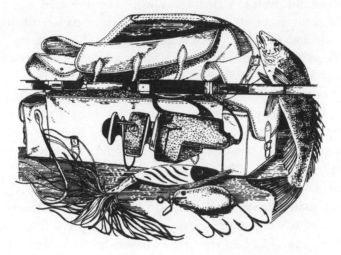

THE DAY at sunrise was quiet and clear. The little bass lake was glassy smooth, and I could see the ripples of surface-feeding fish along the edges of the weed beds that grew out in the shallows. I had no trouble making a decision about the type of lure to use. Everything I could see suggested surface lures. I set up my fly rod, an 8½-foot hollow-glass job that I wanted to try out with bass bugs.

After getting the fly-rod tackle ready, I thought, "It's calm now, but the wind may come up later, as it usually does. If the water gets rough, the bass bugs won't do much good, while top-water plugs will do fine if the bass stay in the shallow water."

So I set up a bait-casting outfit that would handle plugs from ⅜ through ⅝ of an ounce. The only other anglers going out were using minnows, worms, or other natural baits. They'd anchor in some favored spot and stay there, so I wouldn't have anyone else disturbing the shallow water I want to fish with floating lures.

Working my boat within easy casting distance of the first promising place, I stopped quietly and took my time about selecting a lure. It's wise to let things settle down before you cast. Because the lake was well populated with frogs and no large bugs were visible on the water, I tied on a hair frog I'd used for years, usually with excellent results. It was a combination of natural deer hair and deer hair dyed a pale yellow. The lure was light enough so that it cast almost as well as a large, bushy trout fly. Retrieved with slight twitches, it acted much like a live frog.

My boat was parked before a deep indentation in the weed front. There was plenty of surface activity here. I cast the frog well up into the open spot. A fish took before I had time to twitch the lure. It was a small bass, about a pound. I horsed it in and released it.

I waited until I saw another fish surface before I cast again. The fish didn't take immediately, so I let the hair frog rest there a moment or two and then gave it a pull to simulate a frog starting to swim away. The bass then took. It was hooked solidly, but in the lip, so it could be released without injury. This fish, about a 2½-pounder, was a spirited scrapper and it evidently scared off the other fish.

I waited about fifteen minutes and cast well up in the indentation again. I worked the lure back for perhaps twelve feet without getting any rise. I had started to lift the fake frog for another cast, when a really nice bass struck viciously. I played this big fish to a finish with a warm feeling of satisfaction.

My hot spot was quiet again for about ten minutes. Then a slight breeze started moving the boat. I let it drift until the air had become still again. Then I eased the craft back within easy casting range of the weed beds. You can't do good work when you're straining for distance with fly-rod casts.

There was surface action all along the weed bed now. I dropped the hair frog on the water just a few seconds after I saw a bass rise. I let it rest quietly for about thirty seconds and then gave it some movement. Then I let it lie still another twenty or thirty seconds and gave it some more action. Again I let it rest. At that point a good-size bass swallowed the lure. I boated him and two others before fishing conditions changed.

It was a brilliant day, the kind that often comes after showers the preceding evening. I had decided to fish that day for this very reason, for such a weather change, with a rising barometer reading, usually brings fish to the surface to feed. But you may also get a fairly stiff wind as such a day advances. This time the wind started early in the morning, and in a short time the breeze stiffened so that casting with a fly rod was difficult. Besides, the boat began drifting so fast that I couldn't fish the fly-rod lure effectively when I did manage a good cast.

But I'd brought along the bait-casting outfit to cope with the roughening weather and water. The rod was a $5\frac{1}{2}$-footer, made of tubular glass, reasonably limber. The reel was a free-spool, level-wind model, and the line a $9\frac{1}{2}$-pound test monofilament.

I was at a disadvantage because I was alone. When fishing with surface lures of any kind, you can't do a first-class job unless the boat stays in one spot while you're working the lure. If you have a man at the oars or paddle who knows how to keep you placed right for the fishing, you may do right well in rough water. Lacking such a helper, I had a choice of anchoring in a good location, quitting, or changing to underwater lures.

Since it was too early for me to think about quitting and I had no underwater lures with me, I picked out a place where I could anchor within casting range of a good area of underwater weeds. By this time waves four inches high were battering the weed border. To me this suggested a rather large plug and one that would cause considerable surface disturbance when jerked. I picked out a $\frac{5}{8}$-ounce surface lure of this type.

Working the weed border first and gradually circling all around the boat, I had six strikes and hooked two fish. The two bass I hooked came from the weed border. This was understandable, because when fishing this edge I was casting with the wind, so it was easy to keep tension on the line. When fishing against the wind, I'd have short periods of slack-line inertia as I jerked the lure, and the fish in this water struck and then rejected the lure before I could set the hook.

I circled the area with casts again, using the same lure. This time I had two strikes and missed both. One hit came at the weed border, the other out over the sunken weed beds. The one at the border was missed because the boat happened to swing violently just as the fish took; the other bass took when the line was slack.

I changed to another lure—a very old pattern that for years has served me well in all sorts of water. The body of this top-water lure doesn't have any action; the attraction is the metal propeller at the head. The plug itself floats high, and the spinning blade whirls at the slightest touch. It even flashes and whirls in the air while being cast. It revolves and makes a noise being retrieved.

Because the waves were so high by this time, I fished the lure fast enough to make the propeller sing above the sound of wind and waves. In still water, it's best to fish this lure just fast enough to make the blade revolve a few times every twenty seconds or so. But in rough water I have always found it produces best when reeled very fast.

I made the first cast quartering with the wind. I'd retrieved about five feet of line when a bass took and was hooked. Though the boat was swinging from one side to the other, it didn't keep me from hooking the fish because the lure was traveling fast and the bass grabbed it recklessly. I made the next cast quartering into the wind and hooked another bass.

Next I cast directly into the wind, during a lull between strong gusts. The plug had just hit the water when a strong gust hit. I reeled like mad and suddenly got a heavy strike, hooking the best fish of the morning. Now, I believe this fish might have struck some other type of lure, but another sort of lure probably wouldn't have hooked it. With the propeller plug, which can be reeled in steadily without loss of action, I was reeling so fast the fish was automatically hooked.

When I had completed the circle of casts this time, I had hooked and landed two more bass. The wind was getting worse, however, and the waves higher. I tried one more time around, but didn't get another hit. The water was so rough now that fishing was decidedly unpleasant, so I headed for the dock, well satisfied with what I'd already caught.

Now, that was a good morning of surface-lure fishing. I've had some better, but many more that were worse. There are times when you can't get a nibble with surface lures, even though you can see surface-feeding fish. And there are other times when bass that haven't shown on the surface at all will come up to smash a surface lure.

In my experience, it's always worthwhile to give the top-water lures a try in shallow water, even if you don't see fish rising. Of course it would be foolish to fish over deep water with them, and this is usually true even if fish are breaking the surface.

My favorite strategy with surface lures, one I use first when trying out smooth-surfaced water, is to cast to a promising spot and let the lure float motionless for from thirty seconds to a minute. At times I have found it best to wait as long as three minutes before moving the lure. Since seconds pass slowly in such an expectant situation, you're likely to consider twenty or thirty seconds a full minute, and it may take a full minute's pause to get results. Time a few of these waits with your watch to learn how long they are.

Why is it often necessary to let the lure lie still for some time after it hits the water? Well, the splash of the lure may frighten the fish enough to make him dart away several feet or more. If you start to move the lure immediately the fish goes still farther away, and if you persist in retrieving the lure it soon gets out of sight. But if you let the lure lie still for at least a minute, the fish won't run far. It will pause, then turn to look back at the disturbance. If about this time you give the lure movement, say even a slight twitch, the fish will think it live food and return to investigate. But such fish are on the cautious side, so you must avoid excessive disturbance. That is, don't jerk the lure roughly, but make it look alive.

Now suppose you're casting to fish that are rather sleepy and uninterested. If you immediately move the lure away after it alights, such fish will just let it go, giving no response whatever.

[109]

But if you let the lure lie still for a time, twitch it, and let it lie still again, you may arouse the interest of sluggish fish. A few pauses, twitches, and jerks at this time are likely to provoke a strike.

Now we come to the fish that happen to be some distance away from where your lure drops. They may see the slight surface disturbance as your lure hits, but it often won't be pronounced enough to interest them. If you keep working a lure at this place long enough, following the pause, twitch, and jerk routine, you may draw such fish to your bait. It may take a number of casts to do the trick.

Of course, you can't chart the exact location of each fish in advance and judge whether he's sleepy or nervously alert. You simply try one approach after another until you hit on one that works. In some cases you'll be casting to a spot where there are no bass. And, since the fish move about during the day, an area in the shallows that produces lots of action at first may taper off abruptly as a change in weather or other conditions cause the fish to move to deeper water. Surface lures are usually a waste of time when the fish are down deep.

Sometimes a surface lure that's cast out and left motionless long enough will be hit by a bass before you start giving it action. Always be prepared for this. Many fish are missed because the strike comes when you least expect it, at a time when you're feeling that your efforts are useless. Be alert all the time your surface lure is on the water.

Here's another good general tip: after you've given the lure the beginning twitches, pauses, and jerks, work it back to you with a feeling for its particular design. If it's a frog-like lure, try to make it act like a frog. A minnow-like lure should be made to swim like a minnow, especially an injured one. With a lure resembling a moth or other large insect, make it flutter and quiver on the water. A popping or noise-making lure should pop or splash. All that may sound rather obvious, yet I've noticed that most anglers fish all lures about the same way, regardless of the design of the lure.

Often bass need to be teased or shocked into rising to the surface lure. This is particularly true for the discolored waters largemouth bass thrive in. Poppers, plunkers, chuggers, and other such noisy lures are excellent for this. When jerked, they make a noise you can hear and a water disturbance you can see. They will sometimes work on smallmouth as well as largemouth bass, if the smallmouths are in discolored water and feeding on the surface. (By discolored water I mean that which is normally so, not water discolored by excessive rain or some other reason.)

There are scores of different popping bugs, plopping spinning lures, and plunking bait-casting plugs on the market. Most are good, too, if you know how to handle them individually rather than collectively. The secret of their attraction is the disturbance they make when handled properly. I wouldn't think of going bass fishing without some of these noisy surface-disturbing lures along, either in fly-rod, spinning, or bait-casting weights.

Often bass are selective, as is shown by the following experience I had on a California lake. At the start of this piece I told you of a fly-rod-size frog lure I used successfully on an Eastern lake. That deer-hair frog was the first thing I tried on this lake. It was weedy, somewhat like the Eastern lake, but this time my pet frog lure didn't do any good, while a green cork-body popping lure that didn't look or act much like a frog really brought fish to the boat. Perhaps color had something to do with this as well as the popping action.

All morning a friend and I fished that lake steadily without getting a rise. I was using that natural-action yellowish frog lure, and my friend was using a white-and-red popper. At lunch time we stopped to talk with the proprietor of a boat dock on the lake, and he showed us a green cork-body popping frog. He said it was very good on this lake, so I bought several. My friend declined, saying that if his white-and-red bug didn't take them, nothing else would.

After lunch we parked our boat in casting range of a sizable pocket of open water among the weeds near shore. Just then it started to rain. It was a gentle rain of medium-size drops spaced widely apart, and they made a musical murmur as they hit the water. The feel of them on our bodies was delightful, because the day had been hot and the drops dried as they hit our exposed skin and clothes.

My friend stuck to his red-and-white popper, but I tied on one of the new green-frog poppers. Both of us made a cast, waited a minute, then jerked our lures. No response. I gave my lure a few more tugs and still nothing happened.

"It's the same old story," I thought. "If they're not taking, it doesn't matter what you use; you just can't get them."

I took my eyes off the lure and turned to suggest to my friend that we might as well quit. Just then I heard a splash and felt a tug on my rod. I was too surprised to strike, so I didn't hook the fish.

I retrieved the green popper and made a cast to another likely spot. On the third jerk a nice bass struck and was hooked. The rain was coming down a bit harder now, but the suddenly good fishing minimized its discomfort. I took three more bass while my friend did nothing with his white-and-red popper. Then I handed him a green popper, and after he started fishing it he began to take bass.

We had lots of sport until we got soaked to the hide and began to shiver. It occurred to me that I should try some other popper beside the green frog. Maybe the bass had just started to feed when I used the green frog. So I tried a yellow popper. It didn't produce, though my friend took several more bass with the green popper while I was experimenting. By this time the rain had become a downpour, our lines were sinking, and it was getting cold. We quit.

Talking the experience over, we decided the green popping frog had been responsible for our success. But was it the color, the action, or a combination of both that made the lure effective? I'm not sure.

As to frog-like lures, I think the small ones generally work best. The larger size aren't readily taken by the average run of fish, though the bass of "tackle-buster" size may well take a big frog lure if it happens to be in the mood to take anything. Frog lures in small fly-rod and spinning-tackle sizes are all right. For bait-casting tackle I would choose lures other than frog types.

Many fish are more interested in feeding on minnows than on anything else. A crippled minnow struggling at the surface is a particularly attractive dish because it's easy prey. It was this fact that years ago led to the invention of floating, crippled-minnow-action plugs and fly-rod lures. When spinning came into vogue, spinning lures of this type were soon on the market. An injured minnow flounders on the surface, keeps trying to go down, but immediately comes to the top again. The minnow-like surface lure that best duplicates this action will be the one with which you'll catch the most fish.

It's my opinion that the most important thing in surface fishing is selecting the best lure for the time and place. Next is giving the lure you've selected the right action according to its design. This requires an intimacy with each individual lure that you use. That is, you must know it so well that you usually fish it only when it should be fished and handle it so it performs to the best advantage. Once you get to know a lure well, you'll catch more fish with it. Your own personality enters into this, incidentally; the way a lure works will be a joy to one angler and a curse to another.

Often when fishing waters I didn't know, I have gone fishless with my favorite top-water lures while local fishermen did well with some other surface lure. I have always changed to the lure they were using, but never did catch fish with it until I learned to handle it right.

Once you recognize the possibilities of different lures and learn to give them proper action, you'll begin to catch more fish and get more enjoyment from angling. If we anglers would vary our tactics as readily as bass change their range and their moods we'd catch those bass that "just ain't bitin'" about as often as not. Most of us are too loyal to old, established systems—pet lures, patterned retrieves, and favorite places in the waters we fish. That's all well and good, as long as it works. The mistake is in trying to force it on fish when they're obviously not interested. Those are the days when it takes a new approach to catch bass.

I've recently experimented with two such change-of-pace systems that are certainly worth knowing. One is fast trolling, the

strategy I named spoon-plugging when I discussed it in an earlier
chapter. The other is bottom-digging, a way of working a lure so
that it bounces along the bottom, or perhaps is actually dug into
the sand or mud on the bottom with the line pressure and left
resting there for some time. A tug on the line makes it seem to
leap out of hiding then, and bass just can't stand to see it get
away.

Buck Perry of North Carolina sold me on spoon-plugging
with his first demonstrations. I've tested it thoroughly since then,
at times when conventional methods failed, and it's done so well
that I think I can let the facts speak for the system.

Some friends and I fished for bass last summer in Lake Cham-
plain on the New York-Vermont border. Thunderheads were
drifting across the lake when we started fishing near Burlington,
Vermont. It was hot and oppressive as the threatening clouds
boiled up over this beautiful valley between the peaks of the
Adirondacks and the Green Mountains. We suspected we were
in for a storm but we pushed our boat out onto the lake anyway.
The storm soon hit us, first with a rush of wind and quick flurries
of rain, then with a short furious blast. That blew over and left
us in a quiet lull that hinted another outburst was on the way.

The weather was directing our fishing this day. While the
strong wind lasted, we worked a shallow, protected bay. It didn't
produce. Then we took advantage of the lull and ran out to troll
along the shoreline of an island. I got a strike the first pass. That
indicated that trolling was going to get us some fish, once we
worked out the best combination of trolling speed, depth, and
type of lure.

We began experimenting. A small, shallow-running lure
brought some strikes as we trolled near the shore; a deep-running
plug interested the fish in deeper water. So we mulled this over
for a moment and came up with a system the bass readily went
for—a deep-running lure trolled fast in deep water. It worked
best when it actually dug into the bottom occasionally, traveling
the floor of the lake in long bounces.

This unorthodox blend of spoon-plugging and bottom-digging
provoked strikes steadily all the time we used it. We had trouble

with our outboard motor for a while that afternoon and were unable to get enough speed out of it for good spoon-plugging. During that time we didn't get a strike. When the balky motor sputtered back to a fast clip the fish started hitting again.

Two of us tried casting from shore while our outboard was stalled. All we got was one grammar-school smallmouth bass. And we had still another chance to compare our trolling system with other methods when we docked that evening and talked to other fishermen who'd been out. They'd been trolling at the conventional speed, just fast enough to turn a trolling spinner, and none of them had a decent catch. Our fish were not big, but we boated and released so many of them that we lost count.

But don't get the idea that racing around a lake pulling a nickel spoon will always get bass. When you start using it that way, it's just another Old Reliable that's going to fail you when conditions change. This was shown very clearly on a lake in central Florida where successful demonstrations of fast trolling started a lot of anglers using the system. It worked fine in September, when fish were hard to take otherwise, but by January things had changed and those anglers who refused to change their system to suit the bass started getting skunked.

One man in particular complained vehemently in January. He wasn't catching anything at spoon-plugging speeds, but he was just grouching about the system, not changing it. He had yet to learn that cool water required slow trolling, sometimes a lure moving so slowly it was more like jigging on the bottom than trolling. Too, most of the bass had moved to deeper water, out past the shoreline stretches of from two to seven feet deep where most anglers want to fish throughout the year.

This man caught bass when he altered his style to suit the season, but he still wasn't satisfied. He wanted a really big bass. That called for a lure drifted to the bottom on a slack line and worked so that it alternately lay motionless and drifted slowly for a few inches or feet. Those were just general instructions for catching a big bass there at that time of year. Nobody expected the approach to pay off immediately. But this man, armed with the new strategy, went straight out and caught a seven-pounder.

Bottom-digging can be used with several variations. Take the one that we used in western North Carolina during some early spring fishing. We had started by going over the shallows thoroughly and hadn't caught a thing. Then, as we moved to another location, we noticed fish darting out to deeper water from positions right against the shore. Our boat was frightening them for a considerable distance while they were in the shallows, so fast trolling obviously wasn't a sound approach. What to do?

We saw that the bass were congregating along the deep edge of an underwater sandbar that sloped out from the shore. They were skittish, but perhaps we could ease in from deeper water with the boat and get them with long casts. We tried that with a variety of lures, but our routine casts didn't do any good. That's when we tied on deep-running lures and gave bottom-digging a try.

We cast these heavy-lipped spoons right up on the shore, flipped them back onto the submerged sandbar, and slowly dragged them toward us until they were almost buried in the sand. After letting these burrowing lures lie motionless for a moment, we jerked back so that they jumped off the bottom in little spurts of sand. We quickly caught our limits this way.

A minor variation of the bottom-digging technique helped three other anglers take limits in Mississippi in the fall. Two of these men were fishing below a flood-control dam with fly rods and live minnows. They reported the place was lousy with bass, but they had taken only one—"just aren't biting."

A small spoon retrieved rapidly, so that it bumped along the bottom, changed all that. It took forty-five minutes of experimenting to arrive at this system (a larger lure fished the same way did almost as well), but the results were well worth the trouble. The two fellows using minnows switched to small spoons and immediately caught limits by hopping them along the bottom. Another man walked up to investigate and stayed to take his limit by leap-frogging one of the little spoons. When the retrieve was just right, the system worked so well it seemed the stream bed was carpeted with fish. They went crazy for it. When one hooked fish threw the lure, another would slash it as it flew free.

I could list a good many other happy experiences with fast trolling and bottom-digging. I've altered them, combined them, and used them in a variety of ways with good results. If one such combination doesn't work, I move to another kind of water—from the shallows out to deep water, for example. (After a mediocre showing fishing the shallows, Buck Perry and I once followed a deep bar until we were a mile and a half out in the lake. That's where the bass were, and a big lure skipped along the bottom took them left and right.) You have to fish where the fish are to catch them with any system.

Of course there's no point in racking your brain for a novel method of taking bass on those days when they're gobbling up topwater or shallow-running plugs tossed out with conventional casts. If they're going for poppers, flies, or natural bait, feed them what they want and save your ingenuity for those times when you need it. When that happens look the situation over and think it through. There's seldom a time when some approach won't catch bass, and some form of bottom-digging or spoon-plugging will sharpen the appetites of a great many fish that "ain't biting" anything else.

CHAPTER XIII

Surface Bugs and Flies

BASS-BUGGING is a type of fly-rod fishing that was born and raised right here in America. Considering that most fly fishing dates well back into English history, it's a young sport, young enough that as a boy I was among the first to fish these big bugs in this way.

I was born and still live in the Hudson River valley north of New York City, and for years I was the only bass-bugger in a big area of many bass waters and fishermen. Shortly after I was old and prosperous enough to have a bicycle, I got hold of some big, beautiful artificials made of cork, feathers, and deer hair. They were so well tied that I hated to get them wet, but I had a strong urge to try them on bass. I had in mind a lake five miles from home.

My bike had a flat tire when I got up at two thirty a.m. and I'd run out of the rubber plugs used to fix the tire. So I walked to the lake, a shallow one where bass were plentiful and often fed on the surface. It was August—hot and oppressive even at that early hour. A heavy fog hung over the lake when I arrived, although the surrounding land was clear except where coils of mist snaked out from the water. I was the first one on the boat dock, and the wise old fisherman who ran the place had time to talk and examine my long fly rod and bass bugs carefully.

"The bugs look good," he said, "but there ain't been a bass caught here all week—'cept a few on live minnies. Been getting a few pickerel and lots of bluegills, though."

This didn't sound promising, but I'd read a little about the new idea of taking bass with fly-rod bugs and had formed a lot of vivid mental pictures in which bass of great size and earnestness assaulted my bugs. I was going to give them a thorough test.

My first few casts were most discouraging. I was an experienced caster with a light trout rod and small flies, but this combination of long rod and big artificials wrapped line and leader around me a dozen times before I got the hang of it. (Later I learned that, for one thing, my line was much too light for the rod and bug.) I finally improved my timing enough to make decent casts of about thirty-five feet, and this was plenty for this particular water.

But I got no response to any of my casts. Was I handling the bug right? Was it the wrong time of day? Maybe the stuff I'd read about these new bugs was a lot of bunk. Anyway, the hours passed with me still fishless. The fog was long gone and the sun bore down on a lake surface smooth as a mirror. The knowledge that half a dozen old-timers fishing the place with plugs and natural baits were also getting skunked didn't ease my disappointment at all.

I kept trying until by the sun and my stomach I judged it was one p.m. Then I let the boat drift while I opened the lunch I'd packed. As an afterthought I cast the bug out as far as I could and let it trail along with the gentle drift of the boat while I ate. It was a habit I had from bait fishing. But I had so little confidence in the idea that I forgot the rod and bug and puzzled over my frustrating morning.

Before I'd finished my second sandwich I heard the rod and reel bang against the side of the boat. My quick grab barely saved the tackle from going overboard. It was too late to set the hook in the big bass that swirled to the surface and spit out my artificial bug.

Lunch was forgotten. I didn't even take time to put it back in the box, for the incident suggested—and correctly, as it turned out—that if I let the bug rest quietly on the surface for longer periods, or only moved it very slowly, the bass would hit it. They did, and as a result I discovered one of the first principles of bass-bugging: Let your bug rest quietly on the surface for about a minute after each cast and then move or twitch it very gently. It generally ruins your chances to retrieve or move a fly-rod bass bug as quickly as you would a spinner or plug.

When I left the lake that night I had six nice largemouths and would've had quite a few more but for faulty timing on my strikes. The total catch of all the other boats was one whopping bass taken on a surface plug, and four keepers hooked with live bait. I've been a bass-bugging enthusiast ever since.

It was a lonely sort of fishing for several years. Most other anglers considered the system a kind of foolishness, and there was very little published information about bugging for bass. Mostly I learned by trial and error. Certain kinds of water, I discovered, were much better adapted to bass-bugging than others; the shallower waters with lots of weeds or other underwater cover paid off best. I also saw that an artificial bug imitating a bug needed one kind of handling, while a big-size imitation mouse needed another. Sometimes I did better by giving up bugs altogether and fishing with bait or plugs. Other times, when I correctly judged that conditions were right for bugs, I used them to dramatically outscore the anglers using bait and plugs.

My experience on Lake Mead in Nevada was typical. Three of us were fishing from a single boat that was handled by a guide. My two fishing companions were throwing plugs with bait-casting gear and I, though this open water hardly suggested bass bugs, was bass-bugging just to see what would happen.

During five days of calm water I caught most of the bass taken by our party. The best bugging water was close to the rocky cliffs and I had the good fortune to have a guide who would steer me along them slowly enough for the big flies to do their work. After the fifth day the wind came up and my plug-casting companions got even with me, taking fish regularly while my bugs were by and large ignored. There are bug days and plug days, you see. Rough water ordinarily suggests poor bass-bugging. With any surface blown beyond the wavelet stage, you'll probably do better with another system.

A California outing on a lake smooth as a mirror sticks in my mind as one that taught me another bass-bugging lesson. It was beautiful summer weather and the lake shallows were lined with weeds and sunken trees that appeared to me ideal for bass, yet the local people I talked to at the lake tried to discourage me. Bass action had been slow for several weeks.

Briefly, the right kind of bug seemed to turn the trick here. I first cast myself into a lather of sweat without getting a strike on any of my usual patterns. Then I tied on a froggy bug made of green-painted cork, with bucktail legs. A nice bass smacked this oddity on the first cast, and I used it to take five more keepers— this on a day when other fishermen went without a nibble.

And on another California lake further north I learned to cast to pockets and wait patiently for my bug to make an impression on the bass waiting in the nearby shallows. This was another day that started with discouraging results. I spent the morning on a boat where the person rowing never got the knack of placing me in range of a likely spot or moving at just the right—slow and easy—speed. My casts would land and rest quietly for a second or two, then the motion of the boat would drag them over the surface. The bass didn't go for this abrupt action.

Then at noon we went ashore to eat and I walked the bank to where a belt of weeds grew up through shallow water about fifty feet offshore. There were many open pockets of water among the weeds so I stripped off line to try to drop a bug in one of them. My first cast hit the mark and I let it rest motionless there for at least thirty seconds. Then I switched my rod from side to side so the hair-wing bug made just a slight ripple. A good bass had it in an instant.

That same strategy—casting to pockets, waiting, then twitching the bug—was the answer for this lake and this time. It's a consistent producer in many places. As a rule it works better in shallow water, say five feet or less—perhaps a little deeper than five feet if the water is very clear.

Florida bass liked my bugs, too. On one small river there I fished with some plug-casters along a stretch that held a lot of snook as well as black bass. My surface bug hooked bass left and right, but the snook ignored it. The plug-casters got lots of snook but no bass. There was no planning in this; it was just the way it worked out. And all during that trip, which was at a time when the water was low and as clear as it ever gets, floating bass bugs were decidedly the bass-killers supreme in a series of tests that compared them with a wide assortment of other flies and lures.

I could go on telling you how bass bugs catch bass, but let me mention that they also make good catches of northern pike and pickerel. For these two, you need a heavier leader to prevent your bug getting cut off by their sharp teeth. Other than that the strategy is much the same as with bass—assuming, of course, that you always keep your eyes and mind open and vary your approach to meet various conditions.

Perhaps my most surprising catch on a bass bug was an Atlantic salmon. I had fished for ten days on this salmon river, taking a fish periodically with regular salmon flies—standard patterns fished wet. But neither I nor anyone else in our party had been able to hook the bigger fish. Six pounds was our upper limit.

I had had the bass-bug idea for some time before I had the nerve to try it. I knew what our guides would think of offering a salmon such a monstrosity. Eventually I ambled down to the river and cast out a bass bug while the guides were preparing lunch on the shore above my pool. Watching the big artificial drift on the surface I was glad the guides couldn't make out what it was. I have to admit it appeared awkwardly out of place on this water. My first warning was a huge shadow under the bass bug. Then the largest salmon of our trip had my bass bug. I eventually landed him. Having gained social acceptance for my bass bug, I used it to catch several more fish above the six-pound mark before the trip was over.

You can get a great variety of fly-rod-size floating bugs. Some pop when twitched, others wobble or flutter. They may in a general way imitate insects, frogs, mice, or nothing at all. But most of them work, if you handle them right in the proper waters. There are times when nothing works better.

My first actual fly fishing for bass was done long before the surface bugs had gained any foothold among fishermen in general. Since that time, of course, I've become a great rooter for topwater bugs, but because the old-time regulation fly patterns are still useful on occasion and I happened to start fly fishing with them, I'd like to discuss them here.

A smallmouth bass river with its rapids and eddies is perhaps the very best place for using standard wet bass flies. I've always preferred sizes two and four, and for patterns I lean to the following old-timers: Coachman, Black Palmer, Royal Coachman, Grizzly, Black Professor, Parmachene Belle, Brown Palmer with red tag, Silver Doctor, Babcock, Yellow Sally, and Scarlet Ibis.

Let me describe my terminal rig as I make it up now. For average conditions I like a 7½-foot leader tapered from about .019 to .013 with one dropper tippet tied in thirty-five to forty inches from the fly end. For tough conditions I increase the length to nine feet and perhaps cut the taper on the fly end to .012 or less. I always choose a Coachman or Royal Coachman for a dropper fly, chiefly because the white wings are clearly visible under water.

For the tail fly I may use any of the patterns listed above, but I'm inclined to choose the Black Palmer—sometimes with a bright red tail—because it so often does the job. When the black fails, I try the others until I find one that works—or else go through the lot and fail to interest a fish, something that happens to everyone at times.

One quality I consider necessary for a really effective wet bass fly is bulk. It should be heavily dressed so that it looks like a juicy and substantial mouthful. Bass will take a sparsely dressed fly, but they'll go farther out of their way for a bulky job.

The principal working method for this rig is the regular, orthodox across-and-downstream cast followed by the rod-jerk retrieve. Sometimes, however, the best results are obtained by fishing the flies on the surface, making them jump along skittishly throughout the retrieve. If neither of these methods produces, you should use the natural drift, letting the flies travel along as if free of leader and line.

There are limits, of course, to the amount of natural drift that can be achieved, depending on conditions and the skill of the angler. It is the only way you can get depth in moving water without the aid of a sinker. When you have fished the cast naturally to the best of your ability, and it starts to drag, you can retrieve in any style you like—bringing it in fast with a skittish action, reeling it in steadily, or using the hand twist.

Some anglers object to a two-fly rig because the dropper can get you into trouble. A husky bass hooked on one of the flies may snag the other on a log, stick, or weed, or lodge it between two stones. However, I believe that many times the dropper fly gets us extra strikes. Its action is entirely different from that of a fly tied on the end of a leader, and sometimes this is just the ticket for attracting a fish.

Then, too, you often find places where it is advantageous to skip a fly on the surface. Here the dropper fly is invaluable, whether you are fishing a spot where the angler must do all the work or in a current where you can simply hold the rod high and let the surging water toss the fly about. Some of the best river bass have been taken by the simple expedient of holding a dropper fly over a pocket in the rapids.

In some white-water rapids there are pocket holes that contain fish. You can locate these by looking for dark spots amid the foam, and a dancing dropper fly is likely to get results. Sometimes the leader must be adapted to the conditions—that is, the dropper must be in a different position in relation to the end fly, and the dropper tippet may need to be longer. After you have done some of this fishing, you will arrange these things to suit your own taste and needs. Incidentally, I find that the longer the rod, the better you can dance the dropper fly.

This two-fly rig stood me in good stead several years ago on a Wisconsin river. I was fishing from shore, and all the available water was very weedy with only a slight current. After working it hard with a plug and getting no results, I went back to the car for the fly rod. Digging out two well-used No. 4 bass flies tied with reverse wings to act as weed guards, I rigged up a leader with a dropper fly, using a Coachman as the dropper and a Black Gnat as the end, or tail, fly.

Fishing these so that the retrieve brought the flies through the open pockets in the weeds, I was rewarded with one strike after another. Some retrieves brought as many as six strikes without a hooked fish, while at other times the first strike brought a taker to net. Once two bass struck at the same time as the flies touched the water and both were hooked, though one managed to get loose in the ensuing struggle.

My run of luck didn't last long, probably because the hooked fish made such a disturbance while being played. But I landed seven good bass that would have stayed in the river if I had used only the plug that day. And I don't think it was the fly patterns that did the trick; any pattern, I believe, would have done as well, provided it was made so that it could be fished satisfactorily in the weeds.

When the streamer patterns, both feathered and bucktail, came into vogue, they fascinated me just as they did thousands of other fishermen. For some time, in fact, I never used the old two-fly cast or even bothered with surface bugs. I couldn't say how many different patterns I've used through the years. I've taken fish with all of them, and believe that almost any combination of feathers, hair, tinsel, and whatnot will take bass if it is used with the same faith, frequency, and persistence as a favorite lure.

In my opinion a large assortment is definitely unnecessary. On the whole, this type of fly is supposed to represent a minnow, and therefore the patterns that look like different varieties of minnows should be the best for general use. The Erskine is a dandy minnow imitation and so is the Marabou. I like the latter tied with two or three feathers rather than only one, because a single feather gets very sparse-looking when wet. I also like white or very pale yellow marabou, topped with five or six pieces of peacock herl. This dark topping gives a minnow-like effect of a dark back and light bottom. Silver or gold tinsel makes a good body for the marabou feather flies, and in some places the yellow color is very popular.

Combinations of green, white, and silver are excellent in places where the smelt run. I've also found them good where the blue herring predominates, though in this instance I like for the green to have a bluish rather than a yellowish tint. Some makers specialize in these minnow-type flies and they are usually available, especially since suitable hooks are now in good supply.

A long-shank, tapered loop-eye hook of rather stout wire is about the best bet, particularly if the fish are likely to run large. The tapered loop-eye not only makes it possible to finish off with a neat head, but also makes the smoothest eye for tying a leader. Some excellent patterns are the Black Ghost, Gray Ghost, Family Secret, Erskine, Supervisor, Marabou Smelt, Edson-Tiger, Badger Minnow (whitish), Badger Minnow (yellowish), and Furnace or Cochy-bondhu. (The last three are named for the hackle feathers used. The remainder of the fly may be made up to suit the ideas of the maker.)

Since this article is confined to a discussion of simple bugs and flies, we are not concerned with the use of a spinner blade in front of the fly, which is really spinner fishing rather than fly fishing. However, there are two types of wet flies that merit treatment as borderline cases. One is the metal-flange-headed fly, usually tied streamer-fashion; the other is the old-timer with a fairly light propeller head.

The flanged head is supposed to give the fly action in the same way that a similar arrangement gives wiggle to a plug. When the flange is large enough to give noticeable action, you have to be careful in lifting it from the water to make the next cast. Unless you make sure that the flange head is above water before you give the back cast snap, the fly is likely to dive under the water and put a dangerous strain on the rod. Personally, I've never had any better luck with this fly than with the regular streamers or wet flies.

I like to use the spinning-bladed fly mostly as a dropper. When fish need to be coaxed, you can sometimes get them up by making the propeller blade churn the surface. In doing this, you naturally make the fly skip out of the water and flop back, and in other ways act as if it were alive. This often brings results when nothing else will, but believe me, it is hard work and the lazy man won't like it.

Another type of wet fly is either a streamer or a regular fly to represent something besides a minnow, and so fished as a nymph or creeper. One that I've found very effective is a pattern whose original came from a friendly New Zealand correspondent, W. F. Weber. Having mislaid the original name, I call it "Double Trouble" because it's that for both trout and bass.

This fly is actually a double streamer. One set of feathers gives the streamer effect on top of the hook, the other behind it. The original pattern was made of badger-colored feathers—two for the wings and two for the tail—and I've had the best results from this combination. The general idea is too new for me to have tried many different colors.

Double Trouble works well, fished either as a nymph or as a minnow, which adds to its value. I've found it useful for bass in sizes 4 and 6 of regular wet-fly hooks, and the same sizes of heavy streamer hooks. Sometimes I use hooks as large as size 2—and, of course, much smaller sizes than these for average trout fishing.

CHAPTER XIV

Spot Fishing for Bass

Turn the page if you're interested only in quiet, lazy-day bass fishing. This is for anglers who are willing to range water under continual tension, looking for those spots where the bass go wild.

I'm talking about those places where schools of bass or individual fish start a feeding spree that breaks the surface into patches of froth and sends small forage fish flying. You can't accurately predict when or where this will happen. It's the sort of bonanza you must keep prospecting for. Be poised to get into the action fast, once it starts.

Though there's no regular pattern to these surface-feeding flurries, there are shoals and currents where they occur often. It happens when a big school of minnows cruises across a channel or over a shoal, so that bass lying nearby can see and get at them. Largemouths, smallmouths, or white bass often charge the minnows like a pack of wolves, each of the marauders striking viciously and recklessly, jealous of the minnows caught by others. This frantic action may last only a few minutes or go on for nearly an hour. Almost any minnow-like lure tossed into the fray will be hit instantly.

I became addicted to this kind of spot fishing in 1932 while working over a series of small lakes in Wisconsin. One day I was casting from a boat to the shoreline on one of these lakes when I noticed a lot of splashing along the opposite shore. But I was picking up bass with pleasing regularity on my own side, so I didn't investigate. This went on for three days more—the surface boiling across the lake as I worked my favorite shoreline—before I decided to row over and see what was going on.

The lake was a half mile across and my rowing got me there too late—just as the last lone bass ripped the surface and went down. I cast for a long time without the slightest response. Then I made some depth soundings which showed that a deep channel separated the shore from a shoal that ran out into the lake and formed quite an expanse of shallow water. The shoal attracted large schools of minnows, and the bass made periodic raids on the little forage fish. I decided to spend a few days observing this situation.

As it turned out I was in perfect casting range of the shoal when the feeding started next day. It was a sight to behold. An eighth of an acre of water began boiling with minnows, some of them knocked into the air as the bass rushed them. As fast as I could cast, hook, and boat them, I took eight bass, none of them under two pounds, and the largest weighing 3½. I hooked and lost many others. Several times on a single retrieve I hooked and lost one or two fish, and then boated a third that hit my lure before I'd reeled all the way in.

The end came as quickly as a high summer cloud cuts off the brightness of the sun. I stayed there watching for four hours after the final flurry. Nothing happened. After returning to the cabin for lunch I rowed out again. No more splashes, not from then until dusk, when I cast to a good-looking shoreline for half an hour and then quit.

At this point I had seven days left to fish, so I spent them all studying this hot-spot business. Each day during that week there was a concentrated rise about the same time—between nine and ten thirty in the morning. The first two days I boated eight or ten big bass before the action subsided. But the feeding tapered off during the following days. The last day brought just a hurried squall on the surface. Then it was all over.

In the years since then I've fished that same shoal with contradictory results. Sometimes I'd hit an extended rise and catch my limit; on other visits it was a complete flop. The only thing I learned for sure is that it's a kind of bass fishing worth waiting and searching for.

Exploring other waters in other regions, I've learned that most spot fishing for bass follows the same pattern—a lot of blank hours, then minutes of frenzied action. Bass, you see, often leave the shallows and gang up in deep water, where you have to locate them by trolling deep or stillfishing—offering them what they want where they are.

More recently Willie Young, my fishing partner on the Tennessee River in Alabama, introduced me to a somewhat different but equally spectacular kind of spot fishing for bass. A series of dams along the river have created lakes that hold largemouth, smallmouth, and white bass—all of which feed on the surface at times.

Willie and I set out on the Tennessee before daylight, cruising upstream toward Wilson Dam through a fog so thick that we could hear other boats moving cautiously around us without being able to see them. Willie knows this river, however, so we pushed on and anchored at the place he had in mind before there was light enough to see well.

Dawn sneaked in through the fog, so that I didn't realize it was there until I noticed I could see objects in the boat. Then Wilson Dam was silhouetted upstream and I saw with surprise that we were anchored within casting range of a muddy bank. The water flowed smooth and oil-like beneath us, unruffled except by sunken logs and stumps that wrinkled the surface here and there.

"The water's low," said Willie. "When we start running in through the turbines above us we'll get some action."

When the nearby cities wake up, the increased demand for electrical power automatically starts more water down through the turbines, Willie explained. He expected the stripes (white bass) we were after to start hitting as soon as the rising water got down to us. But the townsmen must have been especially sleepy this morning, because we sat there for another hour without seeing any change. I did catch a largemouth, a white bass, and a jack salmon (sauger), with my time-passing casts, but the fishing wasn't as advertised.

I started on a sandwich, poured a cup of tea and invited Willie to eat with me. Willie wasn't interested. "The fish should be here any minute now," he said. "They'll start coming in between those stumps and the shore. And they'll really make things boil."

Hardly five seconds later Willie said, "Here they are," and he barely got the words out before he had a bass on the feather jig he'd cast into the splashing mass.

Willie had a pair of two-pound bass in the boat before I could clear my food out of the way and get my spinning outfit and silver wobbler into play. As I cocked my cast half a dozen little shad minnows were bounced clear of the surface in front of me. I landed the wobbler on the spot. I had a fight on my hands the instant my lure touched the water. It went on like that for some twenty-five minutes before the feeding fracas faded, and by that time Willie and I had taken fourteen husky white bass, the largest about three pounds.

Then Willie called my attention to a place across the river where the dark water was blowing up in little patches of white. We high-balled over there and got into more action just like the first. The fish here were slightly larger and the current swifter. As a result my light spinning rod simply wouldn't subdue them fast enough to match the pace. Willie, with his heavier bait-casting tackle boated three before I brought in my first one. Then the feeding began to subside and soon stopped entirely. But we both had limit catches by then.

The following morning we went looking for smallmouths and found them battering a school of minnows off the point of an island. Casting a white-feather lure with a lead head I quickly boated three smallmouths weighing more than three pounds apiece. And so it went, from place to place and day to day. Once we took eleven smallmouths ranging from three to 7½ pounds. All we caught were full of fight and hard to hold—fish that broke or straightened our hooks, and ripped the hooks out of their mouths.

On my last trip to the Tennessee River, which is one of my favorites for spot fishing, Willie met me with (and how often I've heard it), "You should have been here a few days ago. Things were really happening."

The bass had just about quit working on the surface, but I did get a few that way. And I'll never forget the lunker that boiled up right beside the boat, took the lure I dropped on top of his eruption, and fought his way free. Nor the time when I let my plug drift idly with the current, saw feeding bass suddenly shatter the surface just below it, and let the plug drift into the turmoil. That was when I snagged a bass gone wild.

This kind of fishing will deal you bad days quite often, bad hours consistently. It's always a will-o'-the-wisp sort of search. Yet the sight of bass rising during those vital minutes still makes me tighten up, fumble, drop things—and I'm too old an oldtimer to be easily excited.

Spot fishing for bass is actually a method for casting only to fish that are visibly feeding, rather than making blind offerings to places where you think a bass should be. October is generally a good month for spot fishing, especially in parts of the South.

Typical of spot-fishing activity was the October day Willie Young and I spent cruising the waters below the U.S. Highway 43 bridge in the Muscles Shoals area of the Tennessee River. We had made a run upstream from the bridge at daybreak, hoping to find smallmouth bass chasing minnow schools to the surface. Failing in that, we cruised downstream, acting on Willie's hunch that there might be some action just above the mouth of Cypress Creek. That, of course, is the spot-fishing strategy—cruise, look, and be ready to cast fast and furiously when you get in range of a surface-thrashing school of feeding bass.

But the mouth of Cypress Creek was calm when we got there,

and a dozen or so random casts we made got no response. We ran the creek itself for some distance, scanning the surface expectantly, but still with no results. Then as we cruised back to the mouth of the creek we saw the splashes that raise a spot fisherman's hackles. They were some distance downstream, so Willie opened up the motor.

We got there just too late for the first flurry. All visible feeding had stopped. Willie anchored on the spot and we sat there, waiting. Fifteen minutes passed before anything happened. Then came a spectacular flurry—bass chasing minnows to the surface with frantic rushes that whitened the water among the flooded stumps. We boated three largemouths in short order. Then all was quiet again, bass and bait minnows having moved on, and our top-water plugs came in unnoticed.

We waited and watched again, thinking the school might come back. They did—or others like them—for the surface suddenly broke into white puddles further downstream. Again the motor roared and we got there while the fish were still churning up the surface. We both cast the instant our anchor set and each hooked a largemouth immediately. After we'd boated three more in short order, the place went dead.

This was turning out to be a slow morning, in a way. The periods of action were short, some of the places where the bass commonly surfaced were dead all the time we waited there, and we rushed to several uprisings that were only schools of big shad with no bass among them. But Willie had an ace in the hole. We saw signs of action in front of a precipitous cliff further downstream. They were gone by the time we got there, but Willie announced confidently that this was the place to wait.

Ten minutes passed. We broke out some tea and relaxed. I had a cup to my mouth when it started—and Willie, as usual, had a fish on before I could get my empty cup stowed. In fact, he had a second fish hooked before I got out my first cast. Then we both hooked and fought fish steadily. We took seven largemouths and one smallmouth before this spree ended, and this time Willie had a follow-up idea when the surface feeding stopped.

"The water's running deep along that cliff," he explained, "so the bass may still be after the minnows, only down deep. Let's see what happens with a deep-running lure."

Willie was right. He tied on a deep-runner and took several more good bass. I kept casting a surface lure, just to experiment, and drew a blank during the same period.

We decided to head back to the boat dock then, but were interrupted as we discussed it by some surface action still farther downstream. It was all over by the time we swung up beside the spot, yet we waited a minute, watching. Within casting range beside us was a small bay, its surface smooth and undisturbed when we got there. But we'd no sooner swept our eyes over it than the cove began to boil in several places. We had another ten minutes of fast action with some big fish before the bass went down and we turned toward the dock for good.

We docked at eleven a.m. with a good part of our pleasant October day left to idle through chores and get ready for the next morning's fishing. The Tennessee River area of Alabama is just one of many that afford excellent spot fishing for bass. The state of Tennessee has similar impounded waters that are good. So does the neighboring state of Kentucky.

And so, for that matter, does Ontario, Canada. Lake Traverse in Algonquin Park, Ontario, is a treasure in my memory because of its bass, and spot fishing for them always paid off better for me than casting to places where I thought bass might be.

I got started spot fishing Lake Traverse, as I often do, after a long period of wearing out my arm with fruitless casts to places where the bass either were not hungry or not home. The surface disturbance I eventually sighted was along a flat, sandy beach, the sort of shoreline experienced bass fishermen wouldn't be likely to try. Typically, the action was over by the time I had paddled my canoe to the hot spot. So after I had cast without response a few times I decided to have a look at the place at about the same time the following day.

Sure enough, the bass were rattling the surface at about the same hour a day later. I had a small hair frog rigged on a fly rod, and I caught a three-pound smallmouth on the first cast. Because it was an especially tough fight getting this first one in I didn't get out another cast before the surface feeding ended. But I returned to the same spot about the same time several days later and got in on another surface-feeding spree.

There are certain places, like that one, that seem to furnish consistent action year after year, and they'll often provide good spot fishing when the rest of the same water is practically dead, as far as taking bass with conventional methods goes.

On another trip to Quetico Park, Canada, we found spot fishing a necessity. I don't think we'd have caught a single worthwhile bass by casting blindly along the shorelines. Scouting the water, however, turned up a respectable catch, including a top fish of 5½ pounds. There was a somewhat different twist to some of our spotting, too. Since the water was extremely clear, we could sometimes see schools of bass deep under the surface. We'd move away, let them recover from the slight fright of our spying on them, and then ease back to cast for them. It usually produced a good fish or two.

Another minor variation is cruising slowly and quietly among weedy waters and watching for telltale signs. It's easy to see the weeds move when a bass makes a rush for a minnow, frog, or some lively aquatic food, even though the fish never breaks the surface.

There are also times, alas, when bass will tear up the surface feeding on natural foods and at the same time reject lures with just as much discretion as trout show in taking or refusing a dry fly. Fishing a North Carolina lake, my partner and I rushed to an area where several acres of water were sprinkled with the circles of rising fish. We were both grinning from ear to ear as we approached, but those bass soon changed our expressions. We must have tried twenty different lures, but took only four fish between us.

This whole business bothered me. Once I seemed to have hit the right offering—a silver spoon. It took one fish and got three more hard strikes in rapid succession. Then suddenly they wouldn't touch it. The water was filled with tiny shad minnows and they were moving slowly. We didn't have lures that would duplicate their size and action, or at least none that we could handle on our bait-casting rods.

"A fly rod and my fly box!" I kept thinking. "If only I had my fly outfit."

I still feel sure that would have done it—but that's only what I think, not what I know.

There's still another kind of spot fishing, or a system that sets you up for spot fishing, that can save many a day. I mean the spoon-plugging strategy originated by Buck Perry. Buck trolls a spoon, often at startling speeds, until he gets a strike. If he has to work miles of varied water at different depths before that happens, that's what he does. Then he cruises back to work on the concentration of bass that's likely to be there.

I fished a Georgia lake with Buck recently at a time of year when most anglers there were getting skunked. But Buck's theory is that it's most likely a matter of finding the fish, that they're going to be ganged up somewhere. After lots of searching we found the bass schooled up along a sunken roadbed. And any lure you bounced across that flooded road was very likely to snag a nice largemouth, if it didn't get snagged in the sunken brush.

We'd done lots of racing around before we came back to the dock that evening. You usually do that with spot fishing of any kind. But you'll have lots of days, as we did, when the boys at the dock look at your catch and wonder where and how you got them.

CHAPTER XV

Live Bait for Largemouths

LET'S avoid the endless list of baits largemouth black bass *may* take; the outstanding natural baits for bigmouths are minnows, worms, and frogs. At least that's the response I've had from the thousands of bass I've polled. Through the years and across the country, the fish rate them in that order.

A live minnow is likely to catch a largemouth if it's simply plunked into bass water at random by an angler who sits and waits for a bite. Minnow fishermen who study the water, fish a promising spot for half an hour, and move on if it fails commonly fill their stringers.

Since most largemouth hangouts are laced with aquatic growth, I like to fish minnows with a bobber or float, one rigged to hold my bait far enough off the bottom or out of the tangle that bass can see it. A live minnow will try to hide in weeds or cover. Once it does, you have about the same chance of getting a bite that you'd have dangling a string in the water. An ideal adjustment is to have the surface bobber holding the baitfish just out of reach of underwater cover. Its futile dives are a bass-killing action.

There are lots of ways to hook minnows and strong differences of opinion as to which is best. Probably the most common way is to hook them through the back near the dorsal fin. That's good if you're careful not to hit the spine or another vital spot. With very tender fish which tear off the hook easily, shad minnows, say, a hook run through the head from eye to eye works well. Since fish are nearly immune to pain as humans feel it, the system's not as cruel as it may seem. But my own pet way to hook minnows is through both lips. They live a long time this way, and the hook, because gamefish usually take a minnow head-first, goes into the mouth of the striking fish immediately, giving you a better chance to connect when you yank in response.

Some baitfish will try to stay on the surface, which is perfect for certain waters—shallow or very clear, usually—but useless in others. If you need to force the minnow down, tie a sinker to the end of your leader and hook the minnow about a foot above it on a six- or eight-inch dropper leading out from a swivel or loop. Sometimes it's a good trick to use a small cork on the leader strand holding the hook and bait.

In buying or trapping bait minnows, keep in mind that there are legal restrictions on their use. Goldfish, for instance, are generally unlawful, the reason being that they're a kind of carp and not wanted in game-fish waters. Small catfish are fine baits, if you can use them legally in your state. The young of the common sucker, chub sucker, and northern creek chub all make good, sturdy baits. Bass love the shinier type of minnow, too, but they're delicate and die quickly, especially if you cast or troll them.

Minnows 2 ½ to 3 ½ inches long are good average size for largemouth bass. If it's a case of taking what you can get, as often happens, experiment with them. Using two minnows on one hook sometimes whets a largemouth's appetite. I've had excellent fishing doing this on days when a single minnow was doing a dull business.

Worms, used singly or in gobs, will take bass under many and varied conditions. They're always a good ace in the hole on a fishing trip. My favorite worm combination for largemouths is a big hook—No. 1 to 1/0—with three big worms or nightcrawlers speared on it so that lots of loose ends are left to wave and wiggle. The big hook is needed to keep the point and barb from being so smothered by the worms that it won't bite in on a strike; the big worm bait is the kind of square meal largemouths go for. For single worms, use hooks in sizes 2 to 6. The important thing is to have hooks to fit the various kinds of worms you'll dig or buy.

Since most largemouth waters hold lots of other fish that go for worms, keeping the bait in shape for big bass takes some attention. Small fry will worry and maul the big bait, and nip off the enticing ends of your worms. Add another lively nightcrawler when panfish prune off those squirming ends. It pays. I've taken a few lunker bass on bits of worms impaled on small hooks for the purpose of catching panfish. I believe, however, that those bass horned in simply to take the bait away from the panfish.

Worms are good natural bait for casting, staying on the hook well during the toss and waving in an attractive way as they sink. Drifting or cruising slowly along a shoreline and casting worms to pockets near the bank is one of my favorite approaches. A fly rod with a light (H or G) level line is fine for this. So is spinning tackle. With the fly rod, the best system is stripcasting—stripping coils of smooth-running line off the reel onto the floor of the boat, then shooting that slack out through the guides as you toss out the worms with a swing of the rod. Use a short leader (three to six feet) on the end of your fly line.

Using spinning gear, I want a line heavy enough to handle a rowdy largemouth in the weeds. Monofilament testing up to 8½ pounds handles well after it's wet and stretched by a few casts. It requires no leader. Braided spinning lines of the same test are also good. A short length of leader usually improves their fish-taking. I'd hesitate about heavier spinning lines than these. The extra strength results in stiffness that may be troublesome with a spinning reel. If big bass and heavy weeds make a stronger line necessary, a spinning reel of salt-water size may be needed.

Frogs, third of the big three in natural baits for bass, are easy to capture or buy most places where largemouths are found. And like most baits, anglers have different ideas about them. Some won't use green frogs; others rule out brown ones. Actually, they're both good. A frog matching the color of those in the water you're fishing is a logical choice, but the bass, illogically, prefer a foreign frog at times. Experiment.

Of the many ways to fish frogs, harnessing or hooking them on a weighted, weedless hook is one of the most effective. They're great producers when cast into weed beds, allowed to sink, and then retrieved through the growth.

For surface fishing, a good method is to hook the frog through the skin of one foreleg and cast it gently to a likely spot. Let it swim at will. If it gets to a lily pad or other such haven, let it sit for a while. Pull it off then and let it swim for cover once more. Chances are a largemouth will break up the game before you go much further.

Where the weeds are particularly dense, swimming a frog is of course out of the question, but the solution is simple. Put the frog on a weedless hook and dredge right through the weeds. That sounds crude, but bass have a weakness for frogs and they'll hustle to get them.

Needless to say, none of these three baits has much chance unless it's delivered at the right address. Largemouths ordinarily range through water on the shallow side, from flats that barely cover them to ten-foot depths. But that holds true only in the conventional, weedy, cluttered lakes and streams. Largemouths are also found in deep lakes with little aquatic growth, and there they may be anywhere from the shallow shoreline pockets to channels sixty feet deep.

Bait fishing, I like to explore for bass by letting my boat drift, casting as I go with the bobber on the line above the bait. This system is designed to take them where they usually are—near shore or over shallow shoals farther out. (Those deep-water denizens are another problem.) Put the bobber about 4½ feet above the bait as a starter, determine the direction of the wind and the drift of your boat, and make a cast that will float the bobber and suspended bait through a promising area.

Watch the bobber carefully, just as you would a floating dry fly. A bass may mouth the bait so that the bobber only tips a little. Let the fish take it for a moment and then strike hard. Other bass seem to jerk at the bait in a series of hits and short runs, causing the bobber to dip accordingly. Wait these strikes out, too, and yank hard at the firmest hit you get before the drifting boat makes another cast necessary. When a fish hits with a dash, takes the bobber and keeps going, strike immediately. If it's a slow, steady take that moves the bobber toward you, bring in slack line until you can feel the steady pressure of the fish before setting the hook.

If you hit an especially productive spot by drifting baits in this way, anchor and cast to it until it cools off. Like other still-fishing for largemouths, half an hour is long enough to wait without results. Move on then, probing different depths and areas for another hot spot.

And don't get the idea that bait fishing is just a plodding, work-horse way to catch bass. There are plenty of imaginative stunts in the sport. I once watched a smart bait angler hook a frog by the front leg and then stick a large dry fly of the salmon pattern in the frog's upper lip. Cast out, the frog appeared to have a mouthful of some choice food that it was hurriedly swimming to cover with. The water boiled as several good bass fought for that frog.

I use a version of the same stunt with bait minnows, hooking either a fly or a piece of worm in the minnow's mouth. Sometimes it gets spectacular attention from bass. It may also fail completely. But that's what starts bait-fishing largemouth fans thinking about such tricks in the first place. There are times when even a novice catches fish easily, no matter what method he is using. Live bait will give him a slight advantage over artificials used unskillfully, but will not catch fish for him consistently unless he learns how to use it properly. Consistency in results is the acid test to apply to any method of fishing. It determines whether or not you know the game. It applies to live-bait fishing far more than some artificial-lure purists realize or will admit. The disparaging comment so often heard—"Oh, yes, he caught it on bait"—should be spoken with respect rather than scorn. Bait and artificial-lure fishermen would both benefit if they'd get together and combine the best of each method.

In drift fishing you must become proficient in casting because when the boat drifts fast you should be able to cast far enough forward to make up for the speed of the boat. As the boat approaches the float, retrieve the line, keeping a slight bit of slack. Don't pull against the bait and so create a drag that may spoil your chances.

Turning now to rivers, the best bass baits are minnows, hellgrammites, or crawfish, with the first two preferred. In minnow fishing I use a sinker at the end of my leader and another short leader fastened by a loop or swivel to the main leader. When you cast with this rig the sinker goes to the bottom, and you feel it touch and take hold. After that you merely keep the line taut. The minnow heads upstream and fights the current. If any bass are in the vicinity you'll presently feel a touch. Wait a few moments until you feel that the minnow is well within the bass's mouth; then—strike! Often you'll miss, but after a few hours you acquire an uncanny sense of touch which tells you when to strike, and your percentage of hooked fish will go up.

With hellgrammites you encounter different conditions. A minnow will not hide under rocks, and as long as he stays lively he'll struggle to get away from his "leash." When he tires he heads into the current and still looks natural, even though he's barely moving, provided he's hooked through the lips. But the hellgrammite does not fight the current. It lets the drift carry it until a convenient foothold is found, when it quickly finds its way under cover. In fishing with hellgrammites, therefore, the important thing is to be able to read the water currents. You must know where fish are likely to be, and then cast your hellgrammite into the current in such a way that it will float naturally to that place. It must neither reach bottom until it gets to that spot, nor drift by it so high in the water that the fish will ignore it.

Drifting the bait naturally means it must not be hampered by the line. Slack line is needed. There are several ways to effect this. The simplest is to cast upstream and let the bait drift down on the slack line thus afforded. As the bait drifts you must control its sinking by the way you handle the slack. If the bait is rushing rapidly along, extra slack will slow it up. If it is sinking too fast, then it may be necessary to take up the slack so as to allow it to drift to its objective. A slack-line float may also be achieved by dropping the bait, together with a bunch of loose line already stripped from the reel, into the water at your feet. This is a sloppy device but sometimes it works well.

Then there is the "back flip," which works very well if you stand in a current which leads directly to the location you wish to reach. First, all you do is to let the current take the bait downstream. When it has gone twenty-five feet or so, and is splashing on top of the water, jerk the rod up and toward you. If correctly done, the bait will fall in the water at your feet, and so you get the slack line needed to obtain a natural drift.

Slow trolling is another method used in fishing lakes, and is killing for bass. This is popular with the oldtimers but the younger generation neglects it. No sinker is needed except when using minnows that have a tendency to come to the top instead of seeking bottom, or when fishing in particularly deep water. In slow trolling you let the boat drift or propel it along at about one mile an hour. You let your bait seek bottom and allow it to touch frequently, so that you'll know it's where it will do the most good.

Further to emphasize the need for knowing how to bait fish, let me tell you of the experiences I've had in the bayous of Mississippi. Rarely have I fished them when anything could be accomplished with artificials. I wouldn't use the clumsy cane poles favored there, with which you swing in a bass after hooking it. I found that a 9½- or 10-foot fly rod worked very well—far better than the cane poles.

Of chief importance in fishing those waters with live shrimp is to fish directly against the banks under which bass lie. The bait must not only be close but also sink quickly, so that the fish will see it before the boat drifts past and drags the bait away.

Sometimes, however, water conditions may be such that you must fish "fine and far off," or drift a bait forty to sixty feet to reach a particularly good spot. Because that calls for a rod and reel, I'd often make a good catch while the others—with tackle adapted to only one way of fishing—did poorly. Study of bait fishing will show you there is much to be learned. Try it occasionally. You can make it just about as sporty as you choose.

CHAPTER XVI

The Unruly Esox Family—Mostly About Pickerel

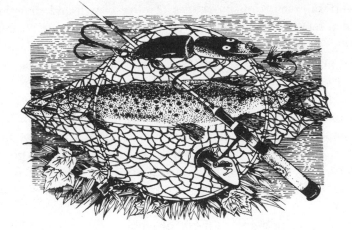

THE *ESOX* family of fresh-water fish is finally winning a social acceptance it has long deserved. One member, the huge and relatively rare muskellunge, has always been considered a worthy game fish, but pickerel and pike, the two smaller relatives, were long scorned by trout and bass fishermen. A lot of old-time anglers considered them trash fish, and many good-sized pike and pickerel have been tossed ashore to rot in the sun.

By my definition, any fish that will readily take artificial lures or flies deserves to be classed as a game fish. That makes all the *Esox* tribe game fish in my book, for a large pike or pickerel will hit a spoon, plug, or artificial fly even more readily than a muskie. And both pike and pickerel will fight as hard, pound for pound, as their larger and better-publicized cousins.

There are several varieties of pickerel, but the one sport fishermen deal with most is the Eastern pickerel, also known as the chain pickerel. Its Latin name is *Esox Niger*. It's common in most of the Eastern states and in some waters as far west as the Ozarks.

Though the average size for Eastern pickerel is about two pounds, some grow as large as ten pounds.

There's only one sure way to tell a pickerel from a pike or muskie. This is by the scales on the cheeks and gill covers. If it's a pickerel both cheeks and opercles (gill covers) will be entirely covered with small scales. The color of this fish varies considerably—from green to many shades of olive brown and sometimes a golden hue. All that I've ever caught have had net or chainlike markings on their bodies.

The pickerel is mostly found in weedy sections of lakes or in the quiet grassy portions of streams. Its favorite food seems to be smaller fish, so minnow-like artificial lures are usually good bets. So are natural and artificial frogs. Actually, I've caught pickerel with almost every kind of natural and artificial bait. Live minnows or crawfish are first-rate pickerel baits. They also go for strips of pork rind, baits cut from the belly of a yellow perch, and skinned frog legs. They'll take nightcrawlers or garden worms.

Pickerel will hit a great variety of wobbling spoons or plugs in both bait-casting and spinning sizes. Be sure that some of the lures you choose for pickerel fishing have hook-guarding devices to shed weeds, for these fish are often found in waters so choked with growth that only weedless lures can be fished effectively.

If you don't have to contend with surface weeds when fishing for pickerel, you may use your favorite bass lures with a reasonable chance of success. However, it's my opinion that spoons spinners, or minnow-like plugs are usually the best and most consistent attractors.

Sometimes you'll find pickerel in very shallow water, water so thin that dorsal fins can be seen breaking the surface. Here they will often take a streamer fly—if you can cast it far enough that they can't see you or your boat and get scared and suspicious. Pickerel are extremely wary and easily spooked when they're in very shallow water. Light spinning tackle is excellent for this shallow-water fishing. Make long casts with spinners, wobbling spoons, weighted flies, or minnow-like plugs.

Pickerel in shallow water provide rare sport. The strikes you get in these places are far more vicious and exciting than those in deep water. What I like best about it is the visual charm. The lure strikes the water. You see a disturbance somewhere near it as a fish starts for it, and then the pronounced V-shaped wake as the pickerel rushes for the lure. The strike is more exciting than the boating of the fish.

I've often taken pickerel in shallow water with large, colorful wet flies, sizes 1/0 down to 2, but on the whole I prefer streamers and bucktails with long-shanked hooks dressed to look minnow-like when being fished. In spinning lures I prefer those which have good action just under the surface and which don't work too deep.

Besides the regular methods of fishing for pickerel with fly, bait, spoons, spinners, and plugs, there's an old method, mostly neglected these days, called skittering. It's practiced with a long cane pole, using a line about the same length as the pole. Using a surface-disturbing lure or some fluttering, dangling bait, you simply maneuver the long cane pole so that the bait or lure dances over the surface of a promising pickerel hangout. Try moving the bait or lure in circles or figure 8's over open pockets in weeds or lily pads.

In some places you can do a fair job of skittering with a long fly rod, but a cane pole from twelve to fifteen feet long is generally better. It gives you the long reach needed to dangle that short line over the possible pockets of water. For years I've been hoping someone would market a lightweight glass rod twelve or fifteen feet long that is either jointed or telescopic so that one could handle it easily when traveling. It would be a fine substitute for the old cane pole, which is sadly neglected because it is so awkward in auto travel.

The Eastern pickerel had much to do with making me an inveterate angler. By the time I was eight I was accompanying my father on his fishing trips, which, since pickerel were the most common and plentiful fish in our local waters, were mostly in quest of these voracious freshwater fighters. This early introduction to the pickerel inoculated me with angling fever so thoroughly that it sometimes caused trouble at school, especially during the magic month of May, when I knew the fish were striking.

My early equipment wasn't very good, and didn't cost very much, but it was effective. My pole—for it was just that—was a sixteen-foot piece of bamboo. I had chosen it from a large bundle, and the taper was true. I used no reel—a line a bit shorter than the pole was tied directly to the tip. As a lure I used a fluted spoon about an inch long, and when the fish wouldn't strike that I used minnows or pork rind with deadly effect. The pole and line I kept hidden along the banks of a nearby stream so that it would be on hand when I went fishing without asking my parents' leave. The spoon and hooks I kept in my pocket at all times, the hooks covered with a home-made cork protector.

My fishing method was simple. I flipped out the spoon or bait with a lifting motion of the long pole, then moved it with a jerky action. The long bamboo pole was ideal for this work. With it I could control the speed, depth, and darting action of the bait to perfection. I've never been able to duplicate this perfect action with any other outfit, and still consider this the best type of rod for pickerel, even though I haven't used one for years.

Of course, my actions after hooking a fish weren't very sportsmanlike. If it was a small one, it would come sailing through the air to land either in the boat or on shore according to where I was fishing. I became quite adept at this method of landing a fish and anything up to 1½ pounds could be placed just where I wished. If the fish was too large to be handled in this manner and there seemed to be danger of breaking the tackle, I would throw the pole into the water, and let the fish tire itself out fighting it. Of course, I didn't get the pleasure of fighting the fish, but it served to start me on my angling career, and taught me where and how to catch pickerel. I think starting at the bottom like this gives you an advantage when you turn to more refined methods.

I've never caught a really large pickerel. The largest I ever landed was about 4½ pounds, and I was quite proud of that. Once I nearly got one which would have been a record for our part of the country. I saw him many times before I hooked him, and then, just when victory was in my grasp, the line broke and I lost him, together with a dobber and part of the line. I was so ashamed of losing him that I never said a word about it to anyone. Some two weeks later, when I was visiting the lake again, the proprietor of the hotel asked me if I'd like to see a really big pickerel. I did, and from the ice box came my fish.

In a daze I heard the hotel man telling about it. "Weighed six pounds, and would have weighed more only he was thin. A man out fishing saw a dobber floating near some weeds, and when he picked it up this critter was on the other end. Don't believe the critter ate a snack since he broke that line. That's why he's so thin."

With as good grace as I could muster I admired the fish and departed. Pickerel of that size are rare. They seldom grow larger than eight pounds and most of them run between one and three pounds.

Pork rind is an excellent bait for pickerel. Either the chunks or strips are satisfactory, but of the two I believe the chunks produce better results. To fish the chunk, cast it out, and let it settle to the bottom. Then start retrieving it with slow jerks. If a fish takes, let him have it a moment or two before setting the hook. Sometimes a fish will grab the end instead of the entire bait, and a premature strike will result in a miss. If you find that the fish will not hang onto the bait when you let him have it for a time, use a tandem hook so that you strike the instant you feel a bite. Many times I have seen pork chunks produce large catches when everything else drew a blank.

Since pickerel like locations where they can lie in wait for passing minnows or other prey, you will find them wherever logs, brush, fallen trees, or weeds form such cover. The best pickerel ponds are usually stumpy and rather shallow, although the fish do well in any water where there are enough small fish for them to feed on. As a rule, they thrive best in lakes where there are no bass. From my own experience I feel bass will gradually exterminate them.

If you are fishing a stumpy pond, and find things a bit slow, try this trick. Select a stump which has a branch projecting from it, and cast your bait so that it drops over the branch. Let it drop to within an inch of the water, and make it swing. If there are any pickerel within eyesight of this swinging bait they will come for it with a rush. Of course, you must pick a spot that will let you guide the line off the branch if you do hook a fish. One day a companion and I took eight nice pickerel by this method when we couldn't get a strike any other way. Frequently I have used the trick with excellent results on bait-shy old fish.

Occasionally you will find ponds in which sunfish or perch make the best bait and, singularly enough, it is usually dead fish which produce the most strikes. Of course, when fishing this dead bait you must give it a bit of action, but when a pickerel takes it, let him have it just as you would a live minnow.

For years I refused to believe that dead sunfish or perch could ever make a better bait than a live minnow. On investigating, I saw a dozen dead yellow perch floating on the surface. As I looked, a large pickerel came up and took one of these. I realized then what had caused the disturbance. The pickerel had killed these perch and was now eating them. The reason was plain enough. Live perch might be difficult to handle because of their powerful, spiny dorsal fins. Dead, they would cause no trouble. However, the lakes in which dead perch can be used are the exception rather than the rule.

You will often find pickerel in very shallow water close to shore. Such places are difficult, because you frighten the fish away before you get within casting distance. If you are sure that pickerel are congregated in such places, work your boat cautiously into an advantageous position, anchor it, and then wait quietly for an hour. Even if you do frighten the fish away it is quite likely they will return if you remain perfectly quiet. Keep your feet from shuffling on the bottom of the boat, and don't stand up. You may talk all you wish.

Once the fish return, a judiciously handled lure will do great execution. Lures or baits for this work should be small, and your terminal tackle should be as fine as possible. Personally I prefer the fly-rod lures for the job. A single gut leader is part of my stock in trade. Of course, I do lose some fish, for the pickerel cut the leader if they swallow the bait or lure. If you insist on using a wire leader, let it be very light twisted bronze wire.

All shallow waters offer an opportunity for the fly fisherman because pickerel will take a fly readily under favorable conditions. Perhaps a streamer is best for all-around work, but at times surface lures will get better results.

One of my pet streamers has a body of silver tinsel. The streamer has, first, two marabou feathers, tied straight along the shank of the hook. Then five strands of peacock herl are tied so that they rest along the top of the marabou feathers, and are about the same length. This gives the striped effect. Underneath the head of the fly is tied a dash of scarlet hackle or bucktail. A fiber from the wing feather of a macaw and a jungle-cock eye tied on each side of the fly completes the job. This fly, I find, is not only good for pickerel but for bass, lake trout, and all other species of trout. For a surface lure, I prefer one which causes considerable disturbance when it is being retrieved. A frog color is good, as is a combination of red and white.

In all this fly fishing, a gut leader will really give you the best results. It should be of heavy caliber, about .017 inches, and of fine quality, so it won't fray or cut easily. The flies should be tied on extra-long-shank hooks to reduce the chances of a fish's getting the gut into its mouth.

On some occasions and in certain waters, plugs will take their quota of pickerel. Almost any of the bass plugs are suitable. The bait-casting spoons and pork-rind lures are excellent for the angler who prefers the short casting rod. The only disadvantage of this outfit, when used for pickerel, is that you cannot give the lures the jerky action so effective on this fish.

Pickerel are inclined to be spasmodic in their feeding. They either feed ravenously or not at all. When they are really off their feed, it is almost impossible to get a strike. When they are feeding, the same fish will strike over and over until he is hooked. But even if pickerel cannot be considered particularly difficult to catch, they do present some problems which makes fishing for them interesting and worthwhile if you use light tackle to give the fish an even chance.

The pike, *Esox Lucius*, is also called northern pike, pickerel, jackfish and other local names. It grows much larger than the pickerel. For instance, a six-pound pickerel would be a sensation, while six-pound pike are common. The pike grows to fifty pounds or more and is usually caught in sizes from three to eight pounds.

Pike vary greatly in fighting resistance. Some will put up a battle that will leave you shaking with excitement; others will come in almost like a log. One of the most exciting fights I've ever had with any pike was with a seven-pounder. This fish was speedy, strong, and fought hard every moment until being landed. On the same day I took a twelve-pounder that made only two good runs and gave up.

The pike is a variety of *Esox* fairly well distributed in northeastern New York, northern New England, in the Great Lakes states, Canada, and Alaska. They have been stocked in other places across the country. To be sure of their identification, examine the cheeks and gill covers (opercles). A pike has no scales on the lower half of the opercles. In color pike range from green or grey-green to olive brown with variations in between. The belly will be whitish. Usually the pike has bean-shaped spots on the sides of the body. These are of a lighter shade than the base color.

The pike is a heavy feeder. Its favorite food seems to be other fish, although a hungry one will take almost anything that comes along. Its habits are similar to the pickerel, but it's often found in much deeper and clearer water than its smaller cousin. For instance, pike range many deep, rocky lakes of the north.

Many folks say that you can't catch pike during hot weather because they lose their teeth then. Research by the University of Michigan contradicts that belief, and hundreds of pike examined at the University of Minnesota showed no sign that they shed all their teeth at any one time. It seems their worn or broken teeth are gradually replaced by new ones.

It's a fact that pike are not caught readily during hot weather, but that's probably because they move to deep water, have an overabundance of food, or a combination of both. I've often had to fish deep for both pike and pickerel during prolonged summer hot spells. For pike tackle I prefer a bait-casting outfit of medium weight using lures of half an ounce and heavier. If the water is free of weeds, stumps, or logs for a good-sized fish to become entangled in during a fight, I like to use a spinning outfit that will handle lighter lures.

Being primarily fish-eaters, pike naturally go for lures that are minnow-like in appearance, fished so they act like a fish. Spoons and spinners are always good in all sizes. When the pike are in very shallow water, surface lures in bait-casting, spinning, and fly-rod sizes may be taken readily. In live bait, nothing can beat minnows of some kind. Suckers make great live bait and so do some varieties of chub. Unless carp are already in the waters being fished, avoid using them for bait. Live carp used for bait often get loose in game-fish waters and eventually increase to the point where they crowd out the game fish.

I've had many exciting experiences with pike. Here are a few highlights:

In Wisconsin I like to fish a chain of three lakes which contain pike, bass, walleyes, and panfish. The lures that work best for me when fishing for pike in these lakes are minnow-like plugs, the type that float when at rest and swim with good action under the water when being retrieved. Pike, chub, yellow perch or sunfish colors seem to do the best job, so I usually depend on one or another of them, according to what I have in my box. I usually have the best luck between the hours of ten a.m. and three p.m. Early morning and late afternoon are good for bass and sometimes walleyes in the lakes I refer to, but the middle of the day is invariably best for pike.

On a typical day on one of these lakes, I get out on the water shortly after daybreak and work the shoreline carefully, picking up a bass or a walleye here and there and, once in a great while, a pike. At about ten a.m. I head for a weedy or stumpy bay to try for pike. I've tried fishing such pike water early and late without much success, but in the middle of the day I usually make out right well.

In the northern part of Minnesota there's a lake noted for large pike. Here I've had some great pike fishing both with surface lures and underwater lures. I remember one season particularly when the pike were very active in the shallows, both in the weed beds and along the rock-bound shores. Day after day we'd cast surface plugs that simulated minnows, mice, frogs, and whatnot—and catch so many fish we'd go back to camp exhausted early each afternoon.

One surface lure worked wonderfully here. It had a spoon blade at the end of the body. Just steady retrieving gave it plenty of action. For anyone who doesn't make out too well with a surface lure that needs to be expertly jerked, this type lure fills a great need.

Getting into Ontario, Canada, where most folks go with the idea of catching muskies, you'll find pike very plentiful. Now muskie fishing can be a slow and tedious job. Good-sized ones don't strike very often. Taking time out now and then to concentrate on pike, which are nearly always present in muskie waters, can provide a sort of rest that revives your spirits.

It was during one of these dull periods when no one was getting muskies that I first tried to catch pike with bass bugs. We'd fished four days with only one muskie coming to the boat. The same results were reported by everyone coming to camp. The muskies had simply quit. It was then that our guide suggested going to an off-beat bay for a solid day at pike. He said that the place was loaded with them.

How right he was. Pike were breaking water all over the bay. After taking a dozen or so on plug and bait-casting tackle, I figured that they could be taken on a fly rod and a bass bug. So I rigged up a fly rod for the purpose. I didn't have much of a bug selection with me and only a few bass-weight leaders. I had six bugs, three of the minnow type and three of the bug type having spread wings. The leaders were 7½ feet long tapering to about .013.

On my first cast with one of the minnow lures, a big bruiser took on the second jerk. I hooked him solidly enough, but at the start of the first run everything suddenly went slack. When I pulled in I found the lure and about five inches of leader gone. It looked like a clean cut of leader by the pike's teeth.

I looked the end of the leader over for any flaws, tied on another minnow bug, immediately was fast to another pike. This one I landed. It weighed about seven pounds. The next cast brought up the biggest pike I'd ever seen. All I did was to see it take, see the fly rod tip strike the water with a swish, and feel a short terrific pull. Then I again pulled in a leader with the lure snipped off. And so it went until I'd lost every one of the six surface bugs of fly-rod size. I did boat two more good pike, a ten-pounder and an eleven-pounder, but there was no sure way to stop them from slicing off my leader with those formidable teeth.

Since then I've often tried bass bugs on the *Esox* family when they were surface feeding, and have sometimes made good catches. I've also failed dismally many times. I found that these fish were seldom spooked by a leader or line, so you could use a very heavy leader on a fly-rod lure or bug. I tried wire leaders, and these were excellent for spinning and bait casting, but they didn't do very well in connection with floating bugs. As a rule, the heaviest monofilament with which you can handle a bug is the best leader for fly-rod work on pike.

The muskellunge is the aristocrat of the *Esox* family. Their distribution is more limited than the pike, and they also average larger in size. As the big ones need a lot of territory to keep them well fed, you won't find a number of them close to each batch of weeds or other good cover, but be prepared for one large one. To tell a muskie from a pike or pickerel, we again come to the infallible cheek-and-gill-cover formula. The muskie has scales only on the upper parts of its cheeks and gill covers. The lower parts are not scaled.

Aside from the fact that they are inclined to make more jumps than their relatives and run heavier in the body for length, members are very much *Esox*. The methods used when fishing for them are the same as those used to take the poor members of the family. At times you may find very large lures the best. You need heavier tackle too,—slightly stiffer rods and stronger lines.

My most memorable experience with muskies concerns a really big fellow that refused to take my lure. There were stories circulating about camp concerning a muskie that had been lost by a number of fishermen. Our guide had been keeping tabs on what was going on, and one day almost at sunset he took my wife and me to the lair of the big fellow. We had the place to ourselves.

The big muskie was holed up at the edge of a wide stretch of open water. The wind was fresh and the clouds threatening. The waves, outside the small, slightly sheltered cove we were in, displayed occasional white caps. My wife, Grace, was jittery. She doesn't like to be out on the open water in bad weather.

Our guide, one of the best we've ever had, put the boat in position for casting to the place where the big fish should be. On the third cast Grace made the big fish follow her plug close to the boat. We could all see it plainly. While my wife was catching her breath from the sight of the monster, I cast and retrieved several times over the water where the fish was. Nothing happened.

Then Grace made her second cast. This time the muskie followed her lure with an open mouth, ready to take. Grace became frightened of the huge fish and reeled very fast, not wanting to hook it. She didn't. Both the guide and I gave her the devil, and I tried again to get the fish to take my lure, which was the same size and pattern as my wife's. But my efforts produced exactly nothing.

Grace didn't want to try again, but we finally persuaded her to do so. Believe it or not, that fish tried to get her lure once more. Grace got panicky and jerked her lure out of the water at the last instant. The charging muskie made such an effort to get the lure that he slammed against the boat. In fact he hit it with such force that it shook us all on our seats.

Thinking perhaps that her lure, supposed to be a duplicate of mine, had slightly different action, I took her outfit and worked the spot carefully. But it was useless. That muskie wanted my wife to catch him. She didn't want to catch him. So we had a stalemate.

Just to complete the story, let me add that two days later another party took this fish, and it weighed more than fifty pounds. Such is the life of an angler.

CHAPTER XVII

Big Pike Will Test Your Skill

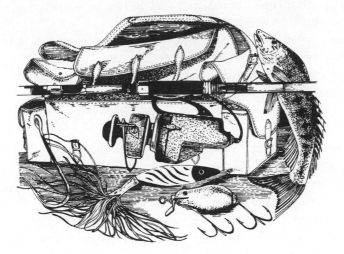

SEVERAL years ago some friends and myself were in the Adirondacks on an alleged trout-fishing expedition, but a severe drought and extreme heat had turned the trip into a card party. Not a trout could we raise, no matter how hard we tried.

We were near the Racquette River, so I suggested trying some pike fishing. The suggestion was greeted with hoots and howls, but after much persuasion George agreed to take the trip with me. He said he would go only to keep me company, certainly not to catch such an easy prey as "snakes," which was his disparaging name for pike.

Having no pike tackle, we took our trout rods and some buck-tail streamer flies. This brought another loud laugh. The gang ridiculed the idea of a pike taking a fly. But their skepticism did not trouble me, because I had frequently taken both pike and pickerel with streamer flies.

On reaching the river, we inquired about the best location for pike. "They ketches 'em mostly in the still water," a native told us, pointing to a quiet, swampy stretch. "But," he added, "they ain't ketchin' any now. Haven't been since the hot spell."

George looked at me quizzically. "Let's try it anyway," I coaxed.

Two hours of casting and trolling netted three small chubs. George was plainly bored and had begun to make stinging remarks.

"Let's try the big pool at the foot of the rapids," I ventured. "This water is lifeless." George grunted to show his disgust.

Nevertheless, I started for the rapids. As we entered the pool, we saw several large fish break water in a quiet eddy at the far side. Excited myself, I noticed a gleam of interest in George's eyes.

"You try for them," I suggested. "I'll hold the boat."

George cast over the fish but nothing happened. He tried many times, retrieving his fly with slow jerks. The pike kept jumping but would not touch his fly.

"So it doesn't take skill to catch 'snakes'?" I remarked.

"Why, they never take flies," retorted George. "What you need for them is live bait. I'm going to quit."

"You wouldn't quit a rising trout without trying several flies and different methods," I said. "If you'll take the advice of a poor pike fisherman, perhaps you'll catch some fish. The minnows in the water have a reddish glint, and swim fast. Why not try that gold-body, rusty-red streamer and fish it fast?"

He did. The fly passed over the scene of activity but nothing happened. George turned to me with a taunt on his lips, but at that moment a fish struck and nearly tore the rod from his hand. The first rush of the pike was swift, and ended in a wild leap. My partner kept too much strain on the line and the leader broke.

"The pike isn't a game fish?" I asked.

"Rats!" he snapped. "Give me another fly."

There are two important fishing facts to be learned from this incident. One is that you should locate feeding or active fish if you expect to catch any; and the other is that it is necessary to present your lure in such a way that the fish receive only an impression of it instead of getting a plain view.

The heat of the still-valley stretches had lowered the vitality of the fish and made them indifferent to food. On the other hand, the water of the pool was kept invigorating by the oxygen picked up at the rapids. Consequently the fish in this section were full of energy, wary, and finicky. A fly worked slowly through them was readily recognized as a fraud, but when it was retrieved at high speed, the pike saw only a streak of red and gold, which suggested a minnow escaping. Therefore they struck.

Where small pike are numerous, anglers are inclined to regard the entire species as a nuisance. They get the name of being easily caught and undesirable. But large pike don't strike any more readily than large fish of any other species. To get them you must use your head and all the skill you possess.

Large pike usually select a location where food is most likely to be plentiful. Most of the larger ones got that way because they were wiser and stronger than their fellows. Let me illustrate with an incident. Last summer we were fishing a wilderness pond. Ordinary fishing over the shallow weed beds brought a great number of small pike to net, but we never saw a fish over six pounds.

"I thought there were large pike in this pond," I said to my guide.

"There are," he insisted, "but you can hardly ever catch them."

"Where are they?" I asked. "I'd like to try them."

"I know where there are several big ones," said the guide.

"One 'uses' over there under that log." He pointed to a place near shore where a large pine tree had fallen into the water. "There's a deep hole under that log an' a lot of squirrels fall into the water. That pike likes red squirrels."

Just then we heard a commotion in the trees above the log. Two red squirrels were fighting so furiously that they lost all caution and came tumbling down, fighting all the way. They dropped into the water with a splash. As they swam to shore there was a swirl of water and one of them disappeared.

"Did you see that!" I gasped. "Just let me cast my plug in there."

"Not too fast," advised my guide. "If you throw that thing in there you'll only make him suspicious. Here's a red squirrel skin I made into a bait. Try that."

"If that pike is as wary as all that," I thought, "I'd best cast the lure to the log and then pull it off." I did this. As the improvised lure struck the water I started working it in an imitation of a swimming squirrel. It must have been a good imitation, because the huge pike struck with a resounding splash.

"I've been after that fish for two years," commented my guide. "Made that bait especially for him, but I never thought of pulling it off that log that way."

It was a simple trick, but simplicity often works on big fish.

"There's where another hangs out." This time my guide pointed to a little rock-bound cove. The water looked deep, and it was— some twenty-five feet. "Ain't never figured out what that fish feeds on regular but expect it's minnies."

"Probably a wobbling spoon would be the best bet," I suggested.

From our position out in the pond I cast to the shore. I worked the cove thoroughly but never got a touch.

"Guess he ain't strikin'," said the guide.

"You're probably right," I admitted, "but tell me, do you know the formation of that bottom?"

"Yes. It's tolerable shallow near shore. Then it slopes out to the deep water."

"Then I think we'd better fish the cove from shore. That pike is hanging deep, and when I cast from the deep water to the shore, the spoon travels so high when I'm retrieving that he doesn't see it. Now, if I cast from shore, I can let the spoon sink to the bottom, and then when I retrieve it will follow along the slope of the bottom instead of away from it. In that way it will be seen by the fish."

This seemed to be drawing things pretty fine but it worked. I got three pike and they were all large fellows. This rule of fishing is of great value. Always, when fish are hanging deep, select your casting position so that when retrieving your lure will follow the contour of the bottom instead of traveling away from it at an angle. Much precious time is wasted by fishing a lure where it can't be seen by a fish. Large pike are as choosy as the most fastidious trout. This is especially true when they are jumping. Although I have made plenty of unsuccessful experiments with pike, the two following incidents show what can be done.

Both incidents took place on the same pond within two days, showing how quickly conditions change. The first day was one of those infernally dead ones. We couldn't get a strike and didn't see a fish move until late in the afternoon. Then the pond became suddenly active. Every large pike in it seemed to be feeding near the surface. Doggedly I went through my whole assortment of plugs and spoons. I fished them in all sorts of ways. My partner even tried live minnows and frogs.

"It's hopeless," I groaned.

"You haven't tried the pork rind."

"Don't believe it will do any good," I replied.

"Then I'll try it," said he.

The pork rind was large and thick. Slitting the ends of one of the largest pieces, he attached it to a small spinner. Just as he got it ready a large pike broke water about twenty feet from the boat. He cast the pork rind over the fish, and started retrieving. The pike followed the lure. We could see his wake on the surface. When the bait was three feet from the boat, the pike suddenly rushed, and hooked himself solidly. My partner's hunch had worked. From then until dark we had some sport.

The second day was full of action. We didn't see a fish jump, but underwater lures brought many strikes from medium-sized fish, and almost any plug or spoon brought results. At five thirty, however, conditions suddenly changed. The pike started to jump but we couldn't get them to take our lures. Our first thought was of the pork rind that had been so successful two days before. The pike would not even look at it. Once again we went through our assortment of lures. I used every one I had, but got no strike.

"Here's a splash plug," said my companion. "I've never caught a fish on it, and don't expect to now, but here goes."

The plug was a bright, rainbow color. It didn't seem that any fish would be fool enough to strike at it, but when my friend started jerking it across the surface of the water, with splashes and great disturbance, he was immediately rewarded by the strike of a huge pike.

I had nothing with me that even remotely resembled that plug. I never thought I would need a lure so atrocious-looking. So all I could do was watch my comrade take pike after pike, while I sat twiddling my thumbs. It was a well-needed lesson. It doesn't pay to get to the point where you think you know what fish will take and what they won't take.

When they jump—and a good many do take to the air—pike are easily lost. This is because the hook will cut through the tender skin around the mouth as if it were so much cheese, yet fail to penetrate the bone. Often in such cases all that holds the fish is the bend of the hook as it curves around a bone, and given the least bit of slack the fish can shake free.

Pike are strong and exceedingly fast on straight runs, though they aren't much on erratic maneuvers. Neither are they capable of prolonged resistance, for the very characteristics that give them speed are a handicap in other ways. The body is round, and narrow for its length. In addition, the dorsal fin is comparatively small and far to the rear. In contrast, the bass has a flat body and large dorsal fin. It's the way he curves these against the water when resisting the rod that gives him such staying power, for by making the water do much of the fighting for him he's able to conserve his strength.

Unlike so many other fish, which congregate in schools, pike are solitary feeders. They want to be alone and so seek out their own individual and separate lairs. Compared with other kinds of game fish they seem to have no fear of shadows, nor do they mind seeing, or being seen by, anglers. Consequently you seldom need to observe any great amount of caution in fishing for them. Their usual method of feeding is to lurk motionless under some convenient cover, or at least against some background of protective coloration, until a luckless minnow or whatever wanders within range. Then they'll dart out, quick as a flash, and swallow the unsuspecting victim.

While all members of the genus *Esox* feed fairly regularly

throughout the year, probably the best seasons to catch them are spring and fall. I would place the peak periods as apple-blossom time, and again when maple leaves turn red in autumn. The actual dates vary, of course, with the latitude; but at such times, where these fish are plentiful, you can almost count on limit catches daily. Unfortunately, these red-letter days do not last long, say two weeks at most. After the spring peak is past the fishing tapers off, to hit bottom during midsummer dog days.

This period of doldrums varies in length and intensity according to the water and the latitude. Where the bloom residue of working lakes is extreme and the weather is sultry and humid, poor fishing may last from six to eight weeks or even more. When there is little or no bloom and where nights are consistently cool, there may be only a slump in activity. After the slow period is over the fish start striking again with increasing tempo until October or November, depending on locality. Later on they can be caught through the ice, for they feed all winter long.

Minnows—five to seven inches long—are perhaps the best live bait for pike. Personally, I prefer sucker and chub minnows for the job, for they live well on the hook, even when the angler is casting. And what's even more important, the fish like them too. Frogs are a close second, if you care to use them. If the fish are feeding among weeds, green frogs will probably prove best; but around stumps and other debris a brown or yellowish variety will likely bring better results.

As a matter of fact, members of the pike family respond so well to artificials that live bait should never be used unless necessary. When the fish are in reasonably shallow water, surface plugs are excellent. Among the best are those which imitate minnows, and those of the disturbance-creating sort. If the fish are in deeper water beyond the shoals and weed beds, you can't go wrong with a spoon lure. As a rule, spoons designed for large bass and muskies work best for good-sized pike. Other good bets are pork chunks and pork-rind lures.

The fly fisherman will find pike very responsive to flies and bugs. Bass bugs that imitate mice, frogs, minnows, and the like are good for surface work. In other cases, try streamers, bucktails, and other lures which simulate a swimming minnow. Sometimes it's best to use a spinner with a sunken fly—preferably Red Ibis, Parmachene Belle, Col. Fuller, or some other equally bright.

One word of caution in choosing your terminal tackle: Pike have sharp teeth and can easily cut any material except wire. So unless you're prepared to lose both fish and lure, be sure to rig up with a wire leader.

On the whole, pike are pretty good fish and deserve more consideration than they're getting from some anglers. In certain areas pike are so unpopular that they're killed and thrown back when caught. The time may come when anglers will suffer for such thoughtlessness.

In this connection I am reminded of a farseeing guide I know— a true conservationist. This fellow operates in the Lake of Woods country, where people go to fish for lake trout and muskies—and are always catching pike on the side. Every time we caught a pike he'd unhook it with great care and put it back. If it was a hefty one he'd often say, "Someday people will rave about fish like that." And then he'd add, in explanation, "Muskie fishing isn't what it used to be, and unless you get off the beaten track it's getting worse. Time may come when I'll have the pike to thank for still making a livelihood at guiding."

An outstanding characteristic of the northern pike is its readiness to strike, which makes it a desirable fish for the average man, who has little enough time to spend at fishing. As long as there are northern pike in the lake, it doesn't matter very much whether the muskies and bass strike, because the pike can be depended on to provide plenty of action.

As with any species, it is the small-size northerns that provide the most action. When they run less than four pounds, they don't amount to much, but fish of this size and up put on a stirring fight if you use tackle light enough to give them a sporting chance. Under normal conditions, many of the ready biters will be in the latter class.

No special rod is needed. Your regular casting rod for bass will be perfectly satisfactory. My own preference is for a five- to 5½-

footer that is not too stiff. Steel or glass rods with bamboo action are probably more satisfactory than split bamboo. Holding large pike from weed beds or snags is tough work, and steel or glass is best for the job. Many times you must troll with a heavy water-resistant spoon. Here again steel and glass rods are the most satisfactory. Nothing is more pleasant to use than a perfectly balanced split-bamboo casting rod, but it has its limitations—if you wish to keep it straight and in good condition.

If you insist on using a split-bamboo casting rod for northern pike, have it fitted with a double set of guides so that you can change the rod around each time you go fishing. This helps somewhat in keeping the rod in good condition. An extra-heavy, split-bamboo bait-casting rod might do, but you will have to sacrifice action and pleasure, both in casting and playing the fish. On the other hand a lightweight steel or glass rod will give you plenty of action, and will stand up under any ordinary strain.

Any multiplying reel will serve for pike, but my recommendation would be a level-winder. I started fishing with a plain multiplying reel, for helpful attachments weren't on the market then. For a long time after they did appear, I refused to use a level-winder because I considered them necessary only for the beginner. I now use this type of reel exclusively, and consider it indispensable for the best work. Proper manipulation of the lure often means the difference between success and failure. With a level-winder you are able to attend to the action of the lure without thinking about how the line is spooling. This is true also when you are playing a large fish. Even if you are reasonably expert in spooling the line without mechanical aid, intense excitement may render you unable to spool properly. A loosely coiled, bunched, or jammed line almost always results in the loss not only of a fish but of a lure as well.

The anti-backlash device built into some reels is not so important. No such device so far designed can possibly brake the speed of the line with the delicacy needed for many conditions. To adapt one to varying conditions, you must be forever adjusting the tension, something you can do automatically when using your own thumb. Of course, if you cannot learn how to thumb your reel without getting bad backlashes, then by all means use the device, but try to do without it if you possibly can.

Do not become discouraged by occasional backlashes. Even oldtimers get them, but usually the ones you get after becoming expert can be untangled in a second or so. Most backlashes occur when you try to force a cast, or when you have seen a fish jump and cast too quickly. In forcing the cast, you whip the rod with too much snap, and at the same time release the thumb pressure because you subconsciously realize that you must thumb lightly to reach the required distance. In making a long cast, do not snap the rod. Give it the needed impetus with a smooth sweep of the arm, thumbing so lightly that you do not retard the line, yet heavily enough to prevent backlashing.

Northern pike will take almost any sort of plug, but at times they show a decided preference for certain colors, sizes, and types. Surface lures are often far more effective than underwater plugs, especially when the fish are near shore or in comparatively shallow water. In really deep water a spoon will probably bring better results. The deeper the water, the less fish bait casting will take, and the more you should concentrate on trolling.

Proof of this was supplied on one occasion when we had fished two miles of shoreline and shallow weed beds without getting a fish, despite the fact that the time of year and conditions were suitable for shallow-water fishing. We decided to cross the lake to try the other shore, which was usually good. On the way over I decided to troll. I was using a new-type 8½-foot bamboo-action rod. My lure was a three-inch spoon with a feather treble-hook. I had let out some sixty feet of line when I got a good strike, and seven minutes later I landed an eight-pound northern pike. As we started off again I released another fifty feet of line and hooked a second and larger fish. From then on, we spent no more time along the shore, but concentrated on water above deeply sunken weed beds. At the end of the day our catch was something to be proud of.

Three weeks later, when we fished the same water again, conditions were quite different. Because we had previously caught so many fish in deep water, we started directly for it. We spent several precious hours trolling, but never caught a single fish. We then went to shore and fished a mile without getting a fish larger than two pounds on our underwater lures. We then retraced our course, and fished with surface lures. That same mile of shore then produced ten good fish, all heavier than ten pounds. The best plug was one at which everyone laughed when they saw it. On water you know is good, it doesn't pay to fish with only one lure, and then leave when you don't get strikes. A different lure may be just the thing you need.

I remember fishing around one small island ten times. The first nine times, two of us fished carefully with eighteen different lures and never got a strike. Because I knew some really large fish were in that water, I hated to leave. We hadn't tried the surface lures because the water was deep right up to the shore. On the tenth time around I decided to give a surface-disturbing plug a chance. It worked. We took four splendid fish, and narrowly missed two others.

Often the best location on the lake is right at camp, but to anglers far-away waters often look fishier. I have known many anglers to travel several miles to fish, only to have poor luck, while others fishing right in front of their camp took fish that turned out to be as big as any taken during the season.

I had this driven home to me many years ago. Immediately in front of our camp was a splendid place for big northerns. However, the water was deep, and it had to be trolled. I was a bit of an artificial-lure purist at the time (I am yet, although I know it's foolish under many circumstances), and when I found the northerns wouldn't take a plug or spoon cast in the regulation way, I went to another bay where I thought they would.

We caught a lot of small fish but we did not see a large one. Just as we got back to camp we saw some other anglers landing. They had two large fish, one a twenty-six-pounder, the other a twenty-two-pounder. Both had been caught within a stone's throw of our camp. They had been taken on a June-bug spinner baited with minnow. In six hours, the bait-fishing anglers had taken six other fair fish.

I didn't mind. I had enjoyed a good day with casting rod and plug. But my friends were chagrined. "Why didn't we stay here and try bait?" they moaned. "We knew the large fish were here. What a rotten break."

That happened many years ago, far more than I like to remember. I don't like bait fishing now any more than I did then, but I do try it frequently just to keep my hand in. Often it is the only effective method to use, and if you really want to catch fish you must sometimes resort to it. I know I would if I had only two weeks' vacation each year and couldn't take fish on artificials during that time.

Though I don't really care for bait fishing, I get tired of plug fishing every now and then, and welcome a day with live bait. There is something about the tug of a fish when it takes a minnow that cannot be duplicated. The suspense is thrilling, and when I get the desire to experience this thrill, nothing else will satisfy me.

If there's a secret to pike fishing—to any lake fishing for that matter—it's this: Fish the water near you thoroughly and carefully. Don't waste too much time racing from one section of the lake to another. Sometimes the fish strike well for an hour or so, and remain inactive for the rest of the day. If you stay in one good location, you will be on hand when these productive periods occur. If you are traveling from one place to another, you will very likely miss these opportunities.

CHAPTER XVIII

Persistence Catches Muskies

THE MUSKELLUNGE, an excellent gamefish, is not widely distributed and for that reason a large proportion of anglers never get a chance at one. Often it would involve an expensive trip to the northern lake country or to Canada, and not everyone can manage it. That's a shame, because every fisherman deserves at least one muskie trip in a lifetime. I speak from experience. My first muskie expedition took place in 1932, after I had saved several years to make it possible, and I've done considerable muskie fishing since.

It takes plenty of food and the right kind of habitat to produce large muskellunge, which may run as heavy as sixty or eighty pounds. You won't find them beside every rock or close to every weed bed. In fact, most of the time you won't find them at all. Even skilled muskie fishermen do not get a fish every time they go out. Frequently, like you or me, they don't even get a strike.

The fact is, muskie fishing is extremely unpredictable. You may get one fish in a week of intensive fishing or you may get several in one day. It is not unusual for a muskie enthusiast to spend his entire vacation without raising a single fish. Yet the sport is so fascinating he'll be back next year trying again.

It's a job that calls for infinite patience. Big muskies are lone wolves; you'll rarely find them in schools. It's common for a large specimen to control a fairly extensive area, where it ranges for food. As long as food remains plentiful and he is not driven out by a bigger fish, he'll stay in those parts until caught. Of course, the shallows sometimes become barren when forage fish go deep. Then the muskies must follow if they are to eat, and they're likely to run into one another. Knowing the fish's plug-ugly disposition, I imagine there must be plenty of competition. At such times an angler's lure—either live or artificial—should get plenty of action in a limited area.

Uncertainty is the keynote of muskie fishing. Some experienced men say that springtime is the most productive, others favor August, while still others prefer mid-autumn, before it gets so cold that only the extremely hardy fish. Evidently one part of the season is as good as another—if the fish are in the mood for taking. One thing is certain: You should plan to have at least seven full days on the water, and from ten to fourteen would be better. A two-week stretch should guarantee you at least one fair muskie unless you are very unlucky.

Choice of tackle also varies. You may get by with a medium-weight bait-casting rod from five to 5½ feet long. Even a light-weight bait caster will handle a muskie all right if you set the hook well—over the barb—when you strike. I prefer a regular muskie caster, which is a heavyweight affair, simply because it will hook the fish better.

It takes a stiff and powerful rod to send the hooks home, and this for two reasons. First, the muskellunge has a tough mouth, and second, most muskie lures are fitted with heavy-wire treble hooks. Why manufacturers insist on them I don't know. Hooks of much lighter wire and with smaller bends would make the hooking of a fish far more certain. If made of high-grade steel they won't give way during the fight. Or single hooks could be used on the lures. In my opinion the treble does not hook and hold fish so well as a single. One hook fights another and the barbs often fail to penetrate.

I lost one of the best muskies I ever encountered because I was using a medium-light bait-casting rod and large, clumsy hooks. This monster took my lure and I figured I had him well hooked, for he remained on the line for five minutes. However, he didn't put up any fight—just swam lazily around. Finally I led him right up to the boat and was just ready to land him when he opened his mouth in a sort of yawn and let the plug slip out. It was obvious that the hooks had never been set.

The fish didn't dash away or cause any fuss, but just sank from sight. I changed plugs and made another cast—a very short one, not more than twenty feet from the boat. As I reeled in I saw a fish following the plug, and it looked like the same one I'd had on. But he wouldn't touch the plug and I changed to another one. Again the muskie followed but did not take. And the same thing happened after two more changes of lures.

At other times I have struck as hard as I could, with complete disregard for my tackle, only to have the fish throw my plug on the first jump, even though I kept my line taut to reduce the chance of vibration dislodging the heavy lure. The one good fish that I hooked and landed with a light rod was taken on a ⅝-ounce bass plug fitted with sharp-pointed light-wire hooks. These, naturally, were much smaller than the hooks found on regular muskie plugs.

As you'll have surmised, I am against the use of heavy, saltwater treble hooks on freshwater plugs unless the angler has tackle heavy enough to send the barbs home. One lure that I use has small, light-wire treble hooks, evidently because the plug itself is quite light and would have poor action with heavy hooks. In any case these finer trebles do hook fish far better than the heavy ones. I believe, though, that a single hook of the right size and weight would do an even better job. At other times, I have removed the trebles from a plug and installed a single with better results. But this, of course, may ruin the action of the lure.

When muskies will take the small, light lures used with spinning outfits, it's not hard to hook them securely. Here the trouble comes in landing them, particularly if you run into water hazards or circumstances that call for a strong arm and a strong line.

In 1949 I took several muskies on a six-foot, 3¾-ounce bamboo spinning rod. I had no difficulty setting the treble hooks of my quarter-ounce lure, because they were small and exceedingly sharp. But I accidentally broke my rod tip and had to swtich to a longer, more limber trout rod. It would not set the hooks as efficiently as the six-footer, and as a result I lost several fish.

To the uninitiated, muskie fishing in a lake can become very boring. It's a matter of casting hour after hour over places where fish are supposed to be hanging out. Since strikes are infrequent, the beginner may lose interest. But one good tussle can make up for the boredom, especially if you win.

Members of the *Esox* clan—muskellunge, pickerel, northern pike—follow lures right up to the boat as they are retrieved. It is a sometimes irritating, sometimes stimulating routine. The devils seem to enjoy your chagrin as they lie near the surface, staring at you with baleful eyes. You get excited and provoked, and long to catch the fish that is defying you. And that is good, for it spurs incentive.

Often you can't do anything with these impudent fish, but there is one stunt that occasionally pays off. When you see a muskie following your lure, speed up the retrieve, making it very fast for the last few feet. Then pick up the lure quickly from the surface and drop it back in the water close to the boat. The instant it touches the surface, start moving it back and forth alongside the hull. Do this with an extremely short line, putting the rod tip down until it almost touches the water.

Watch carefully! If the fish strikes you must set the hooks and release the line almost simultaneously, letting only a second or so elapse between strike and controlled release of the line—that is, with your thumb on it to prevent backlash. If you freeze on the line for an instant too long, it or the rod may break.

In muskie fishing, the twenty-four-pound test line will probably do the best all-around job of bait casting. However, many good anglers use an eighteen or twenty-pound test. The twenty-four-pound, though, gives the average fisherman a margin of safety that he may need. In extremely hazardous waters he might make out better with a thirty-pound line. It must be remembered, however, that when you go above eighteen pounds, casting becomes more difficult. An eight-pound test line is the heaviest I can use with a spinning rod and reel. With lures heavier than a quarter of an ounce, however, some men get by with a ten- or even a twelve-pound line, provided it's not too big in diameter.

Among lures, you may find that practically anything will work if you are at the right spot at the right time. Surface jobs that make a commotion are often great producers. Other times the wounded-minnow type of top-water plug seems to work best. Spoons, both wobbling and spinning, are always in order, and when you put a large bucktail fly behind them they are often better than the regular feathered hooks. You should also have plugs that work under water—some a foot or so down, others that go deeper.

The best natural bait is probably a sucker running ten or eleven inches long. If you cast it, use a minnow harness. For still fishing, a fairly large hook—say 3/o, 2/o, or 1/o—will be about right.

The best muskie fishing I've ever had has been in the Lake of the Woods country of Ontario. It is from this section that most of the prize-winning fish are taken, and many of its lakes are still practically virgin territory, offering unlimited possibilities for the angler with time and money to fish them. I've also had some good muskie fishing in the St. Lawrence River, and many anglers have reported good sport in Chautauqua Lake, New York.

As noted earlier, muskie fishing requires plenty of perseverance and determined application. Many times I've considered one chance at a muskie in several days as pretty good fishing. Several years ago, for example, we went to the Lake of the Woods for the surface lake-trout fishing, which starts sometime between October first and fifteenth. Arriving at the base camp on Sabaskong Bay on September twenty-eighth, we found conditions uncertain. The lakers were still in deep water and, with the exception of "jackfish" or pike, few fish were to be had.

Dissatisfied, we immediately set out for Height of Land, or Kisskuteena Lake, in which as a rule the lakers come up earlier than they do in the big lake. Muskies, while smaller, were always more plentiful. But on this occasion even Kisskuteena failed to produce. The lake trout had not yet arrived in quantities and muskies seemed to have disappeared.

In four days' fishing we took one lake trout and three muskies. The first muskie, a small fish of ten pounds, we took while casting and retrieving a plug in the regulation manner. The second fish was a good one for the water—a twenty-pounder—and was taken while fishing for lake trout from a rock shoal. I had made the cast and was letting my wobbling spoon sink to the bottom before starting the retrieve when the line jerked. Immediately taking up the slack, I subsequently set the hook and eventually landed the fish.

Having had one muskie strike while the spoon was sinking, we tried the stunt again and again. Shortly after this I had another hit from what felt like a good fish, but this time my line broke when I set the hook. Investigation disclosed that the line was cut some three inches above the six-inch wire trace. Evidently the line had coiled around the spoon while it was sinking, and when I put on pressure had cut against the teeth of the fish. A ten-inch trace, or longer, is to be recommended.

On the second day after this incident, my wife took a twenty-three-pounder by the same method, and I have found this method of fishing the wobbling spoon productive on many other occasions. I recommend it as a trick to try when the fishing is poor. Be sure, however, that you watch your line carefully while it is sinking. Otherwise you will get strikes without knowing it.

When we returned to Lake of the Woods we found conditions still poor. Every day or so someone would bring in a good muskie, but as there were about twenty-five anglers at the camp, the fish could not be considered very active. It was during this period that I lost my only chance of the trip to get a record fish, a disappointment caused by a poor reel seat.

The rod was made by one of America's foremost makers, yet it did not have a locking reel seat. As a makeshift I had attached a thumb-screw clamp. Probably this would have been all right if I had set up the screw with a pair of pliers. When the big fish hit, the shock released the thumbscrew, the ring slipped, and my reel dropped to the bottom of the boat. I'll not mention the possible size of the fish because I might exaggerate, but my guide, an old-timer, said it was one of the largest he had ever seen.

For the first two desperate runs, which were away from the boat, I managed to hold him and at the same time tried to get the reel back on the rod. I had almost succeeded when the fish made a lightning rush from the boat. When I tried to save the rod, the reel slipped from my hand, my line became snarled in a backlash and snapped. The moral to this is: Do not buy a bait-casting rod unless it is equipped with a locking reel seat that is practically foolproof.

The reel you expect to use for muskie fishing should be chosen wisely. It should be well-made, dependable, and speedy. Also, in my opinion, it should be a level-winder. For many years, like many oldtimers, I thought that a level-winder was a device needed only by beginners. I've changed my mind. When playing a large fish, your entire attention should be on the fight. You shouldn't have to think about your tackle. A level-winder relieves you of all the worry about even spooling of your line, and that means added security when fighting a stubborn and wily fish.

I shall always remember the experience of a friend of mine. He scoffed at anyone who used a level-winder. "Kid stuff," he called it. Then one day he hooked into the largest fish of his angling career, and during the ensuing fight failed to spool his line prop-erly. It was bunched in some places and loose in others. After a twenty-minute struggle he brought the fish within thirty-five feet of the boat, but could get it no nearer because the line jammed against the reel pillars. He fumed and got red in the face but he couldn't do anything about it. Then the fish took a sudden, vicious run. The line cut down into its loose coils, jammed, and broke. My friend bought a level-winding reel the instant he got back to town and has been using one ever since.

In Canadian waters the favorite lures for muskies seem to be spoons of both the wobbling and spinning kinds, and wobbling plugs on the order of regular bass plugs. In Wisconsin one of my favorite lures is a surface plug, with a spinner blade which kicks up quite a fuss when being retrieved. Personally, I have no favorite plug or spoon where muskies are concerned. I've found them all good at times and none of them effective at others. When the muskies absolutely refuse to strike, I don't think there is anything you can do about it. When they show the least sign of interest, however, I think you can catch them if you have the right lure and fish it in the right way.

This belief is borne out by an incident that occurred on a lake in Wisconsin. In six hours of persistent plugging we had raised just one fish. My wife had spotted this fish and had teased it into striking with the surface plug. Unfortunately, she did not set the hook hard enough and the fish threw the plug on the first jump. Shortly after this she had a fish follow her lure twice. The second time the fish remained in plain sight even after the lure had been taken from the water. My wife continued to play the lure in front of him but he would not grab it.

Deciding to have a try myself, I cast three different lures. Each time the muskie made a slight movement as the lure passed but he would not strike. The fourth lure, however, seemed to be just what he wanted. He took it instantly. The fact that I lost the fish in one of his frantic jumps in no way impairs the value of this lesson in muskie-fishing technique. I've used it successfully many times. Whatever you do, don't give up trying for a fish which follows your lure until you have exhausted all the tricks and lures at your command. I repeat: Such a fish is ready to strike if you present the right lure in the right way.

Unlike brown trout, made angler-wise by the large numbers of men who fish for them, muskies are likely to be more kind to beginners than to experienced fishermen. Often the fellow who is after his first muskie gets a really good specimen, while the old-timer gets nothing. I could give many examples of this, but one stands out.

Several years ago we decided to make an expedition to an isolated lake reputed to have good muskies in it. Out of courtesy we asked some lads who were staying at our camp to go along. Our guide left the boys in a likely-looking spot and we went to another part of the lake. We didn't have a bad day. We took four lake trout, weighing from fourteen to seventeen pounds, but we didn't get a muskie to take out with us. As we approached the place where we were to meet the boys, I saw them rowing out to meet us.

"They're towing something!" I exclaimed.

As we drew closer I could see that they were intensely excited.

"What happened?" I asked.

"We don't know," was the reply, "but we think we've got a muskie."

That's just what it was, and a beauty, too. The scale showed thirty-three pounds.

I think that story well illustrates an angler's chances at muskie fishing. It is an uncertain game and one that requires the utmost perseverance. It gets you, too; pulls you back time after time. Every angler cherishes an ambition to catch a really big one of forty pounds or better. After all these years I'm still hoping to catch mine.

CHAPTER XIX

Walleyes Are a Puzzle

WALLEYES puzzle me. They're good eating fish, but in my opinion, ounce for ounce, the little sunfish shows a more valiant spirit when hooked. Walleyes often run to good size, but the much-abused carp, for example, grows larger. Though they're swift, powerful swimmers capable of holding their own with bass, hooked walleyes often hug the bottom like big eels. Yet this faint-hearted fish has thousands of loyal followers. I know. I'm one of them. Not much is written about the walleye, perhaps because his habits don't stir the imagination, but in the Great Lakes area and in other states where walleyes are plentiful, you don't worry about their valor. You just catch them and enjoy it.

As you probably know, pike-perch is the official name for this fish. State and federal agencies have been trying to establish that name since the 1890's, but local names are still stubbornly holding their own. In part of the South the walleye is called the jack salmon, or simply the jack. In Canada he's a pickerel or dore. Pennsylvania anglers may call walleyes Susquehanna salmon, and they're often known as pike in the Great Lakes states. But walleye is the best and most common name. The fish's big white-rimmed eyes make it a natural.

Whatever you call him, it looks as if the walleye is going to continue to play a big part in U.S. sport fishing. Minnesota alone has been stocking some 825 lakes each year with fry-size walleyes, and they're doing well. In one big lake, formerly confined to northern pike, limit catches of legal-size walleyes were common only three years after the fish were stocked as fry.

Wisconsin is another good walleye state, and there are others with clear-water lakes where walleyes will thrive. They not only increase the fish population in a lake but also ease some of the pressure on the black bass.

Walleyes are prolific spawners. A large female will produce some 400,000 eggs, spawning on either a gravel lake bottom or a pebbly riffle in a tributary stream. Stocked walleyes hold their own by natural reproduction in suitable waters. Only lakes with muddy bottoms or those covering too small an area have been disappointing.

They're a predatory fish and feed in schools like yellow perch, but studies show walleyes eat fewer desirable gamefish than other predatory species do. That's probably due to their feeding habits, which keep them well supplied with trash minnows, crawfish, and larvae of insects, rather than to an active dislike for the young of other game fish. Anyway, they get along in a neighborly way with trout stocked in rivers below some of the new dams and with bass in many lakes.

Fishing for walleyes should fascinate a man who likes guessing games, because walleyes are unpredictable. An experienced fisherman can usually tell in advance where to look for bass, pickerel, pike, muskies, and trout. Not so with walleyes. Sometimes they're in the shallows, sometimes in deep water. They may be hugging the shore or smack in the middle of the lake—and all without apparent rhyme or reason. You just have to find them where they are. Once you get the first one, you're usually in business. Chances are there'll be a whole school there, and they ordinarily stay put long enough for you to really work on them.

In lakes I often start by locating a spot near shore where the water deepens abruptly, leaving a shallow shelf running back to the bank. If the walleyes aren't there, I search them out with some trolling method, avoiding areas with mucky, dirty bottoms. You'll seldom find them there.

It's easier to locate them in streams. Fish the deep, swift water, especially places where an eddy is formed on the sides of a fast current. When you have a strong wind on lake or stream, fish along the rocky lee shores. Minnows seek shelter there, and walleyes follow them in.

In a general way, walleyes move to shallower water as the weather gets colder in the fall. Then they like the water along sandbars and over rocky reefs in rivers or the clean-bottomed bays of a lake. In the spring, they gradually move back to deeper water as it gets warmer. In July and August they'll likely be in thirty to fifty feet of water. But even then they may come into the shallows on a dark rainy day or at night. You can't be sure. A spot that's great fishing one evening may not get you a nibble the next, simply because the school is feeding somewhere else. Keep in mind that walleyes are great travelers. Tagged fish have been caught a hundred miles away a short time after being released.

Since exploratory trolling takes first place in the shaky science of walleye fishing, it's the first system you need to master. Two general rules here are to troll slowly and to get your bait or lure close to the bottom. That puts two factors in your favor from the start, because walleyes are generally close to the bottom and they're lazy about their feeding. They seldom follow a minnow or lure that speeds by as if it would require a strenuous chase. They'll wait for something easier to catch. So use a lure or bait-and-sinker combination that will handle well when trolled slowly near the bottom.

Artificial lures imitating minnows may work well in trolling for walleyes, but several natural baits are consistently successful. Put a sinker on the end of your line and attach a plain hook on a ten- or twenty-inch leader about eighteen inches above the sinker. Bait the hook with worms, crawfish, or a live minnow and troll so that your sinker bounces slowly along the bottom with the baited hook trailing above and behind it. In all trolling, hook live minnows through the lips. They live longer that way.

Another effective rig for trolling is a dipsey sinker trailed by a spinner. The sinker is attached to the end of the line with the spinner below it on a heavy leader about a foot long. Oddly, this outfit doesn't snag up often. The action of the spinner blade seems to lift it off the bottom. You can bait the hook behind your spinner with minnows or other baits with good results. If you use a dead, or nearly dead, minnow, give it a better action by running the hook through its mouth, out through the gills, and through the back behind the dorsal fin. This arrangement also does well with only a sinker and baited hook. The spinner is just an added attraction.

Once you locate a school of walleyes, still fishing may be best. Live minnows get my vote as the best still-fishing bait, but worms, the larger nightcrawlers, and crawfish are also good. Some like live frogs. Whatever your choice, work the bait; don't just let it lie on the bottom. Lifting your sinker off the bottom every minute or so gives the bait just enough action to catch the eye of fish.

When a walleye takes a natural bait it seldom makes a spirited run with it. More often it just mouths the bait or swims away slowly. So let him take it for a while. If he keeps moving off with it or jiggling it in the same spot, snap up your rod tip with a sharp flick of the wrist. Yanking back with a full arm motion can wrench the bait out of his mouth.

Casting takes many walleyes in some places, particularly in fall after cold weather has brought them into shallow water. In the cold-water rivers of the Great Lakes states you may take them while casting for bass and northern pike during the summer. I did just that in Wisconsin during August and September. In fact, my casts took more walleyes than bass and northern pike combined.

Most of the regular bass plugs will take walleyes, but I favor the minnow-like designs. Spoons and spinners are also good, and some of the new spinning lures are excellent. A strip of fish, pork rind, or a worm trailed behind your spoon is always a good teaser with walleyes, and spinning rods handle light baited spoons especially well.

Some of the best casting I've had for these fish has been in the fast waters of big rivers. My favorite lure for that purpose is a feather jig, something that can be bumped along the bottom without snagging. I've fished miles of such rivers without locating a school, but I've also hit hot spots where my limit came in short order. These big river schools will take wet flies and streamers, too, but unless they're in shallow water I prefer the spinning rod with a small spinner or spoon.

Walleye fishing is quite a change for those used to bass and pike. If you haven't tried it you should. Walleyes will continue to puzzle you, but they'll add new interest and pleasure to your fishing.

Walleyes spawn in the spring, usually in April, and are very prolific. Under favorable conditions they grow to a great size. Claims have been made of fifty-pounders, but the largest I can find any printed record of was forty pounds. That fish was caught by Dr. D. C. Estes of Minnesota many years ago, and was mentioned in an article on pike-perch written by A. N. Cheney, an authority, about 1896.

There are three distinct color phases of this fish—gray, yellow, and blue. The gray variety attains the largest size, and it is claimed fish of this color run up to forty pounds. However, usual top weights are ten and fifteen pounds. Fish of this color have the widest distribution and are the most common. The blue variety is the baby of the lot, occasionally reaching a weight of five pounds, but the average is probably less than a pound. These well-defined distinctions in color are supposed to be dependent on age and environment.

The shape of all walleyes is, to get technical, fusiform, which means that it tapers toward each end. The greatest depth at the middle is about one-fifth of the length, with the head long and pointed and occupying a little more than one-quarter of the body length. The mouth is large, and provided not only with bands of short hair-like teeth, but with long, sharp canine teeth located on the jaws and roof of the mouth. The eye is large and glassy. There are two dorsal fins, both high and well separated. The front dorsal contains from twelve to sixteen sharp spines, the rear dorsal from nineteen to twenty-one soft rays. The tail is forked. The body is mottled and marked with indistinct lines.

When you go after most fish, you usually know about where to find them but you never know where you'll find walleyes. I remember an experience at Tupper Lake, New York. We had found a most satisfactory hole, located directly off a rocky point, where the water deepened abruptly close to shore. The fish were deep—at least thirty-five feet down—and every time we sank a weighted live minnow to that depth we immediately got a hit, and usually hooked a fish.

We fished that spot for three days in succession, both in the morning and in the evening, and always quit fishing in an hour or so because we caught so many fish we didn't feel right about catching any more even though we put most of them back. But on the three days immediately following we couldn't get a touch. We couldn't believe that the walleyes had left there, so kept trying although it was a stupid waste of time. When we had only two days left, we started looking for other places where we might find the fish. On the afternoon of the last day, our bad luck continuing, we decided to fish a weedy bay for northern pike. Imagine our surprise when we ran into a bunch of really good-size walleyes which struck our surface plugs just as largemouth bass do.

If you haven't any live bait and can't procure any, you can do the same kind of exploratory trolling described earlier, using a plug instead of a baited hook at the end of your leader. Do not use a plug that sinks. What you want is one that floats when not in action. Your sinker, therefore, must have sufficient weight to offset the buoyancy of the plug. These floating plugs act very much alive when prevented by a sinker from coming to the top of the water. Also, when the sinker snags, as it's certain to do once in a while, the plug will stay above the snag and so the hooks won't get caught.

The more readily your plug responds to movement, the better for this particular kind of fishing, for it must show plenty of action when moving slowly, and slow trolling is a must for walleye fishing. You also should know positively the speed required to bring out the action of the plug used. Remember that the deeper you fish the less speed you'll need to make a plug work properly, for the water pressure helps to bring out the action. Personally, I like this kind of fishing. It really produces, and is easy on lures. By attaching the sinker to a weaker line than the one the lure is on, you may fish bottom thoroughly without much danger of losing anything but an occasional sinker.

And even the sinker is in less danger of being lost when you are using a floating plug because when you get snagged the lure immediately ascends as far as the adjustment will let it, and you may, without danger of getting it snagged along with the sinker, retrace your course in an effort to get the sinker loose. When attempting this, always go back the way you came, and when you are on the other side of the snag it is quite likely that the sinker will come loose without any difficulty.

Whenever you get a hit while fishing bottom this way, with either live bait or artificials, concentrate your efforts on that particular locality for a time, for it is almost certain that you will catch other fish in the same place. However, walleye feeding grounds may be of rather small area, and if they happen to be some distance from shore you can easily lose track of them, and it may take days to find them again.

Therefore, you should mark the spot the instant you get your first strike. Do this by picking out four distinct landmarks, each at a different point of the compass. Then, so you won't forget it, sketch your markers on a piece of paper, setting down the directions and the name of the lake. If you make a habit of drawing such sketch maps, and preserving them, you'll be surprised how helpful they can be.

Probably the most popular bait for walleyes is the June-bug spinner to which is attached a hook baited with a minnow. As a rule this spoon blade is used merely as an attractor, the minnow or other bait trailing some distance behind. Large worms are often better than minnows. Small lamprey eels are also very good walleye bait. Just as when fishing with plugs, keep your trolling speed down, trolling only fast enough to make the spinner revolve.

Fixed-position spoons like the June bug are constructed for this very purpose, and that is the chief reason for their popularity.

Where walleyes are plentiful, you will often catch them when plug fishing for bass along the shore or over shoals and bars. I've fished some lakes where this is a common occurrence. One Wisconsin lake in particular has consistently delivered mixed bags, especially along one certain shore. That shoreline is ideal, heavily wooded, with overhanging branches coming down to within a few feet of the water.

A shallow, weedy shelf runs out from the bank for a short distance, the water ranging from six to twenty-four inches deep. Largemouth bass and northern pike frequent this shelf. At the edge of this ledge the water deepens abruptly—six feet in some spots, twenty-five in others. This deeper water is attractive to walleyes and smallmouth bass, although occasionally an extra-large northern pike is to be found there.

The catch along this shore runs about like this: two largemouth bass, one smallmouth bass, three walleyes, and two northern pike. The smallmouth bass there have proved the least consistent; many times we caught none at all, but the other fish have always been taken unless the fishing was just plain bad. Our best lure along this stretch has been a yellow-perch finish "float-when-not-in-action," wobbling-type plug. Next best is a white plug, with red, gouged-out head and an erratic, darting action. However, except in Wisconsin and Minnesota, I've never had much luck plug fishing for walleyes. In the fall Ed Serely, a friend of mine, has taken many fine strings of large walleyes from his dock on Prairie Lake, Wisconsin, and some wonderful walleye catches are made at that time of year and in that part of the country by casting plugs from the shore.

If walleyes had nothing else to recommend them to anglers, their value as food would cause them to be sought after. Cold, pure water is needed for their best development, and probably that is largely responsible for the firmness, texture, and flavor of their meat. Their flavor is at its best when they are in roe, that is in the late winter, but they are good at any time.

Fried, boiled, broiled, or baked, they are excellent eating. Large fish should be cut into pan-size fillets and fried slowly in a minimum amount of fat. For best flavor, season the meat when cooking. When taken from cold water and baked with the skin on, walleyes take on an exceptionally delicious flavor. For boiling, however, I prefer to skin them, putting the skinned, thoroughly cleaned and seasoned fish in a cheese cloth tied tightly all around to keep the flesh together. In addition to salt and pepper, a bit of thyme and parsley may be added. Yes, the walleye is a fine fish. Those who fish for them know this; those who don't should try it.

CHAPTER XX

The Right Way to Troll

THERE seems to be a widespread idea that trolling is merely a matter of trailing a lure behind a moving boat. If fish hit the moving lure, the angler is having good luck. If there are no strikes, it's a bad day for trolling. At least that's the haphazard style of fishing that some anglers call trolling. Expert trollers, on the other hand, use thoughtful strategies that rely more on skill than luck.

Trolling is an extremely effective way to catch fish, as demonstrated by countless boatmen who hook fish while idly dragging their lures in the water on their way to the dock. Anglers who anchor for still fishing or cast from drifting boats will often catch fish as they move to new positions with a bait, fly, or lure trailing in the water. Those who try to figure out why this happens are on their way toward becoming scientific trollers.

The big advantage of trolling is that it gives more fish an opportunity to see the bait or lure. With casting systems, anglers are swinging their hooks high in the air part of the time, where obviously they won't get any strikes. The trolling fisherman plunks his lure in the water and leaves it there, and his constantly moving boat takes the lure through a great variety of depths and shallows where any fish in a striking mood can get at it. A person can't cover nearly so much water by casting and retrieving, and there's also the possibility that a caster will lift the lure out of water just as a fish is closing in on it.

This is not intended to discredit casting. Many times the fish in a trolling-size lake or river will be concentrated in weed beds or lying in pockets among stumps and snags where a troller can only operate around the edges. Then casting from an anchored or drifting boat may pay bigger dividends. But trolling along the fringe of such tangled waters is a fine way to locate fish, and there are times when repeated passes with a trolled lure will catch more of them than a series of casts from a motionless boat. Trolling through very shallow water sometimes frightens fish that could be taken by casting, but on the whole fish seem less disturbed by a motor than by the splash of a lure.

The science of trolling starts with an understanding of depths in the water you fish—locating holes, shoals, contours of weed beds and submerged stumps or rocks. The troller who knows these things can maneuver his lures until he locates the fish, whereas the novice will either spend his time trolling above the fish or be continually snagging lures on the bottom.

Ordinarily, fish are easiest to catch in moderately shallow water, and trolling, no matter how blindly you use the method, is likely to take more fish from the shallows than casting. In water from two to seven feet deep, a troller may have good luck with surface lures—high-riding spoons, spinners, or surface plugs. If those fail, use lures that run deeper, perhaps adding more sinkers to hold the lures down.

Small lures are best for most shallow-water trolling. I generally use a trolling lure somewhat smaller than the bait-casting lure I'd use in the same situation. In very shallow water I'd start with a lure weighing ⅛ to ⅜ of an ounce and change to increasingly larger lures as I worked into deeper water. A spoon weighing half an ounce is usually big enough for trolling as deep as seven feet.

Fish that are down eight feet or more usually send casters home muttering, "They ain't biting," which is not the right explanation in most cases. Systematic trolling with different lures at ever-increasing depths will usually hook a fair number of the fish that have frustrated casters by going deep.

Trolling in deep water usually requires a tackle rig that will keep the lure a few inches off bottom. If I'm using a sinker for such trolling, I like to feel it bounce on bottom from time to time. My lure will be riding a bit higher than the sinker, and a pass of this sort through an area that holds fish usually will provoke a strike. If I hook one fish, I circle back over the same spot. Chances are there'll be several more there, perhaps a whole school.

Sometimes a troller can park his boat over a school of fish in the depths and do remarkably well by offering them the same type of lure with a casting rod. The vital step in this sort of casting is the long pause after the lure hits the water. A caster will catch very few fish in the depths unless he lets his lure sink all the way to the bottom before starting the retrieve. The advantage of trolling for deep-water fish is that a trolled lure can be kept in motion near the bottom all the time, while a caster's lure spends a lot of time in the air, sinking through the water, or being reeled in through unproductive water.

Another great virtue of trolling is its efficiency in picking up scattered fish in a large body of water. To illustrate, two companions and I once put in some discouraging hours trying to catch trout in a Canadian lake by casting wet flies and spinners, fishing them at various depths in the holes that usually held the larger concentrations of fish.

When the casting failed we decided to troll. One man was trolling a wet fly, the other a spinner, so I chose a small plug that was weighted with a sinker on the line to stay fairly deep. Our idea was to give the fish a choice of three lures. If they showed a decided preference for one, we'd all use it.

Well, we started to catch fish. They were scattered, and trolling located them. In some stretches the spinner seemed to suit them better, but the best producer was the little plug I was trolling. I'm sure that the only reason the plug outclassed the wet fly and spinner was that it would stay closer to the bottom without snagging. My companions were using sinkers ahead of their lures to get depth, but both the wet fly and the spinner, lacking natural buoyancy, would snag when my friends eased them down to the bottom. I could operate right on the bottom, with my sinker bouncing over snags. My little plug, trailing along two feet behind the sinker, was buoyant enough to clear the snags by two or three inches. Thus I was able to fish where the fish were, while my friends mostly hooked snags at that depth.

You can do some good trolling with natural bait, too. With a worm, minnow, or grub on your hook, ease the boat along very slowly, regulating the length of your line so the baited hook is always flirting with the bottom. This is an excellent way to sound out the holes in a lake or large river you're not acquainted with. Once you've learned the bottom contours and located the concentration of fish, you can often work the hot spots with artificial lures and get good results.

Best tackle for trolling? That depends mostly on how deep you need to go. In very shallow water a troller can easily handle fish of moderate size on light bait-casting tackle, spinning rods, even with fly tackle. Shallow-water lures, as I mentioned earlier, should ordinarily be light and small.

As a troller goes into deeper water he usually needs a stiffer rod, heavier line, and larger lures. For depths of twelve to twenty feet, a good average rig would be a stiff bait-casting rod about 6½ feet long or a regular trolling rod of about the same length and weight. Use a sturdy bait-casting reel, or perhaps a trolling reel with a star drag for heavy-duty work. A hundred yards of twenty-pound monofilament or braided line is about right for most moderate-depth trolling. The medium-size spoons that wobble or dart are good at this depth. So are the wobbling plugs. Spinners may do fine, too, but be alert to see that they don't twist your line. Some of them require a keel device ahead of them to prevent twist.

For trolling deeper than twenty feet, a person usually needs large lures—plugs or spoons up to five inches long or long strings

of spinners ahead of a baited hook. This calls for a sturdy trolling reel, line testing twenty pounds or more, and a stiff rod.
Limber rods will be overpowered by heavy lures trolling deep,
and it's important with all trolling that you be able to feel the
action of the lure through the rod. With a wobbling lure, for
example, you should have a rod stiff enough to register the trem-
ors of the wobbling so that you can feel them as you hold the
pole. Limber rods go dead under this weight of heavy lures.

Trolling for lake trout, the angler often has to get down as
deep as a hundred feet. This calls for either a very heavy sinker
on monofilament or braided line, a quick-sinking wire line, or one
of the new leaded nylon lines. Leaded nylon line is a boon for
anglers who do a lot of deep trolling. In addition to its quick-
sinking quality and small diameter, it is dyed so that each twenty
yards of line is a different color—the angler can tell by the color
code how many yards of line he has out.

The matter of color also comes up in choosing trolling lures.
Some scientists say fish only see different colors as various shades
of gray, but I'm convinced by a lifetime of fishing with lures of
various colors that fish will take or reject a lure according to its
hue. In other words, if a red lure is seen by the fish as a certain
shade of gray, there are times when they want that particular
shade of gray that red lures produce. A troller should have lures
in the basic metal colors—copper, nickel, brass—and also in
fish-scale finishes, reds, greens, and combinations of those colors.
I believe the metal colors pay off more consistently in the long
run.

Good trolling reels? That depends so much on the type of
trolling that it's difficult to be positive about the advantages of any
one model. A fly reel on a regular fly rod may be just the thing for
trolling a wet fly on a short line in shallow water. A heavy salt-
water reel is needed for big fish at great depths. Bait-casting reels
are good for most of the work between. A spinning reel can be
pressed into service for trolling, too, and will do a good job with
light lures and fish of moderate size. I'd rule it out only for work
that requires a metal line.

But successful trolling is more a matter of thoughtful experiments with different boat speeds, various fishing depths, and an assortment of lures than of buying a certain type of rod, reel, and line. The masters of this fish-taking system of angling are as meticulous and thoughtful in their style of fishing as those who take their fish with dry flies.

As mentioned earlier, trolling is basically very simple. You simply let a lure of some kind drag behind a moving boat and hope that a fish will take it. Trolling, a small child may hook as many fish as experienced adults in the same boat. But trolling, like most styles of fishing, becomes complicated when used to its fullest potentialities. Let's go a little deeper into the subject of methods and lures in trolling.

Take, for example, the trolling of flies. This method is useful in fishing large, still rivers, lakes, and ponds—places too large to cover by random casting. You may troll successfully with a great variety of flies and make up different combinations of them on one cast.

For trout ponds make up a leader holding two or three wet flies and troll them with both line and leader unweighted. This will sometimes take fish when other methods fail. It also may show up hot spots in the water where you may anchor and cast. Sizes and patterns of effective trolling flies will vary according to local conditions. As a rule, hook sizes 6 through 12 will be a good average. Mix the cast. That is, have flies of both dull and bright patterns on the same leader.

I like to start with a No. 6 or 8 fly of bright pattern, say a Parmachene Belle, Silver Doctor, or Royal Coachman on the end of the leader. For the two droppers I use a gray and a ginger fly, such as Blue Quill and Light Cahill. I prefer sizes 10 and 12 for these droppers. If I get a few strikes to one fly and none to the others, I change the patterns which do not bring any response to something entirely different. I keep changing until I find the most taking combination. Usually the tail fly is taken more often than the droppers. If the droppers take most fish, it's a sure bet that you should change the end fly.

Trolling flies on or near the surface is likely to be most productive when you can see surface activity. The trolling should be done slowly with plenty of line out, say from sixty to eighty feet. A long line is especially important when fishing over shallows where the disturbance of the boat may make the fish momentarily suspicious. I consider a fly rod or a light spinning rod best for this trolling. The less disturbance you make with the boat, the better luck you will have.

If you don't get any response from surface trolling, then try sinking the cast of flies. One of the most effective ways to do this is to place a split shot between each fly. Try BB shot size first. If this doesn't get the flies deep enough, use larger sizes up to the largest, which is buckshot. You can buy special split shot that's made with a rubber core and is easily attached. It doesn't fray or pinch the line or leader as much as regular split shot.

When you fish deep, it may be best to use a streamer or bucktail fly that resembles a minnow for the end or tail fly. And faster trolling may pay off with the fake minnow fly. Real minnows move very quickly when they want to.

Coming to frequent stops and then starting off fast again would make ideal trolling for this type of fly, but such a trolling pace is practically impossible. Vary your trolling pace as much as possible until you find a productive combination. Then stick to it until it stops producing. Trolling with flies is mostly a trout-fishing system, but it often works equally well for bass, landlock salmon, pickerel, and pike. Here are some suggested fly sizes and patterns for fish other than trout:

For landlock salmon, the minnow types are generally most effective. Some good patterns are Black Ghost, Gray Ghost, Mickey Finn, Edson Tiger (both light and dark), Green Ghost, White Marabou, Gray Marabou, or any other pattern that you may think looks like a minnow when thoroughly wet and moving in the water. All the patterns mentioned are well known, and their dressings are available in various books. Sizes of flies should range from as small as No. 10 long shank to as large as No. 4.

Those landlock salmon patterns are also excellent for black bass and the pike family, but use larger sizes, say Nos. 2, 4, and 6 regular shank hooks. Patterns I've found effective for bass are Royal Coachman, Professor, Parmachene Belle, Montreal, Red

Ibis, or any large bee pattern with a fat body of black and yellow chenille. I have also found the Lord Baltimore pattern exceptionally effective at times. Hair flies of various colors and tied on regular-shank hooks in sizes 2, 4, and 6 are also good.

A spinner attached ahead of a fly may give you more confidence in using a fly for trolling, although in my opinion this is spinner trolling, not fly fishing. The spinner should match the size of the fly being used. Use a small blade for a small fly, a large one in front of a large fly.

Spinners have a tendency to twist line, so that when trolling with them it's usually advisable to use extra swivels. Some spinners are so bad at twisting a line that a rudder-shaped sinker or a plastic keel ahead of them will save you much grief. Once a line gets badly twisted, it's such a chore to untangle it that one is tempted to throw the line away.

If the line is simply twisted and not also tangled, take off the line-twisting lure and let the line out carefully behind a fast-moving boat or feed it into a fast current until it unwinds. If the line is tangled and knotted, you need patience, good eyes, and imagination to straighten it. A new line may be the best solution.

When fishing with underwater lures, trolling with a motor is fine. While it's nice to have someone run the boat for you while you troll, you can easily do both things. I know quite a number of fellows who fish that way all the time and make out better than those who have nothing but the trolling to attend to. A rod holder attached to the boat is useful to the solitary troller. It's placed where the angler can reach it quickly. Some trollers simply hold their rods with one hand while the other hand runs the boat.

The trolling reel should ordinarily be drag-set to keep line from going out too fast in case of a heavy strike. The quick rush of line can cause a backlash on the reel spool, and too much slack makes it difficult to set the hook. The thing to learn is sure control of your particular rod and reel, no matter how you're fishing it.

When using a motor, it's best to shut it off the instant a fish is hooked. When rowing, you'll automatically drop the oars when a fish hits. If you're handling the boat and your companion hooks a fish, shut off the motor or drop the oars and reel in your own line to avoid a tangle.

The less stretch a line has, the better it is for trolling. When there's very little stretch you can feel the lure working. Each different lure sends back vibrations that you must learn to know. The lure may pick up a tiny bit of weed or moss on a hook point that will render it ineffectual. Experienced trollers tell by the change in vibration when their lure has trash on it. They reel in and clear the hooks, rather than pull a lure that's lost its fish appeal.

CHAPTER XXI

How to Catch Panfish

OF ALL the fresh-water fishes, yellow perch and bluegills are probably accountable for more pleasurable hours of fishing than any others. Of course those deriving this pleasure are not the rabid bass and trout fishermen, but the large number of anglers who fish mostly for relaxation and for food, and who are satisfied to associate with the lesser lights of piscatorial society.

Generally speaking, perch and bluegills are easy to catch, except when it comes to getting the big ones. Because of this, people who fish for them are often looked upon by trout and bass anglers as lowbrow fishermen. The odd thing about this is that many of the anglers who don't do well with trout and bass are the ones who are most likely to act superior to the panfishermen. And while they may themselves have an urge to catch some of these plebian fish, they don't give it a try because they're afraid of being scorned by the elite, the stars of the trout and bass world.

In my opinion fishing should not be competitive or comparative. Rather it should be contemplative—a sport to build the soul and refresh the mind, so that after a day or more on lake or stream a person goes back to the job of making a living with renewed vigor and new ideas. For this purpose panfish serve just as well as the more popular game fishes. If you get skillful enough to locate and fool large perch or bluegills, you can feel just as proud as the angler who catches a two-pound trout in water where a pound fish is considered big.

Yellow perch were once restricted to southern Canada, New England, and the northern midwest states. Now, as the result of stocking, they're found in nearly all states except a few in the deep South. Since they're wolfish killers of other fish—to the limit of their size and physical powers—these fish are seldom protected by closed seasons and bag limits.

While yellow perch prefer a diet of minnows or other small fish, they also feed on insects and crustaceans. With an adequate food supply they may run to a good size and sometimes be rather difficult to catch. However, it's rare to find them running better than about half a pound. Under ideal conditions they can grow to a weight of four pounds or more, but if you ever catch a two-pounder or better, you're entitled to a little bragging.

As a rule, yellow perch are found in large, quiet streams and in ponds and lakes. Their tendency is to seek deep water, even to thirty feet or more, although the smaller ones usually stay in the shallows near vegetation. However, I've caught large ones while trolling in shallow waters for bass and pickerel.

Good spots to try are areas of weed beds where the water breaks abruptly to greater depth and to a bottom of gravel, rock, or sand. It also pays to investigate water of good depth near pilings, docks, and bridges. Large perch will usually be in the vicinity of forage fish, or where they can grab the unprotected fry of bass and other game fish.

Perch schools usually number from one to three dozen fish. In each group the size of the individual fish will be fairly uniform, a difference of more than two inches in length between the largest and the smallest being uncommon. Perch are spring spawners; sometimes spent females are observed before winter ice has disappeared.

One time while fishing a smallmouth bass lake with chub minnows, my companion took as many perch as bass, with the perch running heavier. Some time later, fishing with ⅝ of an ounce plugs in the same water, we took only one large perch to each eight smallmouths. However, we had many misses which I suspected were yellow perch.

I felt sure that the missed strikes were mostly from perch that couldn't handle our bass-size lures. Later on I went back to test this theory. Using smaller minnows and small spinners on a fly rod, I brought my yellow perch score up to four for each smallmouth. In subsequent experiences with yellow perch, I always did better when using small bait.

Another time a couple of us were fishing for pike in a northeastern lake. Ordinarily pike are ready strikers but on this occasion we couldn't seem to find them. We searched the depths (some thirty feet of water) and experienced many "bunts," or a feeling of something tugging at our lures, but we couldn't connect. Experience told me to try a smaller lure, so I weighted a very small one to get the proper depth. The bunts then became hooked fish—yellow perch averaging about a pound each, with an occasional larger specimen adding an extra thrill.

My most recent experience with yellow perch was in North Carolina. The bass fishing was a bit dull. In some seven hours we'd caught only seven or eight, with the top fish a 4½-pounder. Then we ran into the perch. With the same lure that had taken the largest bass, a deep runner, I hooked a 1½-pound perch while we were drifting downstream. I was surprised to find one in that country, till my companion, Buck Perry, explained they'd been stocked there.

Then we noticed another boat downstream, the occupants of which were taking fish fast—perch, as we found when we inquired. We learned they were using small minnows, but since we had no bait of any kind we started casting with spoons and plugs of bass size. These didn't produce very well, so we changed to small spoons, which did a bit better but not well enough to suit us.

The water where the perch seemed to be congregated was below a dam. For some distance below it the water was quite swift, and we had very little luck in this area, taking only one fish, a bass. Farther downstream the water moved rather sluggishly. In the deepest part of this section we got the most hits, so we decided to let the boat drift over it while dragging the bottom with small wobbling spoons. From then on we took perch readily. There were three requisites: a small spoon that didn't snag easily; fishing the spoon so that it dragged the bottom; and keeping constantly in the active area. If we didn't do all these things we failed to get results.

The active area was comparatively small, perhaps eighty to a hundred feet wide and three hundred long. The bottom must have been literally swarming with perch, judging by the ease with which we caught them. We also picked up some bass at the same time. The tackle for yellow perch should be light to get the fullest enjoyment from fishing for them. A light spinning outfit is perfect.

In natural baits my favorites for perch are worms and small minnows. But if you're willing to take the trouble to get them, the following insects will bring excellent results: meal worms, grasshoppers, all sorts of grubs, nymphs, large flies, and bees. Then there are other natural baits that are good on perch, such as baby crawfish, shrimp, and cut bait—for instance, the meat of mussels and fish cut to the proper size. In artificials I prefer small spoons or spinners, such as those used on average-size trout, but often very small plugs will do a great job.

Now we come to bluegills, with perhaps some exceptions the largest of the sunfishes. In different sections of the country they are called variously blue sunfish, blue perch, bream, pumpkinseed, green sunfish, long-eared sunfish, red-eared sunfish, and sunfish. Then they are known as the western shellcracker in the lower Mississippi Valley and in Florida. All are fair-size fish that will give good sport on suitable tackle, and all taste great.

The methods for catching sunfishes are the same as those for catching perch, with the understanding that you use smaller hooks and smaller baits for the smaller fish. Not that the smaller sunfishes won't try to grab big bait—they will, and I've caught many quarter-pounders when fishing for bass with ⅝- to ¾-ounce plugs. But that isn't the way to fish for them.

Bluegills nest from the middle of May until the end of July. Females are sometimes reported spawning several times in one season. They are very prolific. As with bass (which by the way is a sunfish), the male bluegill makes the nest. After the female lays the eggs the male will chase her away and guard both eggs and young, up to a point. During this spawning and protective season the adult fish becomes very pugnacious. They'll attack anything that approaches the nest, even fish much larger than themselves, and this makes them easy to catch.

Bluegills are considered warm-water fish, and they prefer locations where there is plenty of vegetation growing from mud and sand bottoms. They are found—either native or stocked—from southern Canada southward to the Gulf states and from New England to California.

My personal experience with bluegills and related sunfish dates back some sixty years. While I strayed from the path to concentrate on bigger game, I still love to catch "gills." For their size they're outstanding fighters. Many a half-pound to one-pound bluegill has given me more of a battle than a trout or largemouth bass of equivalent weight on identical tackle.

Quite recently while bass fishing with floating plugs, without success, I noticed rises in several places, and there were numerous splashes around my bass bug. I put on a fine tapered leader, tied on a dry fly, and cast over the next batch of dimples I saw. Seconds later I was fast to a bit of fighting fury that made even my rather heavy fly rod bend beautifully to the water. The fish was a bluegill weighing 1¼ pounds. I caught a number of them that day on the three dry flies I happened to have along—a Blue Dun, a Light Cahill, and a Royal Coachman. The Blue Dun was tops.

Another time I was in Wisconsin with my dad, who was then too old for the more strenuous bait and fly casting. We decided to try for bluegills. There were a lot of them in the lake, and occasionally I'd taken a large one on a bass plug. We gathered a pint of worms and started out.

We tried all the places where we thought the big bluegills might be found, but didn't do very well for the first couple of hours, though we took several small bass and a number of small gills. Then we came to a channel between two islands that was filled with weeds, stumps, and lilypads, but with plenty of open spots where we could fish without getting into difficulties. The surface of the water was like a mirror.

I anchored the boat in a promising spot and made a tentative cast with a large worm, intending to let it sink to the bottom. But it never quite got there. I felt a couple of hard tugs, waited a few seconds and struck, then brought in a one-pound bluegill. We had hit the jackpot. We both took fish after fish, all big ones. But the hot area was very limited, not over twenty feet square. A bait dropped outside it remained unmolested. We took a dozen fish each, then quit.

I've had many pleasant hours of fishing for bluegills with wet flies and nymphs. These fish seem to prefer dull patterns, as a rule, such as March Brown, Blue Dun, or Blue Quill, Cahill, Ginger Quill, Alder, and Gold-Rib Hare's Ear. As for hook size, No. 10 has served me best.

Among the fancy flies I have found Alexandra, McGinty or Bee, and Royal Coachman all excellent. Any dull nymph will do. As a rule, fishing the fly slowly with slight jerks is good practice. So is fishing them at different depths. Start by working the fly just beneath the surface, then gradually let it go deeper before retrieving. Often a split shot above the fly will be needed to get the proper depth. Among natural baits, worms top the list, but grubs, beetles, and any other small bait that may be impaled on a hook will do the job. Remember that although these fish are good little scrappers, they have small mouths, so that unless you use small baits and suitable hooks—not larger than No. 8—you'll miss lots of takes.

While you may take bluegills with a rod and reel that you use for bass, the lighter the tackle the more fun you'll have. I prefer very light fly or spinning tackle. One of my pet bluegill rods is an eight-foot split bamboo weighing two ounces. It's extremely limber, but what fun it gives me when I catch a fish. For the best sport with panfish you should use very light tackle. This may be a light cane pole for some type of fishing, a slender fly rod, or a light spinning rod. Northerners seldom use cane poles but Southerners well know the worth of a nice cane. They choose them with the greatest care for straightness and quality of bamboo, and select different weights and lengths for different kinds of fishing. I've fished with cane poles many times—and like using them, too—though they're awkward to carry in a car.

I remember an old gentleman in Mississippi who always had at least four perfect cane poles on hand—the very light ones eight to ten feet long for panfish, and two heavier ones twelve to fourteen feet long for bass and redfish. Then he'd have some extras for sheepheads, weakfish, and other salt-water fish that ran up the bayous and could be caught on shrimps and cut bait. I suppose cane poles are difficult to find these days. Even in those days it took a lot of selecting. That old fisherman would go through bundles of cane just to find one or two poles that suited him.

My first choice for a panfish bait rod is a nine-foot split bamboo or glass of four to 4¼ ounces. This is long enough for dropping a bait along the edge of weeds and into pockets, and is also good for casting. Strip-casting is used a lot for this work, but in recent years the spinning reels made especially to fit fly rods have come greatly to the front. In stripping, the line must be held or dropped in coils and then cast by shooting it out as the rod is swept forward with a full arm movement. With the fly-rod spinning reel, the line is thrown directly from the reel.

The line for strip-casting should be the best of fly lines—smooth, well-finished, and non-kinky. The size (calibration) should be small, not larger than G-level. The reel for stripping is relatively unimportant, except that it should be well constructed and sturdy. It need not be expensive, but neither should it be junk. There are a good number of medium-priced fly reels on the market that will give good service.

For the fly-rod spinning reel, I prefer four-ounce, five-pound test monofilament line. This is strong enough for any panfishing and gives a bit of extra protection if you hook a larger fish. With a very limber fly rod it's difficult to break even a low-test line if a good bend is kept in the rod. The breakage occurs when the fish gets into weeds or in a snag.

Fitted with a fly reel, the nine-foot rod I recommended as a panfish bait rod will also do a good job of fly casting. However, you will need a line that will fit the rod. A nine-foot 4¼-ounce rod made of split bamboo will work fine with an E-level or H-E-H tapered line. A glass rod of similar weight and length will probably require a heavier line—a D-level or an H-C-H tapered line. If I were choosing a glass rod to be used exclusively for casting flies to panfish, I'd get a limber eight-footer weighing four to 4½ ounces. That rod should balance nicely with an E-level or an H-D-H tapered line.

Incidentally, some fly rods made for small-stream fishing make nice panfish rods. They run about six feet in length and weigh 2½ to 2¾ ounces. I have used a glass one quite a bit and find that an F-level or H-E-H taper works well with it. The rod is too short for satisfactory bait fishing in either lake or stream. Leaders for panfish? Well, you don't need a leader when using monofilament line to fish with bait or hardware lures. A leader is needed for a stripping line. It need not be long or tapered. A 4½-foot piece of four to 4½-pound test monofilament tied on the line end will suffice.

If you buy snelled hooks, the short snell (Leader) that comes with the hook will often be sufficient. For fly fishing a six to 7½-foot leader is needed. A tapered one will work best. For small flies, I'd suggest a taper of .015 to .008. For bugs and larger flies I suggest a stiffer taper, say .017 to .010.

For the panfish spinning outfit I recommend the lightest weight possible simply because it will give the most pleasure. Try a 6½-foot rod of extra-light action. Such a rod should weigh 3.3 to 3.5 ounces. Light as it is, that little spinning rod will handle a bass if you hook one, something quite likely to happen when using spoons, spinners, or plugs of spinning weight to cast for such panfish as perch or crappies in waters that also hold bass.

A six-pound monofilament line is about right for panfish spinning. A line testing two to three pounds will hold panfish, but lines weaken quickly where they're tied to the leader or lure, and the extra diameter also helps handle fish in weeds. If you use lighter weight lures than an eighth of an ounce, however, you need a two, three, or four-pound spinning line to cast them.

The sunfishes are perhaps the most popular panfish. There are nearly thirty varieties of sunfish, but they all have the same basic characteristics, being flat and deep-bodied in relation to their length. The bluegill is probably the most esteemed member of the sunfish family. Good-sized bluegills average from a half to three quarters of a pound in most waters, but in some places they grow to 1¼ pounds and larger. The world-record bluegill, taken from Ketona Lake, Alabama, in 1950, weighed four pounds, twelve ounces.

In my opinion, the bluegill is one of the best fighters in the panfish category. He fights with spirit, speed, and vigor right up to the finish. Good natural baits for bluegills are worms, including nightcrawlers, grubs of any kind, and any kind of larva or nymph that's large enough to go on a No. 6, 8, or 10 hook. Sometimes bluegills will rise to dry flies, but on the whole I find them more ready to take wet flies, streamers, and nymphs.

Some veteran bluegill anglers like very small flies, size 14. I prefer larger ones, occasionally fishing size 12 but more often using size 10. If the fish run large, I'll use No. 8 flies. In spinning lures I prefer the smallest I can get that will cast without the aid of a sinker. However, a fly-weight spoon or spinner fished on a sinker-weighted leader will do a good job if you handle it right.

The shellcracker is another good sunfish. It averages a good size and is full of fight when hooked. I place shellcrackers on a par with bluegills, and I've caught them on the same lures and baits.

The common sunfish, often called pumpkinseed, averages smaller than the bluegill and shellcracker. I've caught sunfish up to three quarters of a pound, but not often and only in a few places, notably the Great Lakes region. They're easier to locate than bluegills and they frequently come close to shore in schools.

The same natural baits and artificials mentioned for bluegills will do just as well for the pumpkinseed, except that you need smaller worms and lures. Sometimes just a tiny piece of worm on the point and barb of a No. 12 hook will take sunfish when more attractive bait fails.

As a group, sunfish could be classed as game fish. I'm a dedicated trout fisherman, yet I must say that a bluegill weighing half a pound usually fights more than a freshly stocked trout of the same weight. When I get to a trout stream and find anglers elbow-to-elbow around a pool, I often find it more enjoyable to go to a lake and see if there are any bluegills in the shallows.

Sunfish are fine-flavored and firm-fleshed. When they're on the small side, I scale them, cut off the head and fins, and then cook as is. If I catch larger ones, I skin them instead of scraping off the scales. Fried to a golden brown and seasoned with salt and pepper while cooking, they make a toothsome meal.

The white perch is found mostly in fresh and brackish waters along the East Coast. When planted in fresh water lakes they grow to a creditable size and do well. Small to medium-size shrimp make excellent white-perch bait. A spinner-and-worm combination for trolling is sometimes effective for white perch in lakes. White perch are splendid scrappers for their size, even small ones being surprisingly peppy. In the pan they're fine.

The black crappie and the white crappie look alike, but anyone accustomed to fishing for them can usually tell the difference. One sure way is to examine the dorsal fin. The black crappie has seven or eight dorsal spines; the white has five or six. The black also has a more highly arched back than the white, and is much darker. It's said that in waters where both species occur, the white crappie frequently dominates the population.

Crappies feed largely on other fish, gobbling up small bass along with minnows, small perch, or any other available fish. They are also partial to nymphs and other larva, particularly those of the dragon and damsel flies. They take worms, grasshoppers, crickets, and the like. While natural baits are often necessary, artificials can be effective on crappies. They will take small plugs, spoons, spinners, small streamers, and wet flies, also plastic baits that imitate the various things they feed on.

Sometimes crappies are hard to locate. On a trip a year or so ago, I couldn't find any crappies for several days, and then hooked a nice one while trolling for bass with a medium-size sun-fish plug. I concentrated on that two-acre area of a backwater bay, and took crappies to my heart's content. None weighed less than a pound and I had a top fish of two pounds.

At the time I was fishing with a bait-casting outfit, and so didn't get the maximum sport from the fishing. I went back the next day with a fly rod, small spinners and flies. Not one strike did I get. Thinking the plug I'd used the day before was what they wanted, I tied it on again. No strikes. Then I tried other lures of this size. It was like fishing in a bathtub. The crappies had left this bay, and they didn't return again during my stay. I'd just been lucky to hit them that one day.

Crappies aren't good fighters, not nearly as good as sunfish. They resist fairly well just after being hooked, but then they usually slide through the water for the rest of the way. For food, though, they rank with the best.

The rock bass and the warmouth bass are similar in appearance, so much so that it's difficult to tell one from the other. The only sure way to identify them is by the spines on the anal fin. The rock bass has six, the warmouth three. Both are often called goggle-eyes or redeyes. Their favorite foods are fishes, insects, and crustaceans, especially crawfish on the part of the rock bass.

They will also hit small to medium-size lures, and I've caught them regularly when casting shorelines for bass with large plugs and spoons. Actually there's no need to fish for rock bass or warmouths with natural bait. They're hungry for artificials.

Both rock bass and the warmouth favor rocky shores, though the warmouth will also range over muddy bottoms. Rock bass definitely prefer clear waters with rocky shores and bars. I've never found rock bass in heavy weeds or submerged brush heaps, or along muddy or clay shores. The original take and the first few pulls of a rock bass are stronger than a bluegill's, but after that the fight becomes disappointing. For eating I consider them inferior to sunfish, perch, or crappies.

The white bass, often called striper because it really is striped, will strike at spoons, bait, and flies. It puts up a great fight, stronger for its size than most other fish, excepting the smallmouth bass and the rainbow trout. White bass are great travelers; tagged fish having been reported covering well over a hundred miles in a short time.

As to eating quality, I don't think much of white bass. The small ones are fair, but I like neither the texture nor the flavor of the larger ones. Of course this is personal taste. Many folks like them very well. Since they run to two pounds in some waters, it doesn't take many to make a meal.

CHAPTER XXII

Catfish and Carp

I COULDN'T forget about catfish if I wanted to. They don't offer the dramatic action many sport fishermen are looking for, yet my mail ever reminds me that the catfish suits thousands of anglers just fine, thank you, and what baits do I recommend?

So let's go catfishing. There are about thirty-five varieties of cats in this country, and among them they reward a lot of fishermen in many ways. The channel cat is quite a fighter. The blue, for one, may grow to a hundred pounds, so that by size alone it's a remarkable trophy. As a result of stocking, some variety of catfish is probably found within easy reach of anglers in all fifty states. In general they're guileless fish and easily caught by relaxing methods. And, finally, a string of cats provides a lot of good eating.

The channel cat is king of the catfish tribe to those who rate the sport of catching fish above the idea of bringing home some meat. There are several varieties of channel cats, but the differences are minor and of little concern to the average fisherman. As a group, channel cats have more slender bodies than other catfish, their tails are deeply forked, and they range in color from a dark blue or slate shade to a light blue or olive hue. These darker colors are on the top and sides of a channel cat, and fade into a creamy white on the belly. Most channel cats have many small, dark spots along their sides.

As their name suggests, channel cats like the channels or currents of a river. They are more inclined to feed during the day than most cats, which are generally nocturnal feeders. I have several times caught channel cats while fishing baits and plugs for bass. One was a six-pounder that took a plug moving about six feet below the surface, and I thought for quite a while I'd hooked a monster smallmouth bass.

Another time I had several days of good channel-cat fishing by drifting crawfish baits in just the same way I'd fish for trout. Except that the water was warmer and less clear, this channel-cat stream had some pools, pockets, and riffles you find in good trout waters, and a crawfish drifted along the bottom through these places was almost sure to be hit by a channel cat weighing one to three pounds. On my light trout tackle, the cats gave me action and thrills aplenty.

The blue catfish is the giant of the clan. I have seen two blues from a Mississippi River tributary that weighed nearly a hundred pounds each. One from the Minnesota River was reported to weigh 160 pounds. Though the blue is much larger than the channel cats, which have a top weight of about twenty-five pounds, the two are much alike in shape and coloration. The main difference is that the blue lacks the black spots found along the sides of the typical channel cat.

As is true of most big catfish, these giant blues are usually taken on trot lines, set lines, or by jugging (a system of drifting baited lines attached to floating jugs or cans). But I prefer the kind of blue-cat fishing my wife and I had on a bass river in Mississippi. Our guide anchored the boat over a deep hole near the bank at lunchtime. I'd been using a fly rod while bass fishing, but this looked like a catfish hole, so I took off the bass plug, and put on a sinker and a hook baited with a lively fresh-water shrimp. I cast upstream and put my pole down to start my lunch.

Before I had a chance to take one good bite of my sandwich, my rod tip started to bend slowly down, as if my bait had snagged on the bottom. I picked up the rod and felt the vibration of a fish taking the bait. I waited a short count and then struck. The result, on my slender fly rod, was an exciting tussle with a 3½-pound blue cat.

My wife and the guide watched me boat this one, and then excitedly baited their own outfits for catfish. In the next hour the three of us boated thirty blue cats, none under two pounds and the largest weighing four pounds. Next day, finding the bass fishing slow, we returned to this hole and had more of the same kind of action. We didn't get as many fish, but this time four of the blue cats we took weighed more than four pounds apiece.

The bullhead is the sort of catfish Easterners know best. It averages quite small, the heaviest variation being the northern brown bullhead, which reaches a top weight of about four pounds. Bullheads have pink or reddish meat, rather than the white flesh common to other catfish. Their tails are roughly square, sometimes slightly rounded, and the body color ranges from yellow to dark blue or black. Some are mottled.

There's nothing exciting about bullheads, unless it's the response of an angler pricked by one of their slightly poisonous spines. They're dull, sluggish fish that favor the muddy bottoms of slow, weedy waters. In fact, the bullhead is such a hardy and insensitive fish that it can dig into the mud when its pond goes dry and stay alive for weeks on end. When the water returns, the bullhead comes out of its dormant state and starts to live like a fish again.

Bullheads will eat most any vegetable or animal matter, and there's very little science in fishing for them. When I decide a meal of French-fried bullheads would hit the spot, I go about dusk to the nearest bullhead waters, sink a bait to the bottom, and haul in the fish when they bite. It's that easy. The only general rules involved are that they feed mostly at dusk or after dusk, that they're on or near the bottom, and that they're attracted by a motionless bait that spreads an odor through the water.

Bullheads from still, shallow, and muddy waters often have a muddy taste. But there's an easy way to correct this with bullheads or any other fish: just dress them and soak in salt water for ten to fifteen hours before cooking.

The flathead catfish, more commonly called the mud cat or yellow cat, has much the same habits as the bullhead. Flatheads, however, grow as big as a hundred pounds. Caught on a set line or trot line—which is the way most whopper flatheads are taken—these giants are just big portions of good meat. Even on sport tackle they're not scrappers in the pound-for-pound sense, but there's a lot of fun in taking a big one on light tackle. I recently saw a fellow hook a twenty-five-pound flathead on light tackle and the skirmish drew quite a crowd. A lot of bass fishermen along the river were watching enviously by the time the big cat was landed.

I could go on listing the different kinds of catfish and pointing out minor variations, but there's a general sameness about the entire clan. They're tough, to the extent that some kinds will swim away calmly after having been frozen alive in a block of ice and shipped a great distance. Sharp, somewhat poisonous spines make little catfish hot potatoes for minnow-chasing gamefish, and comparatively few young cats are found in the stomachs of bass or other predatory fish.

Another common catfish trait is that they seemingly rely a great deal on a sense of taste or smell in searching for food. As a result, catfish anglers have developed an assortment of baits that frankly and potently appeal to fish scavenging for food by smell.

Here are some popular catfish baits gathered from fishermen in different states: A correspondent in Indiana thinks shad entrails are as good a catfish bait as you can use in that state; for channel cats, anglers there like a method known as bobbing. Many of them use long cane poles fitted with guides and reel for this. They rig up a large cork float, a heavy sinker, and a hook baited with a large wad of manure worms. Strategy is to cast upstream into a deep channel and let the bait drift down. (This same system with different baits is very popular on the Colorado River in Texas.) A Kansas catfisherman considers chicken blood a top bait. A local poultry plant supplies it. Anglers hang the clotted blood in a gunny sack overnight to let it drain and stiffen, then cut it into bait chunks and fish it near the bottom. (Mixing feathers or other soft, fibrous material with the fresh blood will make it stay on the hook longer.) Minnows are the basic ingredient for other Kansas baits. Some fishermen there use live minnows, putting two or more on the hook. Others roll dead minnows in corn meal and bury them in a sack for three days. The corn meal absorbs and holds the moisture of the souring minnows, so that they make the kind of odorous baits cats go for. Another system is to mash up a dozen or so soured minnows and a small package of Limburger cheese. The resulting mixture is firm enough to stay on a hook for a long time.

From Nebraska: "We find jackrabbit entrails one of the best catfish baits, especially when the rabbit has been riddled with a shotgun. We put the entrails in a jar with all the blood we can save, add half a cup of sugar, and let the mixture stand in a warm place for three or four days."

From Virginia: "We use oysters quite a lot, especially in water that's not too swift. Raw beef is also good and it stays on the hook better in swift water."

Those are just a few of the hundreds of baits and concoctions used for catfish. But you no doubt get the idea. A lot of people go to a lot of trouble to catch cats.

Some anglers consider the carp a fine fish; others despise it. One fisherman tells you carp are very difficult to catch; a second man says they're a cinch. I think all of these people are right. The carp is all of those things, depending on what you think of it, and how and where you fish.

Disagreements about carp are as old as the history of the species. Various sources say the carp was first brought to this country at dates ranging from 1831 to 1876. But it's reasonably sure that the first major shipment of carp to America was from Germany in 1876. The offspring of those fish spread to many great waters here, and many persons call them German carp to this day. Actually, the stock we got from Germany was probably the result of German imports from Asia, where the carp is a native fish.

Carp are scattered in erratic pattern through lakes and streams all over the country. Their favorite haunts are the still coves of lowland lakes and streams. They like muddy bottoms which they root through in search of food.

The carp is something of a vegetarian, feeding much on the tender portions of aquatic plants, but it will also pick up small animal and insect life on the muddy bottoms. It eats the seeds and fruits of stream-side plants as well as worms, grubs, and the eggs of other fish. Except that it lacks the teeth and the ambition to prey on anything as vigorous as a frog or large minnow, the carp is likely to eat most anything. That's demonstrated by some of the imaginative ingredients in prepared carp baits, which I'll deal with further on.

The carp is also noted for durability. Though I can't personally vouch for this, I have heard of an old custom of hanging carp in cool, damp cellars until they were wanted for eating. These fish supposedly lived for days without a drop of water, and were fed with bread and milk while in storage. I do know from personal experience that the carp rates with the catfish and eel in ability to survive ordeals of weather and water. A lake or stream is in bad shape when carp can't live in it.

It was a school of carp in a muddy Eastern stream that taught me to respect their fighting power. I had located a good number of carp feeding close to the banks of this sluggish and muddy stream on a hot day in August. At the time my interest in carp fishing beat very feebly, but I decided to do some experimenting with these fish. They were close to my home in the Hudson River Valley of New York, so I could work up new baits at the house and quickly drive out to test them.

My tackle for the first carp session was a fly-fishing outfit I ordinarily used for trout. I tied a fine No. 14 hook on the leader, pinched a BB sinker on the leader twelve inches above the hook, and baited with a doughball about the size of a pea. With a swing of the rod I dropped this bait gently into the murky water beside a weed bed. Then I waited, holding the bait still near the bottom.

Nothing happened for twenty minutes, and I was just about convinced my bait had tangled in sunken weeds. Then my line started to move. I struck at once and felt a heavy fish. There was a violent stir under the surface as the startled carp headed for deeper water. My light 3X leader snapped like cotton thread. I put on a heavier leader for a second effort in another hole, but again used a No. 14 hook. A heavy carp took this bait downriver like a record muskie and straightened the little hook when I tried to turn him.

It took a No. 4 hook and heavy leader to land my first carp, an eight-pounder that fought with deep powerful runs. Moving to new spots along the bank, I used the same rig to beach a four-pounder, then lost my hook and leader to a brute of a fish. He started downstream at the sting of the hook. Knowing my tackle would never turn this fish I splashed after him along the marshy shore, but he quickly peeled the thirty yards of line off my reel and snapped the heavy leader as he hit the end of the line.

I spent several days experimenting with the carp in this particular river. They won most of our bouts, but they taught me several things that I've since learned are generally true. First, I saw the need for sturdy tackle. I also learned that patience is a virtue in carp fishing, for they seldom take a bait the minute it sinks into their pool. And I discovered that small baits, provided they generously cover the point and barb of the hook, are not apt to be stolen. Carp often mouth a big bait without being hooked.

I've tangled with carp quite often since those experimental trips. I have caught a few by accident while trying for other fish with artificial flies or small spoons. When concentrating on catching the big mud lovers, I've had good luck with various doughballs, kernels of water-softened grain, small berries, worms, grubs, maggots, and such cut baits as mussels or clams. The cut baits may work better if they're allowed to age to the smelly stage before use.

Best carp tackle? That depends a lot on personal preference. I have a ten-foot fly rod that suits me for carp fishing. Since long casts are seldom needed, my long rod allows me to swing a bait into likely water with a short line. With the tip of the long rod almost straight above the sunken bait, I can feel the slightest nibble and respond with a quick strike. Carp are cautious, nibbling feeders as a rule, and the angler needs tackle with which he can feel the faint tugs and strike quickly.

Spinning or bait-casting outfits will do OK for carp fishing, but they both utilize short rods that handicap the bank fisherman in feeling the carp's cautious nibbles. The fish may be gone by the time the impulse of a strike runs up the line that's cast out with a spinning or bait-casting rig. For boat fishing—where the boat is anchored right over the carp—short rods are fine.

A cane pole is pretty hard to beat for most carp fishing. If you want to keep it simple, get a light cane twelve to fourteen feet long and tie six or eight feet of line to the end of it. The long pole gives the bank fisherman plenty of reach for fishing typical carp water, and the baited hook dangles straight down from the pole tip, allowing the angler to feel a mere touch of pressure on the line. This simple linking of pole and line is death on fish that are nibblers or hit-and-run biters.

How do you play a heavy fish with only six or eight feet of line that's tied to the pole tip? Well, if he's too big to horse in, a lot of cane pole anglers simply toss in the buoyant bamboo and let the fish drag it around. They watch from the bank until the fish tires, then get hold of the pole again and haul in the prize. Often as not, one end of the pole will be in reach of the bank when the fish gives up. Some fishermen fit cane poles with guides and tape a reel to the butt. This simple rig makes an excellent carp-fishing outfit.

With the fly rod I use for carp, I want a reel holding from fifty to a hundred yards of stout line, something testing from ten to eighteen pounds. I like leaders testing six to eight pounds or heavier if the carp run extra large.

Though carp are usually idling near the bottom in fairly deep water, there are times when you'll find them cruising near the surface. These roving schools will often take baits that are cast into the water ahead of them. A spinning outfit shines for this work. A slender quill float attached to the leader will keep a bait at the right depth until cruising fish get at it.

When carp are in deep water, the angler can improve his chances considerably by baiting the hole with doughballs or some other carp food. It's best to do this baiting the day before you plan to fish, so the carp will have time to find the food and gather there in force. If carp are located in a dense weed bed or some other place where it's tough to fish for them, they can frequently be lured out by a trail of bait leading into a better fishing spot.

The question I'm most often asked about carp is, "What's the best bait?" I can only answer that by recommending several *good* carp baits. Each angler has to choose the one that's best for him in the particular water he fishes.

Bread of various types is sometimes very good bait for carp. All that's added is a bit of moisture to work the bread into bait-size balls, and some anglers do this by chewing the bread as they fish. They make it a practice to toss in a lot of extra doughballs to bait the hole. Another simple and efficient doughball is made by boiling corn meal until it is stiff and then mixing in enough cotton batting to make the small pellets stay on the hook.

Russ Krieger of Priest River, Idaho, who learned about carp while living in Kansas, says the following bait formula is sure-fire: Mix a cup of flour with two cups of bran or shorts from a feed store and add a teaspoon of cinnamon. Stir in enough water to make a stiff dough and then drop pellets of the dough into boiling water three or four at a time—dropping in too many at once will cool the water. When the doughballs rise to the top they're ready for use.

Some carp fishermen swear by doughballs made by mixing bread and honey. Others make a paste of white bread slices, white flour, a sprinkling of sugar, and water. The resulting dough is boiled for twenty minutes in a single lump and cut into bait-size chunks after it cools. If the water you fish in is lined with wild berry bushes, try the berries for bait. The carp may be busily feeding on the fruit that naturally drops into the water.

Chunks of boiled potato are a favorite carp bait in some localities. They're wrapped in squares of fine mosquito netting to keep them on the hook. I mentioned earlier that worms, grubs, maggots, and bits of clam or mussel are good at times.

A simple bait endorsed by H. L. Treaster of Johnson City, New York, is canned corn. "I get a can of yellow, whole-kernel corn," he explains, "and toss a portion of it into the carp water before I start fishing. Then I put four kernels of the corn on a No. 4 hook and cast into the hole. Carp gather to feed on the scattered corn, and first thing you know one will grab your baited hook. Just yesterday I caught three carp that were 21½, 22, and 24 inches long."

A final hint for carp fishermen: Try for them in the early spring. As the water first begins to warm, carp that have been dormant all winter come in to shallow water with ravenous appetites. They can be very wary and particular a few weeks later, but the fisherman who's on the spot as they start that spring feeding spree can slay them.

CHAPTER XXIII

Why Not Try Ice Fishing?

A LOT of winter-idle anglers would be ice-fishing fans if they'd try the sport just once. What makes a person eager to leave the fireside and go out to chop fishing holes in the ice of a wind-swept lake? I think it's because we get the real spirit of winter out there. At home, winter is a chore and a hostile force. But on the frozen water it's one of nature's ever-fascinating wonders. There's crackling stillness out there that's unknown in summer. It's a time of barren hardwood trees and dark evergreens. Winter sunlight is subdued and different; there are gray days that may spill down snowflakes to dominate the scene. Ice fishermen see and feel all this, and those attuned to it miss no opportunity to be there.

I include snowstorms in my own pleasant memories of ice fishing. Many times I've neglected the tip-ups over my fishing holes to watch the progress of a storm. The first flakes cause a misty white-ness against the shoreline that becomes whiter and whiter as the snow falls faster. Then the shoreline disappears and you're alone in an all-white world, the flakes softly coating you from head to foot. I like to be there whether the fish are biting or not.

But to enjoy all this you must be properly dressed. Selection of proper clothing comes ahead of tackle and strategy in this kind of fishing. In general, I like to wear two or more light garments rather than a single stiff and heavy one. This is true of socks, underwear, and many outer clothes. The air spaces between layers are the best kind of insulation against cold. With a single thick garment, body moisture has a way of working out to the surface, and cold creeps in through the damp fabric with numbing effect.

I know wool underwear is a standard prescription for cold-weather dress. And it's fine—if you can take it. I can't. It always makes me itchy and uncomfortable. I prefer cotton next to my skin, even though wool is warmer and absorbs moisture better. If I could find some nylon or Dacron longies, I think I'd like them best of all.

Footwear is very important. Two pairs of medium-weight wool socks are a good choice. I also like a combination of a light, neat-fitting sock underneath and a heavy wool one over it. A good fit is needed with all socks to prevent binding or bunching that will impair circulation.

One pair of boots is ordinarily enough if they're lined with felt, fleece, or insulated by built-in air pockets as some of the GI-style winter boots are. Rubber overshoes or arctics worn over comfortable leather shoes or hiking boots will also give you a good cold-weather combination.

As for outer garments, two pairs of pants, if needed, will be warmer than a single pair of the same thickness. The same is true of sweaters, shirts, and coats. And wearing two or more layers of light outer clothing enables you to shed or replace one layer as needed. The weather may change drastically during the day, and chopping holes in the ice, for example, will have you sweating if you do it wearing all the clothes you need to wait quietly for the fish to bite.

Any warm hat with flaps or other ear covering is OK. Warm mittens or well-insulated gloves are necessary. Valuable extras are sunglasses to cope with the glare of the sun on snow and ice, and a neckerchief to fill that gap at the top of your collar. For years I thought the neckerchiefs Westerners wear were mainly for style or eye appeal. But I've learned that they work wonders in sealing in body heat at one of its most chilling escape points, the neck. These days I have a compact, almost weightless silk or nylon neckerchief in my pocket on any fishing trip where I expect a cold snap.

A compass tucked into your pocket can be a life saver if you get caught in a blizzard on a big lake. Without it a man can easily walk in circles for hours.

The tackle needed for ice fishing is simple and relatively inexpensive. Probably the most useful item is the tip-up, a device equipped with a line and a hook for the using of natural or live bait. You set it and when a fish bites it releases the trigger and a signal flag. You rush to it, carefully take hold of the line to see if the fish is still there, guess whether it has had time to get the bait well in its mouth, and then strike. Ice fishing is full of such intriguing uncertainties.

There are various styles of tip-ups, from very simple ones you may easily make yourself to complicated commercial jobs. Actually the cost of ready-made tip-ups is so low that there's little reason to make them except as a hobby. Buy or make tip-ups that will feed line when a fish takes. Otherwise many fish will drop the bait when the line snubs their striking run.

You can also use short rods for ice fishing. Some folks prefer them. Rods of from four to six feet do a good job. As it becomes very tiring and boring to hold a bait in a hole with a rod, I use props to hold mine. This way you can set up two or three baited rods—check to see how many you're legally allowed in that area —and watch them from a reasonable distance. You must be in a position to observe the tip of each rod and get to it quickly when a fish jerks on it. Having a seat with you is a great aid in ice fishing. A good idea is to make a seat on a sled, then use the space under the seat for your tackle, lunch, and whatnot.

Minnows are probably the most useful bait for ice fishing. In most ice-fishing localities you will find someone who makes a business of supplying minnows during the winter. Grubs and worms are good, too. Once you get them in the water they'll live all right but will be sluggish and inactive because of the low water temperature. Here's where the minnows are far superior.

Most minnows stay alive quite well in cold weather and water. I have had good fishing with the tougher minnows, including the salt-water killie that you can carry for an unbelievable time in wet seaweed, but there are some times when only the shiner or its associates in tenderness will tempt the fish you're after. Then you have to pamper your minnows to keep them alive and change baits frequently.

Ordinarily the best winter places to fish will be where you would catch the same fish in spring and fall. If those places fail, try other waters, from the shallows to the depths. I don't go along completely with the theory that because you can't catch any fish "they ain't biting." If you can locate fish, and have the patience and imagination to do some sound experimenting, you'll nearly always catch a few.

Sometimes sulking members of the *Esox* family—pike and pickerel—can be induced to start moving around if you pound the ice near shore or over shallow weed beds. The pounding may cause a temporary panic. But after the fish are awakened completely the panic resolves into an active curiosity. If the fish see your bait then they may take it readily.

Often the best place to cut ice-fishing holes will be over or near big weed growths. To fish these weed forests successfully with minnows, try to place the minnow where it is near enough to think it can reach the weeds to hide, but far enough away so that it can't quite reach them. This keeps the minnow active and at the same time visible to game fish in and about the weeds. Sometimes among the weeds you can locate open pockets. These are often great places to fish, either winter or summer.

Spoons and spinners will take fish below the ice, just the same as they do in open waters. The winter need is for a spoon or spinner that will work effectively when twitched on a very short ice-fishing rod. An artificial should act alive, both when jerked and when it sinks. As with bait, ice-fishing lures usually pay off best when fished down near the bottom.

Once you find a lure that takes fish, stick with it as long as it works. When it doesn't produce any longer, change your style of fishing it. If this doesn't bring results try a lure that's entirely different. Never get to the point where you believe that one particular method of using it is the only good combination.

The most successful ice fishermen are those who do a lot of it and get to know the waters they fish. The wise ones have holes or strategic places all over a given lake or stream. If you are new at the game or don't know the lake, look for holes made by others. Also look for signs of fish having been caught at them. There's a good chance that you will find a hole cut previously by a skilled ice fisherman and strike it rich. For a beginner, it certainly beats new holes at random.

The jigging spoon is sometimes good for pike and walleyes, but it gives its best performance on yellow perch. While the spoon itself is heavy and sinks easily, it must be so constructed that it darts and flutters on the way down. Some anglers prefer nickel-plated spoons; others copper, brass, or a combination of the two metals. Plain block tin makes excellent spoons, not too costly and easy to produce if you start with a good mold. Bright-red yarn wound just above the hook increases the effectiveness of any jigging spoon. (Note: Better consult your game laws about the use of this type of lure.)

To use the spoon, attach a line to a short stick that will hold enough line to take care of various water depths. After adjusting the line so that the spoon reaches almost to the bottom, jerk the spoon upward and then let it settle back. You can vary the speed and length of the jerks to suit different conditions; sometimes it is good to try starting the lure at various distances from the bottom to take care of different feeding ranges. Perch will forage for minnows, which aren't always schooled on the bottom. Since the strike often comes while the spoon is fluttering downward, you must be quick.

The newest form of ice fishing is with a fly. This sport was developed in the Middle West, but I have had success with it in other waters where there are perch, bluegills, and crappies that are willing to feed in wintertime. The fly imitates the larva of an insect. It is constructed and weighted so that it sinks readily, and when worked in up-and-down strokes of an inch or so, the feelers react in a lifelike manner.

For a rod you can get satisfactory results from the tip joint of a fly rod fitted into the grasp, or you can buy an inexpensive outfit designed for the purpose. The latter includes a simple reel that has a cork arbor covered with cotton material. This helps in conditioning the synthetic line.

Best results are obtained with a line of very light leader material, say about two-pound test. If you can't get this in long pieces, you can tie together the forty-four-inch lengths. In fishing, the fly is sunk to within a foot of the bottom and then moved in with short strokes. Work up for several feet if no strikes are forthcoming near the bottom. Most fish are likely to be schooled up in the winter. If you don't get results in five minutes at one hole, move on—unless it has produced a day or so before. In that case, give it thirty minutes.

Sometimes a fish will take without your feeling it. For this reason you should watch the line closely at all times, just as I have so often advised for fishing with regular wet flies. If it acts at all unnaturally between jerks, you may find that you have a fish. But don't strike too hard, or you may come to grief with the light leader material.

One caution about ice fishing: Don't get overheated. Be particularly careful about this when you cut holes. If you work up a sweat and then get chilly again you will be miserable for the rest of the day. There are special ice-cutters that make the job easier, though a regular ice chisel is OK.

There's a lot of gear ice fishermen take along for convenience or cold-weather comfort. You can choose to suit yourself and the occasion, but a skimmer—something to dip the constantly forming ice out of your open holes—is a necessity in freezing weather. It's just a shallow scoop made of screen or wire net. The kitchen department or a hardware or department store will have them, or you can make one by punching holes in a tin pan and bolting on a handle.

Since minnows are the principal natural bait for ice fishing, you need a pail to carry them. I'd get a big one, of at least five-gallon capacity. That'll hold enough minnows to supply three or more anglers for a couple of days of average fishing and it won't freeze up as fast as a smaller pail. You don't need an inner liner or any of the other insulation devices so necessary in warm-weather buckets —just a plain pail of good size, preferably with a lid.

I also recommend a small dip net for scooping bait minnows out of the pail. Some brave anglers do it with bare hands, but it's hardly worth it in zero temperatures, particularly since minnow-size dip nets cost very little. If you're doing such things the hard way, rubbing olive oil into your hands before you go out will ease the sting of the cold water and weather.

A simple depth finder is also valuable in ice fishing. The best place to start fishing a minnow on a tip-up is from six to twelve inches off the bottom, and you can make a simple gadget to locate that level. Tie a loop of line on a sinker or other weight. When you want to find your fishing depth, slip the loop over the hook on your tip-up line and lower it until it hits bottom. Then pull the line up as far as you want to fish above bottom, tie a loop in it, and hang it over the flag trigger. Pull in your tip-up line then, take off the depth finder, and you're ready to bait up and fish. Your baited hook will sink to within the desired distance from the bottom.

Hook sizes 1 and 2 are good for the three-inch minnows that pickerel like. For northern pike you'll need larger minnows and bigger hooks, size 1/0 or 2/0. If you're primarily after perch, use No. 4 or 6 hooks and minnows 1½ to two inches long. The point is to use a hook large enough that it isn't smothered in the bait and yet small enough that it doesn't overweight or shock the hooked minnow too much. Use the finest wire you can get by with in each hook size.

I think that hooking a minnow through the lips or through both eyes gives you an advantage over any other system. They

live longer when hooked this way—especially the lip method—
and a greater percentage of striking fish are hooked. Hooking
them through the eyes sounds like a rugged practice, but minnows don't feel pain as we think of it. An eye-hooked minnow
will be lively for quite a while. With tender-fleshed ones, it's probably the best way.

After you've picked a starting point, chop your first hole
(make them round and twelve to eighteen inches wide) and set
your first tip-up near shore, over water two or three feet deep.
From that hole make a rude half-circle out in the lake and back
to shore again with as many tip-ups as the law allows, setting them
twenty-five to thirty feet apart. If the sets near shore get better
results within half an hour, move some of the others in to the
adjacent shoreline. If the action is on the sets farther out, spread
out.

It's wise, by the way, to walk gently over very shallow sets,
especially if the ice is thin, and answer a "flag-up" summons as
softly as you can. With the ice exceptionally clear and the skies
bright, it'll probably be useless to work the shallows unless the
fish are very unwary. Under conditions like those you're usually
forced to deeper water or to where the ice itself is clouded or
covered with snow. Fishing over deeper water doesn't call for
such precautions.

When fishing off a point of land, it's best to follow its underwater contour by placing tip-ups as close as six feet apart, steadily
advancing outward if you don't get results near shore. Go out to
a depth of eight feet or more when fishing for eastern chain
pickerel. For perch and walleyes this doesn't count. They're
where you find them.

Sometimes you'll find enough hot spots to make all your legally
allowable tip-ups productive. If you do, and others on the ice are
near enough to observe you, you may get swamped by competition. Chances are your new neighbors won't hurt your fishing,
though—unless they chop new holes within elbow length of your
operation. Your holes—and some of theirs—will go on producing
after the fish recover from the commotion of the new onslaught.

Don't, however, expect any hole to yield fish indefinitely. Ice-fishing action will ebb and flow throughout the day, no matter how hot the spot.

Strikes on tip-ups have to be handled in different ways depending on what kind of fish is taking the bait. The members of the pike (*Esox*) family, which includes the Eastern chain pickerel, will usually grab a minnow quickly, run to a more secluded spot, and then stop to swallow the captured tidbit. If you strike on that first run you often miss the fish. And the same fish may not come back for another minnow after having one rudely yanked from its mouth. You want the tip-up rigged so that it will spool out the line with little resistance during that first run. Strike back a moment after the run stops.

Yellow perch are quick-gulp strikers. If you wait for them to run and then swallow the bait you won't catch many. You've got to be quick on the trigger with perch.

You can see the guessing game that confronts the ice angler who's getting strikes from pike and perch through the same holes. Quick strikes miss most of the pike and pickerel; slow strikes miss the perch. But there is a solution other than good guessing: Perch usually frequent deeper water than the pike, say depths ranging from fifteen to thirty-five feet. This, plus their snappy strikes, make them vulnerable to anglers who use artificials and concentrate on perch.

If winter's boring you, head for the ice and try one or all of these systems. They'll give you some bright hours of angling before the spring seasons open.

CHAPTER XXIV

Tricks You Ought to Know

THERE are certain basic fishing principles which will consistently produce results for anglers who follow them. I do not
pretend to know them all, by a long shot, but the ones I am going
to discuss are among the most important, and are easy to put into
use.

Perhaps the most glaring fault of many anglers is the careless
way they approach a spot they propose to fish. Far too many
otherwise competent performers have the bad habit of rushing
right up to within casting distance of every choice, deep hole,
without realizing that by this action they not only pass up a good
deal of possibly fine water en route, but also ruin it for hours
afterwards.

Such anglers will charge along through these in-between
stretches, never even trying to fish them. They continue these
tactics—or lack of tactics—until the inevitable happens. Frightened by their approach, a big fish darts out of an exposed, shal-

low-water station, and a rueful fisherman says, "Golly, what a whopper I scared out that time."

In the past I have been quite an offender in this respect myself. It is so easy to pass up intermediate water when you are pushing on to a favorite hole, or perhaps trying to get within casting distance of a fish rising far out in the stream. Now I try to remember that the best fishing is often to be found close at hand. I have learned from experience that it pays to make haste slowly. Look for fish in the unlikely places—for those are the ones that will be skipped by the boys who concentrate on holes only.

Some feeding trout and bass frequent the shallows, where food is often plentiful and easy to collect. But remember that the scanty protection afforded fish feeding in shallows makes them unusually wary. When you come upon them suddenly it is only natural for them to rush to the safety of deeper waters. Unfortunately, a badly frightened fish will often communicate its fears to the others it joins in some under-the-bank sanctuary. Keep this in mind the next time you are in a hurry to get to a red-hot pool. You may be ruining it before you get to it. Haste along a trout stream seldom pays dividends.

On the other hand, you can never go wrong when you proceed with exaggerated caution. Unless you send desperately frightened fish into them, the deep holes will keep till you get there. A trout scared from shallows by the cast of a fly will bring no contagious excitement to other fish it may join in the deeper water of a pool. However, trout scared by the boisterous advance of a careless angler will remain nervous for some time.

Please do not misunderstand me here. There are certain conditions and types of water where speedy fishing will produce best results, but when working a stream where most of the water is on the quiet side—then, in my estimation, you should proceed with the greatest caution unless you know every shallow-water feeding station well. In the latter case, of course, much valuable time may be saved by skipping the barren spots.

Sometimes treating the shallows with the respect that I have indicated can be embarrassing. Witness what happened to me one day when I had approached what looked like a good spot on my knees, and was busy dapping a fly over the top of the grass to the water below. In the middle of this operation a deep voice boomed behind me:

"Shucks, you can't get any fish where you're fishing. There's only a mite of water there. The fish are on t'other side."

I arose and looked. Sure enough, there was only an inch or so of water along the entire grassy bank. Mumbling some rather lame explanations I left for a more secluded place. But that same day, using those same tactics, I did manage to take three good browns, none of which weighed less than 1 ½ pounds.

Ever since, when fishing unknown streams, it has been my practice to sneak up to any water which couldn't be studied from a distance. Results have been so gratifying that I feel the point is worth emphasizing, particularly as my entire object in writing fishing articles is to set forth ideas which can help anglers put more fish in their creels.

As another illustration of the value of this practice, consider the case of a certain Western stream where my luck, upon first fishing it, was exceedingly poor. I was out with some friends who knew the water, and we caught plenty of small to medium-size fish in the deep sections. However, we kept scaring a number of large fish on our approaches to these deep sections, and that bothered me.

On the whole, the banks of this stream were flat, and the water was slow-moving. Often, while fishing that first time, I saw big trout dash from banks where the water averaged four to eight inches in depth. Later, when I was able to fish alone and sneak up on these spots, I invariably creeled a good fish and sometimes more, depending on the amount of disturbance created while playing the trout. From then on it was easy to take fish from the stream—as long as I remained limber enough to walk on my knees and occasionally fish from a prone position.

A point to remember about deep holes is that, unlike the shallows, they can usually be approached fairly recklessly. However, when with care and caution you fish shallows adjoining deep water, you are definitely safeguarding your chances of success in the deeper water when you reach it—unless somebody else comes

FISHING WITH RAY BERGMAN

along, ignoring your ethical rights, to ruin both his and your own chances by acting like a bull in a china shop.

Generally bass are not nearly so wary as trout, but on occasion they can be exceedingly skittish, especially when feeding in the shallows. Under such conditions, use just as much caution as when fishing for trout; otherwise you will be treated to the sight of departing wakes as the bass rush for deep water.

The smooth water at the tails of pools and eddies is often productive, if you know how to fish it without putting the fish down. Sometimes such places can be worked at some distance from the side, although this is frequently impracticable because of the background, or because snags jut out of the water. It is often possible to get at these spots by using a slack downstream cast so that the fly or lure can drift down to the fish without drag. After the natural float of the fly has run out, retrieving with twitches and jerks can produce good results. Sometimes a very slow retrieve is effective.

With the dry fly, I have had best luck by creeping up to the tail of the pool or eddy, keeping low so as not to disturb the feeding fish, and then dropping the fly with a short cast just above the rises. Doing this eliminates most of the reasons for failure to take fish from such locations. If you keep down low enough, the rapids will hide you from the trout. And being close enough to make short casts means that you won't have to show much leader.

Let me elaborate a bit on this technique, as it is very important. Many times when I have spotted trout rising in the smooth-topped water just above rapids or riffles, I have approached from below—on foot if the stream was deep yet wadable, or on my knees if shallow—and thus eased myself into a low, close position from which it was simple to make a short cast to the feeding fish. This method has put some large trout in my basket.

To do the job successfully, you must be close enough so that after the cast has been made, you can keep pace with the speed of the retrieve by raising the rod tip as the fly drifts rapidly toward you. Often the rise will come just as the fly reaches the lip of the rapids, and failure will result unless you are in full control, with practically a taut line. A trout can spit a fly out in a twinkling.

This technique of working smooth water from below is well worth mastering.

Quiet, still stretches often contain many fish which are sometimes most difficult to catch. Here, a dry fly or a surface bug will often frighten instead of attract trout. When floaters do not bring results quickly, common sense suggests that you change to a wet fly and fish below the surface. While it is quite possible that the cast of a sinking fly will alarm fish just as much as the cast of a dry, remember that as soon as your offering begins to settle to the bottom it will attract attention—even though you impart no action at all.

The fish will be wary to start with, but when the commotion caused by the cast subsides and is not repeated, they'll get over their momentary fright quickly. Then upon seeing the fly or nymph sink slowly, they will become interested. By the time the fly reaches bottom—if not before—a few of the fish may be curious enough to investigate at close quarters. When this does not occur, lift the fly gently from the bottom and give the lightest of twitches as the hand-twist retrieve begins. This often brings results. However, this is not always true, for on many occasions the rather fast twitching of a fan-wing Royal Coachman on the quietest and clearest of waters has produced excellent fishing for me. It pays to experiment a little.

On the whole, trout seem to fear a sunken leader or line far less than when it is floating on the surface. In this connection, it is important to remember that, once over their fright, trout will generally commence feeding again on the bottom first, and it will be some time before they rise, or move back to the shallows. It seems they feel most secure in deep water; in shallow water they are susceptible to shadows, movements, and unnatural disturbances.

This trait is not so apparent in bass. Provided they do not sense your presence, they are most susceptible to surface-disturber lures, regardless of the fuss caused by the connecting line and leader. On many occasions top-water chuggers, plunkers, and splashes will bring quick action from bass when underwater lures elicit no response. But even here the surface disturbance should not be overdone. Show me a fellow who has no luck fishing top-water bugs, and I'll show you a man who works them entirely too fast.

Too many anglers never fish seriously behind waterfalls—even the tiny ones so common in any fast-water, rock-filled stream. Perhaps they go by surface appearances, without considering the basic setup of most waterfalls—for behind each one there is usually a gouged-out backwater, which acts as a natural repository for food. Small minnows usually frequent these backwash areas, and these are an added attraction to the game fish which you seek.

Bait is usually the best medicine for behind-the-falls work, although flies and other lures will work if you can manipulate them properly, and feel your strikes. The important thing is to keep your bait behind the falls long enough for a fish to see and take it. Weight is usually necessary to accomplish this, the correct amount depending on both the type and size of bait or lure used, and the depth and pull of the water.

If your offering persists in shooting downstream, then you definitely need more weight. In many instances, when the falls are on the heavy side, you will have to push the rod right through them, then throw the bait with an underhand motion. A steel or glass rod should be used instead of a bamboo one if you are going to do much of this work.

Scattered through streams and lakes wherever you fish will be a number of small holes or shelter locations where a good fish or two will make their headquarters. When fishing is good, it matters little if you skip these places. For one reason or another, they are usually tough to get at anyway, so you pass them by.

It is desirable, though, to try them on days when the more obvious places fail to produce. In fast water it is easy to tell where these positions are—just look in the white and tumbling water for the dark-surface areas. It will be quieter and perhaps deeper, and trout lurk in such spots because food is washed into them or along the outer edges, where it can be seen and seized. Also the fish can rest in comfort without battling the current all the time.

A short line is called for here, for the rough water surrounding the hole means that you can get up close to it without fear of detection, and then be in a good position to work it thoroughly. Further, the short line makes it easy for you to control your offering effectively. You can float a dry fly or manipulate a spinner in the manner intended for these lures—a feat that is almost impossible when fishing a long line in fast water.

Often a trout which will ignore flies floated over it will rise to a fly dangled provocatively from the side of a rock. Thus presented, the fly has the advantage of being free from conflicting currents which interfere with the natural drift of a cast fly. Also, the dapped fly touches the water lightly for brief intervals, and most of the time no leader shows at all—and so is deadly. Be sure, though, to keep well hidden.

A variation of this dapping process may be used on fast runs where the very-short-line presentation is impossible. Tie a rather heavy wet fly to the point of a nine-foot leader, then attach a dry fly or two for droppers. About eighteen inches between the droppers would be good spacing.

Now get in position so you can reach the desired spot with your lures. Make a cast, and when the tail fly has got a good purchase in the current, jump the dry flies so that they dance over the surface. This is a lot of fun in itself, and when you take time to do the job thoroughly, quite a few fish should rise as a reward for your efforts.

To me, the most important things about fishing are those apparently insignificant trifles which most anglers look upon as accidents or bits of luck. Two anglers, fishing the same water with similar flies, may be equally skillful. Yet one will take a number of trout while the other fails to get a rise. Have you ever stopped to analyze such an occurrence? Or have you simply called the incident luck and let it go at that?

For years, I fondly entertained the idea that such happenings were due to luck. It was an easy way to alibi my failure and to soothe my ruffled dignity. But one day I woke up. I stopped to consider why I didn't catch fish while a companion did. To my surprise I found that luck hadn't had a thing to do with it. My failure had been caused by overlooking small details.

This truth came to me on the Esopus eighteen years ago. A friend and I were fishing a long, glassy glide. Trout were rising freely but they were particular about the lures they took. My companion finally found a fly they would take and told me. I put one on but could not take a fish. Meanwhile, my friend took trout with exasperating regularity. Finally I couldn't stand it any longer.

"Jim," I said, "these trout won't take my fly. Let me try those fish where you are. You come up here."

We exchanged places. Jim continued to get fish. I still failed. For once I did not call the incident luck. I decided that my fishing lacked something. I stopped fishing and went up to watch Jim. At first I could not see that his methods differed from mine. Then, suddenly, I realized that when he made his cast he put a curve in his line, a deep loop which caused his fly to drop on the water some distance downstream from the upper curve of the line. His fly was floating over the rising fish in advance of the line and leader. That was the reason for Jim's success.

I made it a point to learn how to cast a curve and, when I got the knack of it, I found that I could take many trout from locations where previously I couldn't get a rise. The incident ended my crude alibis of "luck." From then on I figured that my failures at times when someone else was getting trout were due to a lack of knowledge. I began, at every opportunity, to compare the successful tactics with my own unsuccessful methods. It was the real starting point of my career as an angler.

Another thing I learned after several years of haphazard fly-fishing is small but very important. It is to use great care when lifting the fly from the water for another cast. To "rip" the water when doing this is bad practice and should be avoided. This is a common fault with beginners and scares many trout which otherwise might rise.

For a long time, when floating my fly over a rising fish or a likely-looking pocket, it had been my practice to lift the fly the instant it got a few feet below the fish, so that I could get in another cast. I figured that the more often I got a fly over a fish the better were my chances for getting a rise. Theoretically this seems like good fly-fishing practice. Practically it doesn't always work out. Trout don't always take a fly at exactly the spot where you saw them rise. Many times they will follow it for a considerable distance downstream, probably looking it over and calculating the advisability of taking it. A premature lift of the fly is sure to discourage them. If the angler will let the fly float down to within a few feet of him, he will improve his chances a hundredfold. It is always wise to make the cast from a point outside the possible feeding range of a fish and never make the lift until the fly has reached the end of this possible range.

If you are fishing across instead of upstream, you should not lift the fly the instant it has passed the rising trout. Instead of this, let the fly float well past the fish, as far as it will float without dragging. At times it is good practice to let the fly go with the current even after it has begun to drag and sinks. Often I have taken good fish below me when the sunken fly was curving around to come taut against the line. Of course, the latter part of this method is wet-fly fishing but, in my opinion, we must often resort to the wet fly if we want to get the most out of fishing.

Years ago I employed successfully a method of fly fishing which was not orthodox and which I no longer use. It was the wet-dry method. On the end of a nine-foot leader I used a nymph or cut-down wet fly. On the dropper above this I tied another wet fly. On the top loop I tied a large dry fly. The cast was made the same as when dry-fly fishing, either up, or up and across stream. It kept me on my mettle to fish this cast, since it was necessary to watch not only the floating fly but to see the flash of a fish striking one of the sunken flies. Because I might fail to see the rise of a fish to the sunken flies, I had also to watch for the slight twitch of the line or floating fly. If no strike was forthcoming by the time the flies reached a point opposite me, I let them continue on their way, trying to keep the dry fly on the surface as long as possible. After the dry fly had been dragged under, the flies were still allowed to travel until the section of water being fished was thoroughly covered.

On the retrieve I brought the flies upstream by several methods, sometimes slowly and without jerks, sometimes fast with emphatic jerks, and sometimes in such a way that the flies skipped on the surface. If all rises came to the dry fly, I discarded the wet-fly method and resorted to dry-fly fishing entirely. But if the fish took the wet flies I followed the wet-fly method throughout the day.

It was surprising how effective this method was and how it sharpened my wits. There were so many things to watch for, so much attention needed to know when I had a strike. Of recent years I have become so much of a one-method-at-a-time angler that I have discontinued this wet-dry system but I still consider it a dandy. Only last summer I saw an illustration of this. The water was low and the general report from anglers was, "Nothing doing." And yet one fellow was catching trout; good ones, too. I got in touch with him and found that, though he didn't call it that, he was using the wet-dry method.

The value of nymphs and wet flies is far greater than you might suppose. It is true that dry-fly fishing is exciting and more pleasurable, but my main reason for fishing a dry fly so much is because it is the easiest and simplest way to fish. Now don't get up in arms. I love dry-fly fishing as much as the purist. Nevertheless I contend that successful angling with wet fly and nymph requires more skill and finesse than dry-fly fishing.

In dry-fly fishing, the fly is always in sight. We know, therefore, exactly what it is doing and whether our fishing is faulty. In wet-fly fishing our flies are usually under the surface and out of sight. We must learn how to fish them in a manner that appeals to the trout. Often this requires the floating of the sunken fly without drag. Sometimes a slight movement without appreciable drag is needed, at other times a series of quick jerks will work best, and often the simple holding of the flies in the current is the secret.

There are many little tricks necessary to successful wet-fly and nymph fishing, intuitive manipulation of rod, line, and fly, which lead trout to strike. The entire game is complicated and requires considerable thought and study. Even the art of striking a fish is subtle. Often a clever wet-fly man is at a loss to explain how he knows when a fish takes or why he strikes at some particular moment. Most of this skill comes from keen observation and quick, accurate reactions to delicate influences.

As the fly floats along, out of sight in the water, the senses of the angler are keyed to a fine pitch. Suddenly he is conscious of a rise, and strikes. The hint may have been given him by the appearance of a fish so faint as to seem like a trick of the imagination, the line may have twitched slightly, or may have acted in a manner a little different from its usual behavior. So elusive, so slight are these indications that many anglers, who give wet-fly fishing a half-hearted try, are never aware of their existence.

Last season I stopped to watch an angler fishing a wet fly. Even while I watched he had three rises which he never even suspected. Finally he quit and came up to have a chat.

"New at the wet-fly game?" I asked.

"No. I've played it for years but never had much luck except up north. It's dull compared to dry-fly fishing. Nothing but luck if you get a fish."

"You had several strikes in that run," I remarked.

"What are you talking about?" he demanded. "I never felt a thing."

"Of course you didn't," I said soothingly. "The strikes didn't carry through the slack line enough to be felt. But you had them nevertheless. Just get back in there and try again. When I call 'strike' you do it."

He missed four fish but connected with the fifth.

"Didn't you see that last fish flash when he took?" I asked.

"Yes," he answered, "but I thought it was imagination."

Always keep keyed up to the highest pitch when fishing wet flies. Strike at the slightest provocation, whenever the impulse comes. Don't wait for obvious, easily seen indications. Be guided by impressions. Sometimes you may strike to the flash of a bird flying overhead, a sudden shaft of sunlight through the trees, even to the flash of a floating twig or leaf. But more often than not you will connect with a fish. These subtle touches are the essence of successful fly fishing. Without them you can never get the most out of your fishing.

It does not pay to be governed too much by rules. It is all right to say that trout will not take a dry fly that drags but it doesn't pay *always* to fish a fly without drag. Perhaps we are not always sure just when a fly appears to the trout to be floating naturally.

Often, when orthodox methods fail, a seemingly atrocious action on the part of our fly brings a strike. Then again the best way to get a strike in still water may be to move the fly, twitching it slightly. No matter how skillfully we do this, we cannot make it look to human eyes like a natural and live insect. Yet fish will frequently strike a fly handled in this way. One thing that helps in such cases is a leader that sinks. Here is a little kink which helps:

Soak the leader in a solution of one part vinegar and five parts water. Then rub with a rag treated with salt. This not only helps the leader sink but reduces the flash of the gut. Always remember that a leader which is under the surface is less noticeable and causes the trout less concern than one floating on the surface.

Keep in mind that the little things count all the time. If you get a fish by some odd thing you do, remember it and use it again. Those are the things that enable you to catch more fish.

CHAPTER XXV

How Well Can Fish See?

LIKE most anglers, I have always been interested in the subject of fish's vision, and for many years, as I fished, I have observed and made notes of incidents that seemed to have some bearing on the subject. Also, I have read much that anglers and scientists have written about it. I am setting down here what I have learned from these sources, offering, though, a warning that what I shall say is not the final answer.

The whole business offers a fascinating field for speculation, and one on which most anglers have strong and conflicting opinions. You can get into a lively debate at any time, any place where fishermen gather, by making any one of the following statements: Fish have (or have not) keen vision. They have (or have not) keen color sense. They are (or are not) sensitive to the form of an object like an artificial fly.

So far as I know, all the experiments that have been made to ascertain just what and how a fish sees have necessarily been based on the assumption that it sees and reacts to what it sees pretty

[239]

much as we humans do. Perhaps so; but let's mull the thing over a bit. Let's just consider simple things, easy to witness and to verify.

Obviously throughout the normal course of its life a fish is looking through water. But when the human eye is in direct contact with water, vision is blurred. So the nearest we can come to approximating the conditions under which a fish sees is to stand outside a glass-walled water tank and look through three mediums at once—air, glass, and water—to some object floating in or on the water. Thus, at least insofar as seeing in water is concerned, the eye of the fish must be different from that of man.

To think otherwise is to assume that a fish has blurred vision, and so is incapable of distinguishing faults in our flies, in their delivery, and whatnot; but those are the very things that we, in varying degree, unanimously agree that they do distinguish. Therefore we must believe that a fish has keen eyesight in its natural medium—water. That being so, we may well reason that because man has poor vision in water, unless given artificial aid, experiments with glass tanks to find out how a fish sees may not be conclusive.

We may also reasonably suspect that a fish has poor vision when in the air, as in jumping—perhaps even poorer than that of man in water, since the fish has no eyelids to shut out the glare. Then, too, when a fish is looking through water up into the air, the laws of light refraction, that is, the bending of the rays as they penetrate the water, doubtless come into play. It seems safe to assume that its vision is also influenced by the clarity and other characteristics of the water. This is the case—in reverse, of course —with man as he looks from air into water.

Another significant difference between fish and man is the placement of the eyes. Man's eyes are in the front of his head. They operate and focus in unison so that the vision is stereoscopic, which means that when both eyes see an object they combine into a single image. But the fish's eyes are on the sides and operate independently. What's more, they are connected with the brain individually, whereas human eyes are connected to both sides of the brain. Both eyes of a fish can focus at the same time on one object directly in front; but because each one has its own distinct connection with the brain, it is reasonable to suppose that the eyes of a fish can operate separately and thus permit the fish to observe two entirely unrelated images at the same time. For instance, it is quite possible that while one eye is watching your fly floating nearby, the other eye may be looking in a different direction—perhaps at a minnow, or at some suspicious object such as the legs of an approaching fisherman.

As to the keenness of a fish's eyesight, all of us can bear witness. I need only to mention the way a fish will take a tiny fly in fast water on a dark night. But this keenness of vision has its limitations. To human eyes, at least, few of the popular trout flies, even when supposed to imitate closely some natural insect, actually do so; and many artificials—the Royal Coachman, for instance—are not intended as imitations at all. Yet both types are readily taken at times.

And if we should succeed in tying a fly that was the spit and image of a natural stream insect, there would still be the hook to give it an unnatural appearance. In fact, some fly tyers, in an effort to achieve an exact copy of the natural fly, tie the artificial very sparsely, thus exposing most of the hook. Yet these flies are successful.

Then, too, there are the low-water types of salmon wet flies which also take fish. Here we have the greatest possible exposure of the hook consistent with the dressing required. If a fish can distinguish the difference between a No. 8 and a No. 12 fly (and it surely can), it stands to reason that it can also see the hook to which the fly is tied. Thus, while it is certain that fish have keen eyesight, we must conclude that they are indifferent to certain minor details, and to such an unnatural appendage as a hook. Otherwise they would reject the fly.

We all know, however, that when a lure picks up a bit of weed or other foreign matter the fish will almost never take it. We also know that we can get much closer to fish feeding in deep water than to shallow-water feeders. But what if any relation these puzzling facts bear to the vision of fish is something that can be pondered far into the night.

How good is the color perception of fish? On that question there is a wide difference of opinion among anglers. Some maintain that fish are absolutely color-blind, seeing only in different tones of gray; others claim that fish distinguish colors exactly as the normal human eye does; and there are all degrees of belief between.

If fish *do* see all colors just as shades of gray, then obviously any color you can name must correspond to some shade of gray in the fish's "color chart." So you might assume that a fly of red and green and blue, say, and one tied with their gray counterparts would be all the same to a fish. But, strange to say, either that doesn't seem to be the case or nobody has found exactly the right combination of grays. Somewhere I read how an angler of an inquiring turn of mind tried an experiment of this nature. He was fishing in the north country for brook trout, and they were taking a Parmachene Belle, which as you know is scarlet and white with a yellow wool body, silver ribbing, and black tip. To see what would happen he substituted a gray fly which matched pretty closely the one that had been producing, and although the new fly bore shades of gray that varied from mist to almost black, he got no results at all with it. Of course, all colors look different in different lights. And for us, as darkness deepens, color becomes less and less distinguishable until in time it is completely smothered by the dark.

Here again we come to another difference between the vision of fish and of humans. For with fish, especially trout and certain other species, color apparently is never completely blacked out. This has been demonstrated many times. For instance, when fishing at night we often find that trout will select one fly but refuse others. Sometimes, even on the darkest night, they will unerringly choose between flies which differ only by a shade or two in the color of the hackle, body, or wing.

This suggests the thought that what is absolute darkness to us isn't even the dimness of twilight to some fish; that even on the blackest night they see so well that they easily distinguish not only contrasting colors but even minor variations of shade. We must then conclude that fish not only can differentiate between colors (whether they do so as we do or in some other way is immaterial here) but that they also are extremely sensitive to them.

The degree of intensity of light affects colors. It may be, then, that it is only when fish see our artificial flies in certain positions and in certain lights that the flies look acceptable to them. Such a hypothesis would account for many of our failures as well as for our successes.

Naturally the degree of light intensity in relation to various backgrounds calls for innumerable combinations in the color and design of artificial flies if we are to match the exquisite creations of nature. Whether the vast array of available lure and fly patterns is necessary, or could be reduced drastically, remains a subject for argument which will probably go on till doomsday.

To sum up: 1. Gamefish have keen sight. 2. Even so, they seem singularly to ignore the hooks and other incongruities present in all artificials. This is fortunate, because these are the very things that cannot be dispensed with. 3. Fish have color perception. They seem extremely sensitive to slight variations in shades. 4. Fish also are choosy as to size (and to textures, too, by the way). In brief, *color*, *size*, and *material* seem to be the important factors in fish lures. Hooks may be ignored.

As to what colors, sizes, and materials to use, that depends on the place, time, weather, season, and angler. No general rules, no specific recommendations, can be laid down. Individual experiment by trial-and-error methods gives the answers here. If in your own experience you have found that certain flies or lures are consistent producers, by all means keep on using them at such times and places and under such conditions as they continue to be successful for you. But when these tried and true favorites do not produce, it's time to try something else.

Along these same lines, for many years skilled fishermen have faithfully followed the rule never to fish with the sun at their backs. The idea, of course, is to prevent their shadow from falling on the water. I, too, long accepted that rule as infallible but now have learned that it should be modified to meet certain needs.

It is important, of course, that your shadow should not fall upon the water you're fishing, and so advertise your presence to the fish. But when your shadow is short, as it will be when the sun is high, or when you can keep it off the water by one means or another, it is often to your advantage to fish with the sun at your back.

To do so, however, is so contrary to the usual experience and training that careful analysis is necessary to justify it. Let us consider, then, the sunlight's effect on human eyes. When it strikes them directly it dazzles and blinds, but as you turn them away from the sun the vision becomes clearer and clearer until every object is seen in sharp relief. If you look at a stream against the sunlight it is difficult to perceive any detail at all, even when you move your eyes slowly to one side or the other away from the direct rays. Now if you go to the opposite bank and look at the stream with the sun at your back, everything stands out clearly.

If this is true of you, isn't it also true of a fish in the water, watching for flies drifting downstream on the surface? That is the thought that struck me when I first gave this question careful consideration. My reasoning was as follows: "If the sun, shining in my eyes, makes it difficult or impossible to see details clearly, why isn't the trout's vision similarly blurred under such conditions— and if it is, why shouldn't there be just one right spot to place a fly so that even a wary, wise, and selective fish will be fooled by it? For if its vision is thus blurred, it should not be able to distinguish between the natural fly and the artificial."

I was convinced that my reasoning was right. The problem then was to test it. My experiments have continued for at least fifteen years. I've proved to my own satisfaction that by floating a fly where sunshine blurs a fish's vision the angler has a definite advantage, for the fish is then more likely to mistake an artificial for a natural fly. The productive area lies between the "blind spot" where the fish receives the full glare of the sunlight and that area where crystal-clear vision begins. For the sake of brevity let us call that area the "window of blurred vision."

Here are two experiences that are typical of the many I've had which bear out the correctness of my theory. While these adventures were with trout, the same principle applies to other species of fish angled for with surface flies and lures and under similar conditions.

My first experience literally was thrust upon me. Fishing had been so good that there seemed to be no need for theory or experiment. I started my fishing at seven a.m., when the trout were rising to natural flies in a desultory fashion. They proved so willing to go for an artificial that if one spot offered difficulties I could shift to another spot nearby without changing position, and soon have a trout on the line. These fish were not large—they ran from ten to fourteen inches—but they were well worth taking.

While fishing in this rather careless way I spied a steadily recurring dimple in the limpid, slow-moving, and oily glide a little upstream from where I stood. I cast to it several times without response, so turned to other more obliging fish. I was about ready to move along to the next good stretch of fishing water when that dimple again arrested my attention. I can't tell how I knew it but suddenly I was sure that I was watching the rise of a steadily feeding trout of large size.

With that realization my heart started to thump, and for a moment or two I was as much a victim of buck fever as any beginner. Luckily I had enough sense to keep from casting until those fevered moments had passed. The spot where the fish was rising could be covered perfectly from where I stood, so I started working on the fish from there. However, he took not the slightest notice of my offerings! Why? Not because I had frightened him, for he continued rising as steady as clockwork. The flies on the water were small, and colored somewhat like gun metal. I tried all my No. 18 patterns in blue-bronze, blue, and combinations of both colors, but even on the small-size hook they looked monstrous compared with the midges being taken by the trout.

I knew the trouble couldn't be drag. The spot required only an easy cast, there was no wind to speak of, and all the water in the slight current between me and the fish was moving at the same speed. Except for size the flies looked as natural to me as did the actual hatch, yet the fish took the living midges in front of and behind the artificial, sometimes so close to it that only by keeping my nerves under strict control was I able to resist striking. Had I struck, of course, the fish would not have risen again.

I had been working on my blurred-vision theory for years, yet now I'd forgotten what I'd learned! It never occurred to me that the cause of my present failure might be that I was casting to a spot where the trout could tell instantly that my flies were phony.

Then I realized that I was fishing from a position where the sun was shining in my face. This meant that my fly was floating in the clearest possible window of vision. Should I cast beyond the trout to put the fly on the other side of him, the leader would almost certainly put him down. Now was the time to put my window-of-blurred-vision to the test once more. I carefully changed my position, which meant going some distance below, crossing over, then up the opposite bank to water that could be waded, yet was not so close to the fish as to scare him.

From my position, with the sun at my back, I had much clearer vision, and although the water between me and the trout had currents of varying speeds, a slack-line cast probably would provide the needed length of dragless drift. Because now I had become light-conscious I studied the situation intently before making a cast. I wanted the fly to land on my side of the fish and directly in his window of blurred vision. Next I had to figure out the direct line from sun to trout which would tell about where that window would be.

It is seldom possible to hit that window without many trials, but this time I struck it just right. The fly dropped lightly, drifted a bare three inches, then disappeared in the center of a suction dimple. I raised the rod and off the trout went in that first exciting run so typical of a sizeable brownie. As he weighed in at a full 3½ pounds I felt that the time spent in figuring out that particular problem was well worth while.

The second incident took place on a slow-moving meadow stream. Late in the afternoon I had come to a long, deep run where the water flowed due north. I was on the east bank because I had just fished upstream through a stretch which could not be covered from the west bank. This particular run, some two hundred feet long, was something to see. Trout—lots of trout—were rising in the main current all along the stretch. There were various species of flies on the water, mostly ginger or gray in color—in terms of artificials—ranging in size from 12's to 18's.

I worked over those trout for an hour from the east bank of the stream. All I got were two half-hearted rises. These trout were as choosy as they come. They refused flies that seemed to me to be very good imitations of the naturals, yet the two short rises I had both came to large fan-wings which did not resemble the naturals in the least.

Now I thought again of the blurred-vision window. Possibly these fish could be fooled if I fished from the opposite side. In this instance it took half an hour of precious time to get to the desired spot. By that time the sun was low enough in the west to make a very real shadow problem. Fortunately the bank was high enough and the water sufficiently shallow near its foot so that I could avoid casting a shadow by wading on my knees. I did so without wasting any more time.

My success was not spectacular but it was quite good enough. I took six fish, each weighing at least 1¼ pounds, before the sun left the water. After that I couldn't get a trout to rise, even though they continued feeding on the naturals with the same abandon as before.

This experiment convinced me that the sunlight was a controlling factor on that particular stretch of water and at that time of day. The fish I caught couldn't detect the artificiality of my fly as it passed over the water making up the window of blurred vision; but as soon as the sunshine left the water they were no longer fooled.

I realize that fish aren't always so selective. If they were, fishing would be tough indeed. I am sure, however, that at times trout become extra-hard to please after the sun has left the water. It is obviously impossible to work out all the angles of my theory exactly. Thus its importance as an aid to fishermen is problematical, but it does seem to explain certain bothersome problems which otherwise remain unanswered.

For instance, consider those not infrequent occasions when two anglers of equal ability fish the same current of water from opposite sides of a pool. One man catches trout consistently, while the other gets none or only a few. If this happens when the sun is on the water, the window of blurred vision may be responsible for the difference between success and failure.

There are times, of course, when trout take best in shady places or on dark days. There are times, too, when my sunshine theory doesn't seem to hold. But keep it in mind when fishing with a dry fly, in the sunshine, particularly on glassy runs, oily-looking glides, limpid still pools—places where often you will find the trout selective and scary—and it will likely work to your advantage.

CHAPTER XXVI

Balanced Tackle

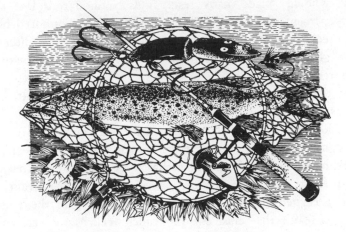

FLY FISHING is probably the final refinement in angling. In no other fishing is the balance of tackle so vital. This is the system that really lets you test the limits of your equipment and skill.

Tackle balance is easy enough to define. It simply means a combination of fly rod, reel, and line that works best for the person using it. Getting that is quite a different thing, because tackle balanced perfectly for one man may not work for another. And it takes some knowhow and experimenting to fit the first man. Different leaders and flies complicate things still further, enough so that it's wise to first make peace with your basic equipment. Flies and leaders need chapters of their own.

First get the right rod for the kind of fishing you'll do. Bamboo, glass, and steel are the common materials used in making fly rods. All three are good, but they're different enough that you'll want to know how to make a choice. It boils down to this: Split-bamboo rods, first in the hearts of fly fishermen for years, are still a good choice if you get high-quality bamboo. The new glass rods, offering more for the money, have just about crowded medium and low-priced bamboos off the market.

In one way, both steel and glass are better than bamboo. A. E. Low, who has made many tests, finds bamboo rods lose about thirty percent of their original action after three hundred hours' use. Steel rods lose only about 1½ percent. His tests didn't include glass rods, but it's a good bet they'd compare favorably with steel.

Of the three materials, glass requires the least care. It won't rust as steel does, and heat and water have no effect upon it, as they do with ordinary bamboo. There are, however, bakelite-impregnated bamboo rods that are impervious to live steam, salt water, and sun. They're about as hardy as glass, except that glass better resists permanent bends, or sets, from undue strain. Still it's not ruggedness that keeps quality bamboos in the running with glass—it's that elusive thing called feel. Many veteran anglers say nothing has it like bamboo.

But how do you select a balanced rod? Well, the best way is to rig several rods with lines that fit them and make practice casts. Unfortunately, few dealers can offer such service. Next best is to mount a reel on the rod, run out line through the guides, and whip the rod gently back and forth. Watch how it bends. It should have an evenly graduated bend right down to the hand grip—a wide bend at the tip that decreases until it's barely visible just ahead of the grip. It should have a live feel, as if it were just the right compromise between limberness and stiffness to whip out the line. If this system's out, tie a one-ounce weight to the rod tip and swing it gently, checking for the feel just described.

The entire rod should come into play when casting for distance, so pick a rod with the best hand grip. Standard is about six to 6½ inches long. Grips 7½ inches long for short rods and up to nine for long rods work better. They allow you to shift your hand up and down the grip, changing the balance of your rod as you vary your casts. Get a slender grip. Even large, strong hands soon tire from using one too thick. As for shape, none shifts in the hand better than the cigar taper. Poorest is the style that flares out at each end, though that doesn't matter much with a very short grip. If you fish all over the map, trying wide, open streams and narrow, brushy ones in turn, two rods are needed— one long and one short. Where your angling is limited to one stream or type of stream, one rod will do.

For medium to small streams my choice is a 7½-foot rod with medium action (neither too stiff nor too whippy), one weighing from 3½ to four ounces. (Weight is not a true indication of the size of the body of the rod, because fittings—guides, windings, reel seats—vary.) Forgetting the weight, I prefer a rod for these streams that's stiff enough to handle a tapered silk or nylon line calibrating .040 or .039 inches, measuring at the thickest part of the line. This is size HEH. Some nylon lines are lighter than silk and would require a size larger (HDH) to give you the same weight balance on your rod. You can also use an eight-foot rod of comparable action with the lines just listed. Either it or the 7½-footer are good choices for most Eastern trout streams. Balanced with those lines, they'll give you easy casts up to forty-five feet, and that's usually all you need to fish Eastern streams.

For wide streams where you have room to handle a long rod, as is the case on many Western waters, the best choice is an 8½ to 9½-foot rod. It's also a valuable rod for Eastern anglers who work lakes or use bass bugs and heavy streamers occasionally. Then you need that extra length and power. A rod in this class should weigh between 4½ and 5¾ ounces. Balance it with an HCH double-taper light nylon line or with HDH in silk or heavy nylon. A forward-taper line to fit it would range from HCF in light nylon to HDF in silk, which averages a little heavier than nylon in the same size.

Get a rod with real power and punch if you do a lot of fly fishing for bass or steelheads. With bass, you need it not only to cast large, air-resisting bass bugs, but also to set hooks in their tough mouths. For steelhead fishing, that power is necessary to make the long casts often required. My choices are a nine-foot, six-ounce bamboo for steelheads and a 9½-foot, 5¾-ounce bamboo for bass. They don't have to be bamboo rods, of course. It just happens I've never tried a glass rod in those lengths that suited me as well. My 9½-foot bass rod is a little more limber than may be ideal, yet it has a lot of life and lays a pretty bass bug. A little heavier rod in that length is good insurance if you really need to lay out a long line, as fishermen on Western steelhead and trout streams commonly do.

A fly rod for salmon, steelheads, or other such heavy fish will be much easier to handle while playing a fish if it has an independent handle that fits onto the main grip behind the reel seat. These long rods exert a lot of leverage against hand and arm, holding them with a single grip. The extra handle's an arm-saver.

You'll read and hear about ultra-light tackle, of course—two-ounce rods and the like. They're fine, too, but you want to know why you're getting one before you lay out the cash. About the only reason for them is the added sport of playing a fish on delicate tackle. I often use an eight-foot, two-ounce rod for strip casting worms and minnows. You can get a lot of satisfaction out of fly fishing with other such special rigs. Just don't jump to the conclusion that they're recommended for over-all efficiency. Your personal temperament and requirements should guide you.

There are a lot of good fly reels, many of them inexpensive. Regardless of price or style, look for these features: General durability—it's poor economy to buy a cheap reel that will fail when you're playing the big one; simple construction that allows you to clean and adjust the reel without a lot of tools and trouble; ample line capacity—enough that a fine fly won't be bunched and scraped during the hasty reeling you'll do fighting a heavy fish.

Single-action, hand-cranked fly reels are the most dependable models. Automatic reels, popular with many, are handier but more cantankerous. I've been on two or three trips to high-altitude waters where automatics were freezing up tight during sudden squalls. Single-actions weren't bothered. Automatics are also easier balked by sand, hard knocks, and general abuse, and they're somewhat heavier and bulkier than manual reels. On the other hand, an automatic, which operates off a coil spring, will gather in slack line or retrieve a fly at the flick of your finger. Fish sometimes go for the fast, steady retrieve possible with an automatic. It's also an easy way to keep a tight line while fighting a fast fish.

A drag is a help with a single-action reel. I like those with a friction clutch that allows you to keep reeling while a big fish is taking out line. The second the pressure lessens enough—according to how the drag is set—your line reels in. When the spool is linked directly to the reel handle, a hard-running fish may spin the handle out of your hand and free itself on the resulting slack line, or the leader may be broken when you excitedly clamp down on the spinning handle. Some fly fishermen play fish by giving line and stripping it in with their free hand, but I'll warn you that can result in fish-losing kinks if the fish makes a run and catches you with any considerable amount of loose line dangling at your feet.

For salmon, steelheads, or other husky fly takers, be sure to get a reel of excellent quality and large line capacity. They'll take out lots of line, often with a rush that's destructive to second-rate reels. Lose one of those big silver prizes because of a cheap reel and you'll never forgive yourself for your false economy.

A reel that will hold twenty-five yards of level or thirty yards of double-taper line is enough for average trout and bass fishing. The heavy front-taper or torpedo lines usually sell in lengths of about forty yards, so allow a little extra space if you plan to use one. If you're after heavy, long-running fish, allow still more space for backing. This is a thin, strong line spliced to the fly line to extend its fish-fighting length. It saves the expense of padding your reel with more fly line than you can cast. A 3½-inch reel with a 9/16-inch drum will hold a heavy tapered line and some backing nicely. You can go a little smaller if you use only level or smaller tapered lines without backing, but there's no particular advantage in it, and a larger spool has the added virtue of keeping the fly line from taking a set in tight little coils if it's left wound on the reel for some time.

The line is a very important part of your fly-fishing tackle. Basically, there are three types: level, double-taper, and forward-taper—the latter also called tadpole, torpedo, three-diameter, and bug-taper. These last are made in many variations, but the main idea is to have the bulk and weight of the line in the forward portion so that it will pull the lighter running, or shooting, portion of the line through the guides when the heavy portion is flipped through the air for a long cast.

Usual length of a level line is twenty-five yards, although it often comes with four twenty-five-yard coils connected so that you may get a longer continuous length if you like. Double-tapers commonly come in thirty-yard lengths; forward tapers forty. Level fly lines are plenty good for small brooks where you need to make only short casts. The heavier ones are also suitable for bass-bugging or wet-fly fishing. But on the whole I think tapered lines do all fly fishing a little better. As usual, you pay more for them.

I think double-taper lines are at their best when used to make delicate casts at comparatively short range, say twenty to forty-five feet. They'll easily cast farther, but I'd go to a forward-taper if longer casts were to be a regular thing. Casting for a distance is the forward-taper's long suit.

Ranked according to cost, level lines are cheapest, double-tapers next, and forward-tapers most expensive of all. The only reason for the double construction on the double-taper, by the way, is the economy of being able to use both ends in turn to cast with, switching ends when one becomes shortened or worn.

Fly lines are made of silk, nylon, and glass fiber. Because finishes won't penetrate nylon as they do silk, some nylon finishes crack quickly. Nylon also stretches enough to damage the finish. But nylon has been improved of late. I've seen new nylon finishes that seem to be very durable. Nylon lines are good floaters, too, which makes them good dry-fly lines.

With the exception of one superb hollow silk line, hand-finished and very expensive, I prefer nylon for dry-fly and surface bug fishing. For wet flies I like a silk line, particularly if the flies have to be well under the surface to get results. If you fish both wet and dry flies, the most satisfactory system is to carry two lines on separate reels—one for each purpose. Otherwise you're always battling a line that floats when you want it to sink or dives to the bottom when you want it on top. The exception here is greased-line wet-fly fishing, working a wet fly or nymph just inches under the surface. That takes a good floating line.

There's one fishing outfit that will handle anything from sunfish to steelheads with reasonable efficiency. It will serve you on narrow brooks, wide rivers, lakes, or ponds. It will cope with high water or low, and adjust to the changing demands of spring, summer, and fall. I'm talking about a spinning outfit.

This doesn't mean that spinning tackle will do a better job of fly fishing, say, than tackle designed specifically to handle flies. Nor will it outclass a trolling rod and reel when it comes to fishing heavy lures behind a moving boat. Yet the spinning outfit would be a fine choice for a person who had to do both these jobs with a single rig. There's nothing more versatile than a properly managed set of spinning tackle.

Although European anglers were using primitive spinning reels in the 1800's, spinning in the United States got a slow and halting start. Spinning was just about established here when World War II stopped the mass production of fishing tackle. There were no imports, and American manufacturers were busy with war contracts. Spinning tackle and publicity about it nearly disappeared.

After the war, spinning started off with a zoom. New spinning rods and reels appeared, and with them new lures of weights and shapes particularly suited to the tackle. Articles and books were written about the tackle—some of the early claims bordering on the fabulous.

The reason spinning took hold so quickly was that newcomers to angling could catch fish with it at once, something that rarely happened when beginners set out with conventional fly or bait-casting tackle. In my opinion, spinning equipment has bred more new anglers in a few years than other tackle has accounted for since sport fishing in this country began. Today the person shopping for spinning tackle has a multitude of styles and models to choose from. The only trick is in getting separate items—rod, reel, line, and lure—that form a well-balanced unit.

Here's my idea of a general-purpose spinning outfit for fresh-water fishing: The rod should be 6½ feet long and of medium action—neither too stiff nor too limber. Most spinning rods are made of fiberglass these days, though it's possible to get fine—but rather expensive—spinning rods made of split bamboo. Either material will do an excellent job in a rod of quality workmanship. Price is a fair guide to quality. Get the best you can afford.

Modern spinning reels are a good deal alike, despite differences in outward appearances. Some have hoods covering the spool and pickup bail; others are open. Handles and adjustment devices vary too, but they generally do the same jobs in about the same way.

Whatever model you choose, be sure the line-holding spool can be removed quickly and replaced with an identical spool holding lighter or heavier line. Be sure the reel has a dependable drag device that can be adjusted to match the strength of lines ranging from three to ten-pound test. The reel should be sturdy and well-made in all respects.

You should have at least three spools filled with different-size lines. When using a spinning lure weighing, say, three quarters of an ounce or more, you may be able to cast quite well with a line calibrating as thick as .012, which should test from eight to ten pounds. Unless a line of this calibration is very soft, you may have difficulty casting a lure as light as three eighths of an ounce. This is one of the main difficulties attending the use of the spinning reels. The thicker lines tend to be stiff, and this stiffness may make them flip off the spool in coils that jam in the guides of the rod. I wouldn't use a spinning line thicker than .011 calibration for ordinary fresh-water fishing. This may range from six to eight pounds in test. Of course, different brands vary.

For the heavier lures, fill one spool with a line calibrating .011 or .012. This heavy line is very good for deep trolling, and will make you fairly well equipped for casting lures that weigh as much as five eighths of an ounce.

Regular spinning tackle is ideal for casting lures ranging from an eighth to a quarter of an ounce. It was designed for such light lures. For the quarter-ounce lures, a spool filled with line calibrating .010 or even as light as .009 (four- to seven-pound test) will perform nicely. The .009 line will also cast one eighth-ounce lures well if they're of a type that will cast easily.

Some lures cut through the air with little resistance; others fight the air, making casting quite a problem. And the answer doesn't lie in using only the lures that cast like bullets. Many times the lures that are hard to cast are just the ones the fish will take.

You can cast light, wind-resistant lures better with very thin line, but you must use discretion here, being careful not to use a line that's too fragile for the stiffness of the rod. For the 6½-foot all-around spinning rod, I prefer .008 line, which is approximately five-pound test. For the general-duty outfit, I consider lines thinner than .008 calibration too frail. However, these lighter lines will serve nicely when using special lightweight spinning rods and reels.

You can really make out well with a single spinning outfit if you have extra spools filled with different size lines. This is a great convenience to the traveling fisherman who wants to take a single outfit on a trip that might lead to a variety of fishing opportunities. It's a money-saver for the angler who must budget carefully in buying fishing tackle.

The angler who consistently uses heavy lures and deals with large fish will do better with a salt-water spinning outfit than with lighter all-around spinning tackle. In my experience, tackle of salt-water weight is needed to give top performance with the class of lures ranging from ¼ to ½ to ¾ of an ounce.

The all-around spinning outfit is also less than perfect for lures weighing an eighth of an ounce or less. To handle these fragile fish attractors with maximum efficiency you need a whippy, light-action spinning rod and line as thin as .005, which will test two or three pounds. You can also get a light-weight spinning reel designed to match the light rod and line.

Some light-tackle fans use spinning lines that test no more than a pound and a half and claim that it's strong enough, but it hasn't worked out that way for me. I'll admit that such thin line makes longer casts, and no doubt it's superior for fooling very wary fish. But in my experience it breaks too easily after a bit of use, especially when you're playing big fish in snaggy waters or where they must be worked back to you upstream in a strong current. Personally, I consider .006 about the finest line needed for spinning, and it's more practical than anything smaller. All lines lose strength in use, and the finer they are the quicker deterioration sets in.

When using light-weight lures and low-test lines, I find that a fly rod mounted with spinning guides is a splendid tool. For this you really need a fly-rod-type spinning reel, which is designed to fit a fly-rod reel seat. However, a regular spinning reel can be used. I've often done well using a regular spinning reel on a fly rod having only the ordinary fly-rod guides. The point is that you will do best if you have exactly the right equipment.

We must also consider fly fishing with a spinning rod and reel. There are two gadgets that make this reasonably practical. One is the plastic ball float, a small transparent ball into which water may be put to bring it to the desired weight. Top weight with the ball completely filled is about a quarter of an ounce. The one I like best is globular and about three quarters of an inch in diameter. On the water it looks like a bubble.

This casting bubble is tied to the end of the spinning line. Then a short dropper tippet, say from four to five inches long, is tied to the line about five inches above the bubble. The distance I've suggested, as well as the length of the tippet, places the fly close to the bubble float. Some fishermen think that the fly so close to the float will deter fish from striking. In my experience it hasn't. But if you feel different about this, place the tippet farther up the line from the bubble.

The second fly-casting rig for spinning tackle can hardly be called a gadget, although it actually serves as one. It's a fifteen-foot length of tapered fly line which you tie to the end of your regular spinning line. It weighs about a quarter of an ounce, and so serves as a casting weight in place of a lure, a bubble, or a sinker. To the end of this short tapered line you attach a leader six to nine feet long, with the fly on the end of the leader. As this fly line and leader will range from twenty-one to twenty-four feet long, you can readily understand that it's quite different from casting a quarter-ounce lure. However, there are some anglers who consider the rig tops in performance.

You need a long spinning rod or perhaps a regular fly rod equipped with spinning-type guides to do the best job of casting flies with the fifteen-foot length of fly line on the end of a mono-filament spinning line. At the start of the cast, all the fly line should be worked out through the rod guides—until the end of its fifteen-foot length is just beyond the rod tip. Then, with the spinning rod held in front of you in about a ten-o'clock position, raise it sharply to one o'clock to toss the twenty feet of fly line and leader combined into the air behind you. When line and leader straighten behind you, drive the rod forward to deliver the cast to the water. One finger of the rod hand holds the spinning line on the reel spool until the air-borne line starts to straighten on the forward toss. At that point you release the line at the reel to let it shoot through the guides and add distance to the cast. It takes practice to get the feel of fly fishing with a spinning rod, whether you use the plastic bubble for casting weight or tie on a length of fly line.

There isn't any doubt in my mind that spinning tackle, rigged in one way or another, will frequently take fish that can't be reached or fooled with other gear. A spinning rig is ideal for the one-outfit angler. And the fellow who owns and uses a dozen different fly rods would catch a lot more fish if he added one spinning outfit to his collection.

However, though the fixed-spool spinning reel has won the hearts and fancy of many members of the angling fraternity in recent years, I'm of the opinion that spinning tackle will not do certain jobs as well as the standard bait-casting outfits that use revolving-spool reels.

It's continually being claimed that the lighter the weight of tackle you use the more pleasure you'll derive from catching a fish. This is true to a degree. But I believe you get the most pleasure from fishing when you have tackle that reasonably matches the average size of the fish. With small fish ultra-light tackle may well give you the most satisfaction. If the fish run medium to large, then standard-weight tackle will probably give you the most sport. But if the fish are extra large, you need tackle sturdy enough to feel that you are playing the fish rather than letting it play you.

When casting monofilament line, you don't need a separate leader between line and lure, because the entire line acts as a leader. You may tie the line directly to the lure. A snap connector tied on the end of the line is handy for changing lures. When using spinners or other lures that spin when being retrieved or trolled, a snap swivel or a snap and a couple of swivels may be necessary.

Without swivels tied ahead of them, some lures will twist the line. This can cause considerable annoyance, plus rendering the spinner nearly useless as a fish attractor. Use the smallest snaps and swivels you can for the size of the lure. The balance on some modern lures is so precise that using a heavy swivel and snap may ruin the lure's action. Watch this carefully. It may easily make a difference in the success of your fishing.

When out for sharp-toothed fish, such as pickerel, northern pike, muskies, and walleyes, a short wire leader is advisable. You may catch dozens of these fish without losing one because of no wire trace, but sooner or later you're going to lose a good one. I've lost a large number of pike by failing to use a short wire trace. As a matter of fact, I've had several big fellows cut off a six-inch trace by taking the lure very deep or making a sudden turn and cutting off the line just above the trace. As a rule, however, a four- to six-inch trace with a snap and swivel will stop such casualties and will also prevent line twisting. You can now buy wire traces which are almost as invisible as monofilament. They are light-color wire (stainless steel) wound with nylon. For most fresh-water fishing, I find the twelve-pound test wire-and-nylon about right. I either use four- or six-inch lengths according to the fish I'm angling for.

For bait-casting lures you may use any of the great variety in the stores that weigh from three eighths to a full ounce. I consider bait-casting tackle tops for lures ranging from three eighths to three quarters of an ounce. Most practical anglers are more accurate in casting lures with bait-casting tackle than with spinning tackle.

CHAPTER XXVII

Best Natural Baits

THE FIRST trout I ever caught fell for a worm on opening day in early April. Today, fifty-eight years later, I still think
that worms are as good a bait as an angler can have for early season fishing.

In addition to their general appeal to fish, worms are easy to
obtain and so simple to use that the most awkward beginner can
often take fish with them. Worms are the secret weapons of those
small boys who use willow poles and string lines to outclass adult
anglers armed with two hundred dollars worth of tackle. You
don't need intricate tackle to fish a worm effectively. In fact, the
one-piece cane pole that so many anglers used years ago is still a
good rig for a lot of worm fishing.

There's a fiberglass rod on the market now that has the old
cane pole's advantages of length, springy strength, and low price
without being awkward to transport in a car. The fiberglass
counterpart of the cane pole is jointed so it will telescope to a
length short enough to fit into a car trunk.

I have two of these rods. One is thirteen feet long, the other fourteen. I find them great for fishing worms and other natural baits. All you need to do to rig a cane pole or its glass counterpart is to tie ten to fifteen feet of line to the rod tip and add a short piece of leader with a baited hook on it.

The long cane or glass pole is a poor choice for fishing brushy streams, turbulent rivers, or for wading. It's ideal for small meadow streams and ponds. Fishing a meadow stream, the long pole lets you stay back far enough from the bank to be hidden from the fish. This keeps them from becoming scared or suspicious. On ponds the long rod puts the bait out far enough to attract the fish feeding or cruising fifteen to twenty feet from shore. Or you can stay back out of sight and drop the bait close to the bank where good fish often come in to feed when no danger threatens. This is possible with the long pole, although impractical with any other outfit.

A light spinning outfit is excellent for most natural-bait fishing. By a light outfit I mean a limber 6½-foot to 7½-foot spinning rod, a good quality-spinning reel, and a line of .011 calibration or less. Personally I prefer six- to eight-pound test monofilament line for average trout fishing with worms or minnows. That size monofilament usually calibrates from .010 to .011. Larger calibration than .011 will not cast well with light tackle unless you use a heavy sinker.

If the water is very clear and without much current and the fish are wary, then I'd suggest monofilament line as thin as .007, which should test 3½ to four pounds. You can break the very fine stuff, say two-to three-pound test, by striking hard at a fish as small as one pound. It's for the devotee of ultra-light tackle, the highly skilled angler.

I like a fly rod for worm and minnow fishing in streams that must be waded to be covered properly. In the old days one had to use a single-action fly reel, a braided fly line, and a leader for this, but today one may use a spinning reel built especially for fly rods and filled with one of the monofilament lines already suggested. In my opinion, a fly rod equipped with a fly-rod spinning reel and a thin monofilament line is about tops for handling lightweight natural baits when you need to fish without a sinker.

There isn't any outfit that ideally serves all needs. A cane pole or telescope glass counterpart will be best for some conditions; a 6½- to 7½-foot spinning rod with a suitable reel and line will no doubt be best for average conditions, and the fly rod with spinning reel will be most acceptable for some persons and for some special conditions. I use them all, according to the need and my fancy at the time.

Now to the question of choosing a worm to fish with that tackle. There are several kinds of earthworms, commonly called angling or fishing worms. Probably best known of the clan is the night crawler. The name comes from the fact that these worms come to the surface at night in favorable weather, which means warm and wet weather. These worms are gathered after dark with the aid of a flashlight. When it gets very wet, they'll spread out all over a lawn and are easy to catch. At other times it takes skill and patience to gather a good supply.

The flashlight shouldn't have too bright a beam. (If it's very bright, cover the lens with a piece of thin cloth.) A glaring beam of light thrown about carelessly will scare the crawlers back into their holes. I wait until it has been dark for at least two hours. If there hasn't been much rain, I first test places where night crawlers are usually plentiful, using utmost caution in displaying the light and in walking. The softer you walk the better your chances. If I can't spot any in favored areas I give up and wait for a rain or perhaps water the lawn thoroughly the next afternoon and try again that night.

If conditions are favorable I step softly and move the light very slowly over the ground before me. When I see anything that looks like a worm, even the end of one, I hold steady until I can tell which is the tail end. Then I grab the thicker head end gently with my thumb and forefinger. Usually the worm has its tail in the hole and will start squirming. If you simply hold with firm gentleness the tail will squirm loose in a matter of seconds. If you hold too tightly or pull, there's a good chance that the worm will break. This is still a usable bait worm but it will not remain so very long in a bait container, although it may survive if left on the wet grass.

I usually release such injured worms. Put in a can of uninjured worms they soon die and contaminate the good ones. Sometimes, though, it's difficult to catch night crawlers, and when they're scarce I usually keep the injured ones, but I find it pays to place them in a separate can. Use up the injured worms first.

In some soils you'll find a small to medium-size worm that's rather pale in color compared with the night crawler. It's a firm-fleshed and lively worm, and in my opinion about the best for trout bait. I've dug these worms from banks of trout streams and in some gardens. When I can find this variety without too much trouble I'll use them before any other. Another worm that's good, although on the small side, is the one found near the manure piles that are around a barn or stable.

A compost pile is also a good place to dig worms. And you can buy them. Sporting-goods stores have them, and some bait dealers even sell them by mail. There are worm farms which make a business of raising and shipping worms to anglers.

Because night crawlers are large worms, a rather large hook is suggested for them. Size 6 is a happy medium, and the finer the wire of the hook the better, because it will injure the worm less. Sometimes two night crawlers on a hook work better than one. Many times I've had fish go for this big dish when they didn't seem to be interested in a single worm.

However, the reverse has also been true. My suggestion is to start fishing with one worm. If that doesn't work try two or even as many as three. If you go to that extreme, use a size 4 hook. It will do a better job of holding the large bait and you will also have a better chance of hooking the striking fish. However, the use of more than one night crawler at a time is not recommended unless the fish run fairly large, say from one pound upwards. For average stream trout a single worm is usually enough.

Under some conditions, such as fast or very deep water, a weight may be necessary to get the worm down to the fish. In recent years some intriguing sinkers have come on the market.

These are made with a rubber core, which makes for easy attaching and releasing without injuring the leader or line as badly as ordinary pinch-on sinkers. Some anglers prefer using a thin strip of lead, winding it on leader or line. Personally, I prefer the rubber-core split shot. But don't use any sinker at all if you can get the depth required with the bait itself.

When using large night crawlers you'll rarely need any additional weight in the average trout stream, especially if you fish the bait upstream. If fishing downstream in fast water, it may be absolutely necessary to use a sinker, sometimes one heavier than a large split shot.

On the whole, fishing a worm or minnow upstream will produce better than fishing them downstream. However, you must learn to take in slack line so the bait doesn't get snagged and be able to tell when a fish takes by watching your line. Otherwise you'll do better letting the bait drift with the current. Often quartering cross-stream fishing will be best.

Worms are about the easiest of all natural live baits to carry along for fishing and to keep for future use. Some ordinary soil in a can will keep a day's supply in good shape. In fact, I've used a single quart can of worms for several days, simply by keeping them from getting too hot. I've kept a month's supply in good condition by putting them in a wooden box filled with wet moss and keeping the box where it was cool. About the best way to carry them while wading is to use a belt bait box. These are available at any tackle store.

If you wish to keep an entire season's supply of worms to use as you need them, this can be done in two ways. If you have a cool cellar, a box of sufficient size filled with sod, loam, and moss in alternate layers will give you plenty of lively bait at times when other fellows are unable to get them. A burlap bag saturated with molasses or cane syrup and kept moist will serve as a food supply. You just place this on top of the last layer of sod and soil. Keep the burlap cover wet, but not soaking wet. If it's so wet that the water leaks freely through the bottom it will prove injurious to your stock.

Either bore tiny holes in the bottom of the box or remove

the regular bottom and cover with a fine-mesh rust-proof screen. Make sure holes or wire mesh are small enough to prevent worms from escaping. Also make sure that the box is tight otherwise. This same sort of box may be sunk in the yard if you have a reasonably shady spot. In this case the edges of the box should not be more than two inches above the surface and the top should be covered with fine-mesh wire to protect the worms from birds and rodents.

In recent years special worm-keeping preparations have appeared on the market. Instead of using moss, soil, or sod, you fill the box with the commercial mixture, following the instructions given. From my experience and that of friends, this material is very good. It is simple to use and the cost is most reasonable.

Minnows are excellent bait for nearly all fresh-water game fish. However, it's quite a problem keeping them alive, either at home, while transporting them to the fishing place, or while fishing with them. For home-keeping one needs running water and a large container. Even then it's a tough job to keep them in good condition.

For transporting live minnows in your car, one of the modern minnow buckets will be fine. Some have "breather" containers which mostly eliminate the constant need of aeration. Without one of these, you must aerate the water in the bucket at frequent intervals by dipping out water and pouring it back into the pail again. Do this from a height above the bucket sufficient to bring in enough oxygen, at least eight inches. If you use new water instead of the water already in the container, then you don't need to pour it back from a distance. But the new water should be approximately the same temperature as the water in the bucket or it will injure the minnows.

The modern buckets will keep minnows in good condition for considerable time. They're far superior to tin or galvanized pails that were used in the past. The warmer the weather the more aeration minnows need. When the air is cool to cold they need little attention, even in a metal pail. Just don't leave them in a car that's parked in the blazing sun.

In hot weather putting ice in the water before you start traveling will aid in keeping minnows in good condition. However, care must be taken when using ice. If you change the temperature of the water too quickly it may kill the fish. Let the first ice cube dissolve, then add two more—and so on until the needed amount of ice is in the pail.

You must reverse the process when changing from cold to warm. For instance, the water in a pond or stream may be much warmer than the water in your iced bucket. To hook a cold minnow and immediately start fishing with it in warm water is to have a bait that will quickly be sluggish or dead. The change in temperature here is accomplished by adding the lake or stream water to the bucket in small quantities and at about ten-minute intervals. The process may take up to half an hour if the difference in temperature is considerable, perhaps only fifteen minutes if the difference is slight. No matter how long it takes it will pay dividends in the way of lively minnows that will catch fish. The point is to avoid sudden shock. Minnows are delicate.

It's a chore to carry live minnows when stream fishing without a boat. For wading, where you are almost continually on the go, a small bucket tied to your belt or wader harness is about the best bet. Have the cord long enough to dangle the bucket in the water at all times, even when wading shallow streams. Usually the splashing of the water into the cover of the bucket and the continual movement will keep the water inside the pail in good condition, but each time you use a new bait look to see that the rest of the minnows are in good condition. If not, aerate with fresh water.

For trout fishing, small minnows are usually best, say those about two to 2¼ inches long. This same size is also good for sunfish and perch. Use the same tackle I suggested for worms. A size 8 fine-wire hook is about right for the small minnows. If using three- to 3½-inch baits, then I'd suggest a size 6 fine-wire hook. I recommend fine wire because it's less shocking to the bait.

When using small minnows, I think there are two ways that are really sound for hooking them. One is hooking through both lips—for fishing in moving water. The other good hooking area is in front or back of the dorsal fin—for fishing in still waters, ponds, and lakes. Slow trolling in lakes and ponds calls for the both-lips hooking method.

For most stream fishing with minnows, perhaps an across- or across-and-downstream cast, letting the bait drift as naturally as possible is as good a method as any. But casting a small minnow is difficult without the aid of a sinker and when casting mostly across stream a sinker can hang on the bottom rather quickly unless you know how to handle it. If the water is deep and swift you won't have any trouble, although you may need a heavy sinker. Only testing can determine the right weight, so you should always carry an assortment of sinkers in different sizes from split BB shot to sinkers as heavy as three eighths of an ounce. Experiment until you get the weight best for the particular condition.

In fast water I've often had my best worm and minnow fishing when I've been able to stand in a place where the bait would drift down directly before me into the place where the fish were feeding or resting. For still-water minnow fishing, especially in large stream pools, or in ponds and lakes, I've made out best when using a float and a split shot. The float is used to keep the minnow from getting into a hiding spot at the bottom, the split shot is used to keep the minnow from surfacing.

When bait fishing, one usually fishes deep. If the fish are surface feeding it's rarely necessary to use natural bait. Artificials will usually do the best then, besides being easier to fish. A fresh dead minnow will do as well as a live one if it acts alive enough for a game fish to take it. When stream fishing in active water, the flow of the water will give it enough action to simulate life. In lake fishing it's usually necessary to give the dead minnow some movement to make it seem alive. However, there are times when game fish will take a dead minnow even when it acts dead, as long as it is fresh.

In streams, preserved minnows will sometimes take fish. This is because in swift water game fish strike quickly in order to capture their prey. In still water they don't have to grab quickly. They can look a bait over carefully before taking it.

On the whole, I consider natural live bait or recently deceased minnows better than preserved minnows. I believe this is mostly because of odor and taste. Preserved minnows are not the same as naturals. If you doubt this just smell and taste the preserved product. I've done that. An odor that displeases may prevent a fish from taking. A taste that the fish doesn't like may prevent it from taking hold firmly enough so that you can hook it. It's only when fake baits are fished with speed in quiet waters or fished in very fast currents that they produce as well as naturals. Under such conditions they sometimes produce better than the real thing.

CHAPTER XXVIII

Some Deadly Lures

Repairing fishing lures on a winter evening should be a calm and relaxing pursuit. I start out that way, but I can't get far without picking out some lure that has an exciting history. I'm emotional about deer-hair bass bugs, for instance. It's impossible for me to repair one without being caught up in dreams of times when I cast this lure with fingers that were clumsy with tension.

We were making a float trip on one of the smaller rivers in the Ozarks. I started out fishing with a spinning rod, using small plugs, spinners, and spoons. These took bass but only small ones. At noon while the guide and my wife were cooking the meal, I rigged up my fly rod and tied a spread-wing deer-hair bass bug on the leader. Then I walked to the head of a deep pool upstream. I'd fished this pool with a spinner while we drifted down, but hadn't had a strike.

I cast the deer-hair bug to the far side of an eddy and started working it across. At the start of the fifth retrieve a bass struck hard and was solidly hooked. It was a good fish—a 3½-pound smallmouth. On the next cast I hooked another almost as large. As I landed it, loud calls from downstream told me lunch was ready.

Needless to say, I kept fishing with a fly rod and this deer-hair bug from then on. For two more days the weather stayed fair and dry, and the bass bug continued to produce, the largest fish being a four-pound largemouth. There were plenty of scrappy fish weighing one to two pounds. Each night we tented on clean gravel bars beneath spectacular bluffs and chatted of past experiences.

The fourth day started out fine. The sun rose bright and the weather was mild. As we left the campsite I noticed a bank of smooth, dark clouds close to the southwestern horizon. But the bass were hitting and the west was hidden most of the time behind the bluffs, so I forgot about the approach of a storm until I noticed the sun had stopped shining and our guide was heading in to a likely gravel bar.

"Better get camp set up before it starts raining," he said.

We were all set and finished with lunch when the rain came. We spent most of the afternoon in the big tent. The rain stopped before sunset, so we had a dry dinner and an hour or so of good fishing before turning in.

I awoke at dawn and saw a leaden sky which threatened a downpour. We rushed breakfast, packed the boat, put on rain dress, and started early. We'd just got over the shoals below the gravel bar when the rain started. My wife soon got discouraged with fishing and huddled under a tarpaulin. I think I'd have done the same, except that just then the bass seemed to go berserk. Every time that deer-hair bug hit the water a good fish would smash it.

We hurried along and I had action all the way. At noon it was still pouring rain and the river started rising. Then the river started to color with silt, and the fish stopped taking. When we came to a deep eddy which hadn't started to cloud up I'd take fish, but there was no action wherever the dirty water had worked in. By one thirty the entire stream was the color of milky coffee and not a fish struck.

"Guess we might as well quit," said the guide, and I agreed.

"There's a place we can get out about two hours downstream

from here," he added, "and I can walk to a telephone and call for the truck."

The two-hour run downstream seemed five hours long, and we were downright miserable when we reached the muddy road that led to the river's edge. It wasn't a regular pickup place; simply a farm lane used to water stock.

Our guide told us it would take him at least an hour to phone and return so before leaving he built a rip-roaring fire. Soon, despite the rain, we were feeling quite chipper. The rain moderated after a while, so I explored the grub box and whipped up a meal. Seasoned with pure water from the sky and sparks from the fire, this food was wonderful. We even regretted having canceled the rest of the float. But by the time the truck picked us up, we were glad we'd decided to quit.

That's just one of the trips the deer-hair bass bug brings to mind. You can handle the smaller bugs with fly tackle. Light spinning tackle will cast the heavier ones. The deer-hair bugs, fished on the surface, are not an accurate imitation of any living creature fish feed on, but they're dependable bass-slayers in water all over the country.

The first spinning lure that recalled a fishing adventure was an underwater wobbler shaped like a tiny boomerang. We were in New England. It was windy all of the time, raining about half the time. Fly fishing was poor. Here and there we hit a concentration of trout that responded to sunken wet flies, but many of the locations that were usually good produced nothing.

On the fourth day, with the weather getting worse, I changed to a spinning outfit. At first I used spinners, then wobbling spoons. The spoons took some fish but couldn't be called top performers.

We'd worked the bait up to a shoal that was some distance from shore. I fished around the shoal with the metal baits without getting a hit. I was about ready to quit, but this shoal was well known as a hangout of good-sized brookies so I hated to give up. Instead, I looked through my tackle box and picked out one of the boomerang-shaped plugs, a small one, mostly yellow.

To fish this place right, it was necessary to cast against the wind toward a large stump that marked the hot spot. The curved lure was a bit light for the job, so I put a sinker on the line just ahead of it.

The stump was about thirty-five feet away and on my first cast I tossed the lure out three feet beyond it, snagging the stump. I tried to jiggle the plug loose, but the line broke. The plug was held on the surface by the length of broken line wedged in the stump and the action of the waves and wind kept the lure active. We could have gone over to rescue the lure, but that would have meant going directly over the fishing spot. Besides, the plug seemed secure enough so we figured we could get it after quitting.

I had several other plugs of the same basic design, so I tried on one of silver or aluminum color. This time I cast farther off the side of the stump. I'd reeled in about three feet when I connected with a nice brook trout. The next cast to the same spot netted another. I was just about ready to make a third cast when a splash occurred close to the stump, and the "hung" yellow plug disappeared. A trout had taken it.

For the next half hour the brook trout in this spot went wild over the silvery boomerang lure. Then they suddenly quit. It may have been because we'd spooked them or it may have been because of the weather change. A storm sent us back to camp.

Boomerang plugs (that's only a loose descriptive name) are made in various weights, sizes, and slight differences in action. Regardless of make, every one I've tried has been an excellent fish-taker. In my opinion, a few lures of this shape should be in every angler's tackle box. Trout, bass, pickerel—most any game fish—will hit them.

While I personally favor fly or bait-casting tackle for surface lures, there were a few top-water spinning lures in my assortment that reminded me of enjoyable experiences. One was a weedless popper plug weighing a quarter of an ounce. The body was plastic, the hook single, and the rear end was feathered.

We were fishing an extremely weedy creek arm of an Alabama lake. At the time, I didn't have a weedless lure suitable for the condition, so I turned to spinning simply because the only weedless floating lure I had was of spinning-tackle weight. Bass were flopping directly in the thickest of the weeds, and casts of non-weedless lures to the edges of the weeds didn't make for much action. What was needed was a lure that could be fished right in the weeds.

On my first cast to a tiny pocket in the weeds, I hooked a fine bass. I'd moved the lure six inches into the weeds bordering the open pocket and was resting it on the edge of a lily pad when the fish opened his big mouth and took it.

The rest of that day was one I'll never forget—because I had a lure that could be fished where the bass were feeding. I could cast it recklessly into tall, grassy weeds without getting hung, and then cautiously work it through them. There weren't many chances to make the lure pop, but that didn't make any difference. I believe that any lure that could be fished through these weeds without getting hung would have proved productive.

Sometimes, as I retrieved, the plug would climb up a stalk until the grass bent from the weight and dropped the lure. Time after time a bass would smash the plug when it dropped from a tall stalk. Of course I missed dozens of strikes and lost many hooked bass, but I caught all I wanted, thanks to this efficient weedless lure. All anglers and tackle manufacturers should remember the importance of well-made and workable weedless lures. Where waters are very weedy such baits are a must if one hopes to catch fish.

There are two other surface spinning lures that made my memory work overtime. I've used both with good results ever since they came on the market. This particular incident includes both of them being used at the same time.

One, which I shall name the splasher minnow, was made so that it was always on its flat side when being fished. It represented a struggling minnow. The plug weighed a quarter of an ounce and had a small propeller at each end. The action was made by giving it twitches or reeling it fast a few inches at a time. This made the spinner blades splash. It always stayed completely on the surface.

The other plug, which I shall name the dying minnow, was a torpedo-shaped job of the same weight. It had one propeller blade at the rear end. This lure floated when not in action, but most of the body stayed underwater. Only the head remained on the surface. When this lure was jerked it gave the effect of a minnow thrusting its head above water.

I was fishing a shallow-water section of a Wisconsin lake. Ordinarily the fish in this lake responded reasonably well to bass bugs and bait-casting plugs, but this time they didn't. I'd spent the entire morning with them without getting a strike.

I chose a stump-cluttered bay for the afternoon fishing. I fished this water thoroughly, half the time with a plug and the other half with a bass bug. No luck. I was about ready to quit when a good-size bass rolled in the very place where I'd made my last cast with a large surface plug that they usually liked.

Seeing that bass roll revived my falling spirits. I wondered if smaller lures would be better. Fortunately, I had a spinning outfit with me. I quickly assembled it and tied on the quarter-ounce splasher minnow. I cast it to the spot where the bass had surfaced and after twitching it a few times hooked a good bass. I figured I'd caught the bass that rolled. But several casts later another bass took. I kept working the place for some time, but had no action other than several investigating rises.

I tried four more known good spots and from each one took one bass. There were many interested customers that rose for a close look. I hadn't done badly, having landed six nice fish, but I wasn't satisfied.

The bass that seemed willing to take, but wouldn't, bothered me. The dying minnow was my next experiment. A bass took it on the first cast. I retraced my earlier route and fished each place again, this time with the dying minnow. In each one I took a bass, and after that got only inquisitive responses. This made my total catch eleven good fish.

By this time the sun had long since set, so I quit, but I couldn't help wondering whether using another small lure of different action and perhaps color wouldn't have taken more fish if I'd retraced again. I don't know, but I think the experience shows that a change in lures can sometimes increase your catch.

Several years back a lure with a new sunfish shape came on the market. Made in weights suitable for both bait casting and spinning, it proved very effective. I was sold on this underwater plug the first time I tried it. I liked the way it handled, and I liked the way fish liked it. Whenever I used it I never got skunked. The sunfish-shaped lure featured in the following two experiences weighed a half ounce and was 2 ½ inches long.

The New York lake was small and mostly shallow. It was also very weedy and stumpy, and from what I'd been told good-size pickerel could be caught in it. We got there early in the morning, and started fishing supposedly sure-fire spots at once. Yet by lunch not one of us had caught a fish large enough to make a good bait for the size pickerel we hoped to catch.

It was about two thirty before we got started again. Again no action. The most killing lure for the lake was said to be a popular red-and-white spoon. It was an old-timer, much imitated, and has always been good for pike, pickerel, muskies, and bass. I'd fished it all morning and for the first half hour in the afternoon. Then I started trying other lures—which didn't produce any better.

The first of the flat-nosed sunfish lures I tied on had a finish the color of a yellow perch, a choice I made because perch were plentiful in this lake. The yellow-finish lure took the first keeper pickerel of the day. Then it hooked another that cut my thin monofilament leader with its teeth and made off with the plug. (I should have been using a short wire trace to cope with these sharp teeth.)

I tied on another sunfish plug of silver color, linking it to my casting line with a length of wire leader. This was what the pickerel wanted. At a time when fishing was generally poor, this lure took several good fish—pickerel that refused other offerings. I have had equally good luck with the sunfish lure on bass. It's the sort of ace-in-the-hole plug that deserves a place in your tackle box.

CHAPTER XXIX

Fish Like Small Lures

UNTIL spinning reels became common, the use of small hardware lures was extremely limited. Some anglers used fly rods to cast small spinners or tiny plugs, but small lures were awkward to handle with fly tackle.

Though I often made a good catch by fly-rodding a small plug or spoon, I much preferred fishing with flies or even some kind of natural bait—for the simple reason that I disliked the crippled casts and clumsy retrieves that were a part of fishing hardware on a fly rod. My small spoons, spinners, and plugs were seldom brought out until I'd tried and failed with flies and natural bait.

Some of the lures weighing three eighths of an ounce or less could be cast fairly well with a long, whippy bait-casting rod. However, it took a lot of practice to learn to do good light-lure work with the early bait reels, and the long bait rods needed were expensive and hard to find. For these reasons light lures were neglected.

Without a shadow of a doubt it was the modern spinning reel that brought small artificial lures into the limelight. Here was a reel with which one could cast lures as small as a quarter of an ounce with the greatest of ease. With the right combination of rod, reel, and line, spinning gear would even cast lures as light as a sixteenth of an ounce—if the ultra-light lures were constructed so that they didn't offer too much air resistance. This business of fighting the air is a major factor in casting. It's the difference in air resistance that makes one lure tough to cast while another of the same weight goes out like a bullet.

There was still a dearth of light lures on the market for some time after the advent of the spinning reel. The small lures offered were good, but the assortment was so limited it was difficult to acquire a collection varied enough to cope with different fish, water, and fishing conditions.

That's no longer the case. Now tackle stores are full of light lures of various shapes, colors, and actions. In choosing an assortment, keep in mind that lures of the same weight vary in three important ways—shape, action, and color. The more solid and compact shapes will cast farther because they meet with less air resistance. But the very compact lures tend to be sluggish in action when reeled through the water—and that action is a major factor in getting fish to strike.

I think color is important, too. Though certain scientific tests have shown that fish are "color-blind" by human standards, game fish continue to hit lures of one color while rejecting others that are exactly the same except for color. Red, as humans see it, may be just a shade of gray to a trout, yet there are days when the fish wants the particular shade of gray that red represents. So get lures that vary in color as well as in shape and action.

A trip to a Montana trout stream taught me one of my more dramatic lessons about the effectiveness of the proper light-weight lures. I arrived there in early September and found weather as nice as any fly fisherman could ask for. However, the trout were cool toward the flies I offered. Fishing all day with either wet or dry flies would produce only four or five fair-size fish. Since I could see plenty of big trout in the stream, these results didn't please me at all. When one travels more than two thousand miles, as I had, one hopes for a limit catch or a fish of lunker size.

I'd fished this same stream several times before when dry flies had been outstandingly successful, so I was puzzled. First I thought the size or pattern of fly was the trouble, so I systematically tested a wide range of patterns and colors in sizes 8 through 22. The sizes from 14 through 16 produced best in dull patterns, such as Blue Quill, Red Quill, and Adams. However, it was with these that I took as many as five fish. When using others the score dropped to four, often to three fish. The results with wet flies were about the same.

I finally decided not to be stubborn about fly fishing and spent the last ten days of my stay fishing with a light spinning outfit. Because a curved, fish-shape spoon in silver finish had worked well for me at other times, I tied this on first. This spoon weighs only an eighth of an ounce, the metal blade being 1⅝ inches long, not including the treble hook dangling from the end. It casts nicely and has good action when fished slowly or reasonably fast.

I thought I'd get immediate results with this spoon, but I didn't. For one thing, it didn't get deep enough when fished at the speed that gave it the best action. So I attached another lure of the same pattern and color but weighing ¼ of an ounce. It went deeper but I still didn't get any response.

I changed to a brass and then to a copper spoon. Still no strikes. Two weeks previously, when I was fishing a river in Colorado, these same lures in copper and brass had done the best job of any in my assortment. But this Montana stream was swifter and deeper. Even with the quarter-ounce spoon I touched the bottom of the stream only occasionally. Feeling that depth was necessary, I changed to another make of wobbling spoon. This was a chunky and rather small lure for its quarter-ounce weight. It sank quickly.

But even though this nickel-color spoon went down just about right and bumped the tops of the rocks when handled at good fishing speed, I didn't get any strikes. Remembering the Colorado experience, where brass and copper colors had been needed in the fish-shape spoons, I changed to copper in this instance. That did the trick. I took trout from every run and pool I fished with the copper-colored spoon. I also tried brass, which was fair, but the trout were not interested in silver or nickel.

Now, lest you think that copper and brass are always best colors, let me tell you what happened at a small lake only a few miles away from the Montana stream. I'd been taking nice rainbows from the lake with wet flies and Wooly Worms, but there were some good fish working too far out to be reached with a fly. I decided to use a spoon and spinning tackle to get out there.

Because the copper color had done so well in the stream, I tried it first, using the fish-shape spoon. It took a couple of fish during some hundred casts and retrieves. When I changed to a silver spoon of identical proportions I hooked about twenty nice trout in quick order. The four I kept ranged from 1¼ to 3¼ pounds.

In my opinion, there's no doubt that both color and action of lures as well as size have a bearing on whether or not you catch fish. It's also my opinion that there's no point in making any set rules from year to year or even month to month for any particular water. Never get the idea that a lure you consider tops in waters you know well will be just as good in waters new to you. Often they are, but you can't count on it. Weather, condition of the water, extent to which the waters have been fished, and the natural food supply all have a bearing on how fish will react. Always be ready to experiment, both in your method of fishing and the lures you select.

Generally, the best colors for certain waters remain fairly constant. That is, the fish in some lake or stream may consistently take the silver or nickel lures better than others. This applies to all other basic colors, yellow or red, say. But don't take this as gospel. Sometimes a change in color is just what is needed to catch the fish.

A tiny plug of aluminum color broke my four-day run of bad luck on a trip to Canadian brook-trout waters. Flies had failed, and so had a variety of spoons and spinners that I'd cast from all angles and worked at various depths.

I was about to give up when I found the little aluminum color plug among my streamer flies. It was about 1¼ inches long and no heavier than a streamer fly—so light that I had to put a sinker on the leader about twenty inches above it to get the lure out with my spinning outfit.

The water was about eight feet deep, current speed two miles an hour, the skies cloudy, the air cold. I first fished the plug downstream, then down and across, then across, then across and upstream. I did this systematically and completely, fishing to each direction many times and varying the speed of the retrieve to reach various depths. I didn't get a single strike for all my efforts.

My ace-in-the-hole was an upstream cast, a thirty-five-foot toss into the main current that led directly down to our canoe. I retrieved line just fast enough to make the plug wiggle. When the deep-running lure was almost to the canoe I felt a hard snub and was fast to a nice brook trout. After the first fish was netted, I repeated the cast and hooked another good fish. In about twenty more casts I hooked and played to a finish eight brookies weighing from 1½ to three pounds each. All were hooked near the bottom and close to the canoe.

Friends of mine fishing with fly rods from another canoe tried the same lure in a different color, unweighted. They couldn't get any response. I believe that here the complicated combination needed for success was the right lure, the right length of cast, and the right depth of the lure at the right spot. Perhaps color had something to do with it, too, but I'm not sure. While I was fighting one stubborn fish, a friend cast his yellow plug close to my hooked fish as it came near the surface. Immediately he hooked a trout.

That suggests that the color yellow was a factor in interesting the trout my friend hooked, but the truth is that his fish would probably have hit anything that moved near the fish I was playing. Many fish, brook trout included, are competitive about grabbing bits of food adrift in the current, and a fish fighting to get free of a lure often gives other fish the idea that it is struggling with a choice morsel of food. Other fish rushing in to try for a share of the spoils will commonly take most any fly or lure that's dropped close to the hooked fish.

You can make this pay off by making a quick and accurate cast to an area where your partner is playing a fish. Such a cast must be timed just right, for the fish investigating the tussle usually turn back when their captured kinsman breaks the surface. It's not good manners, of course, to make a cast that might hook your partner's line and cause him to lose his fish.

Frequently you need to fish very deep or make long casts with a small and buoyant lure. This is when you need a spinning or casting outfit and a suitable sinker. Many times I have fished one of these fly-weight lures very deep by using sinkers of two ounces or more to get it down to the fish. Sometimes these small and buoyant lures, held down with a sinker, will score more when larger and heavier lures reaching the same depths fail. That's not a fixed rule, though. The larger and heavier lures will often take fish while the smaller ones are ignored.

The small lure fisherman should always go fishing supplied with a variety of sinkers, both in weight and in style. The weights needed could run from buckshot to more than two ounces. By styles I mean split shot, lead-wire, clinch-on, swivel, dipsey, egg, or others. The point is to have a good assortment.

In fishing very light fly-rod plugs and spinners with aid of a sinker, you inevitably encounter unpleasant casting conditions. With either spinning or bait-casting tackle, the length of leader material needed between the sinker and lure makes the casting much more difficult than when casting a spinning-weight lure of from an eighth to three eighths of an ounce direct from the rod tip. The sinker travels faster than the fly-weight lure and leader attached to it, and this is what causes the trouble.

To cast this rig you must change your regular casting style. Instead of using the snappy forearm-and-wrist movement, as in casting a lure directly from the rod tip, make the cast with a rather slow sweeping motion, using the entire arm. That's a great help in keeping the sinker and lure from tangling in the leader that separates them.

One of the first spinning lures that came from France at the time when spinning tackle was new in this country has remained one of my favorites. I regret to say, however, that the American copies of this excellent lure don't compare in action or workmanship with the originals. Some do quite well, others don't. Some you can adjust so that you can get by. At times I have bought as many as a dozen to get three that performed to please me. Yet the good ones are so good that I wouldn't think of going light-lure fishing without them.

The lure I mean is approximately 2½ inches long, the spoon portion three quarters of an inch long and of a modified spade shape, the body made of synthetic or natural rubber tubing and about a quarter of an inch thick. Some are made with a tuft of bright red wool as a tail, some without any tail. I've bought them with both treble hook and single hook, which are set rigid to the body. I prefer single to treble hooks.

With the lure I'm talking about, as with all spoons and spinners, I find a need for three basic colors of metal in the spoon or blade portion of the lure—nickel, brass, and copper. For bodies I favor pale amber or pale yellow for all-around use, although I occasionally find other colors necessary. If you can't find exactly the combination of blade and body I have mentioned, try any available. The style of this lure is good enough to rate a test in most any color. As with most spinning lures, especially those of a quarter of an ounce, this French design is good for bass or trout, not to mention pickerel, pike, and others.

In my opinion there's a decided need for more lures made with one hook solidly attached to the lure. When fishing snaggy, rocky water—the kind of place where many fish feed—you need a lure that will scrape bottom without snagging. Lures with loose-hanging treble hooks are the worst snaggers; lures with single hooks rigidly attached to ride point up the best for bouncing over obstacles.

If you can't find anything but treble-hook lures in your box, cut off one or two shanks of the trebles for bottom fishing. Test before cutting to see which shank or shanks should be cut by running the lure in water where you can see how the treble hook rides. The two hooks that point toward bottom should be cut; they snag most frequently. If two of the barbs run upright and one down, then cut off only the one that runs down. Small lures are both plentiful on the market and definitely appeal to game fish. Try them.

CHAPTER XXX

Pay-Off Flies

A SIZE 14 Adams tumbled out of a box of dry flies I was inspecting on a recent winter day. Flattened and bedraggled, the fly wasn't much to look at, but it recalled a day of trout fishing when the little Adams was a joy to behold.

This happened on a river that meandered through open, natural meadows and patches of woods. The water had plenty of movement, running quite fast here and there but slowing down in places to a speed ideal for fishing small dry flies. There was one pool just below a sharp bend that particularly intrigued me. There were plenty of good fish there. I'd spotted them by peeking cautiously over the bank and occasionally had seen them rising en masse in the current.

But it was a difficult spot to fish with a dry fly. I'd tried it a dozen times without success. I couldn't get a float of more than a few inches without a drag. But I kept at it, trying casts from one location and another until one day I got in the right spot. It was about ten a.m., the wind very slow, the sky blue, and the air cool. There had been a light coating of frost on the meadow at dawn.

As the little Adams started drifting on my first cast I knew I'd at last hit a good position. It floated some eight to ten inches as smoothly as a natural. Then it disappeared under the surface so gently that I actually thought it had simply sunk. But long experience has taught me never to take things for granted. I struck lightly the instant the fly disappeared, and was thrilled by the feel of a heavy trout on the hook.

It took considerable time to play and land the fish, for I had to completely exhaust the scrapper before I could reach down from my precarious ledge 2½ feet above the water and get him in my hand. If I'd moved from where I was casting, or made any undue disturbance, it would have spooked the rest of the trout. That first fish was a brown trout that several hours later weighed three pounds ten ounces. I dispatched it with a heavy blow on the head and pushed it back into the grass behind me.

It was just the beginning of two hours of remarkable dry-fly fishing. I kept count of the fish hooked and played up to twelve, and then forgot to continue. Most of the fish were released. I lost four size 14 Adams flies that were swallowed so deeply I deliberately snapped the leader rather than keep the fish or make a commotion getting the hook loose. When the fish stopped rising, I found that I'd kept four trout, not one under three pounds. All in all, I must have caught twenty trout, none under three quarters of a pound, most from one to 1¼ pounds. Do you wonder that I had memories when I took the Adams flies out to recondition them? They have served me well almost everywhere that I've fished for trout.

Before I got through reconditioning this one box of dry flies I'd reviewed fishing experiences from coast to coast. I came across the Light Cahill that was especially productive on Eastern trout waters, the Royal Coachman that served me well wherever I fished, the bivisibles in brown, gray, and badger that had often been the best patterns to use, and the variants of spiders that so often made good days out of bad ones.

The variants intrigued me the very first time I saw them. Actually, they were nothing but spiders with tails and stubby wings. The stubby wings seemed to improve the over-all balance and appearance of the fly, and it also hooked a greater percentage of fish than the spider. The spiders I'd used always received plenty of attention from trout, but many of the fish just bumped the long-hackled spiders and turned away.

Sight of one variant pattern in my collection of winter-stored flies took me back to a perfect fly-fishing day. The sky was unclouded blue. There was a mere suggestion of a breeze, a high and slowly rising barometer. The trout were rising in ideal water, taking naturals from the surface with great enthusiasm.

"It's a cinch," I exclaimed the moment I looked over the beautiful stretch of dry-fly water.

The batch of natural bugs was mixed, ginger-colored insects and gray ones. The naturals were so small that size 16 flies tied with short hackles looked large in comparison. But I had plenty of smaller flies that should match the hatch very well. I started out with a size 20 Light Cahill, switched to Blue Dun, Blue Quill, and Quill Gordon. All to no avail, even though I was fishing carefully with a ten-foot leader tapered to a hair-thin 8X end.

The trout would rise all around my offerings, sometimes so close they drowned them, but I never felt a tug. The water was easy to fish without drag. I never put a fish down. Yet I could hook nothing but the foolish undersize youngsters that will hit most anything. I'd released half a dozen of these.

"It's evident that they don't like regular flies," I mused. "A variant? Might as well try one. It can't do any worse than the patterns I've been using."

Since there were ginger-colored natural flies on the stream, I chose a ginger variant. I wanted a size 14 but found I didn't have anything smaller than a 12. I tied it on and went back downstream to where I'd started fishing three hours earlier. Trout were still rising but not as much as before. Yet they took the ginger variant recklessly. By the time I'd covered the stretch a second time I'd taken all the keeper-size trout I wanted and released a good many.

Another point should be stressed here. When using the size 18 and 20 flies, you'll remember that I had a ten-foot leader tapered to 2X or .009—a much shorter and heavier leader. I did this because a long-hackled fly is very difficult to cast with a very long and finely pointed leader. The air resistance on a large, fluffy fly calls for a heavier leader. I bring that point out for a definite purpose: to show that using a leader that fits the fly is of more importance than having one extremely long and thin. A big fly doesn't act right on a spider-web leader.

When my dry flies had been washed clean, steamed over a teakettle to fluff out the hackle, and returned to their mothproof containers, I began inspecting the boxes that held wet flies and streamers.

While dry flies need to be in fairly good repair, a bedraggled wet fly or streamer will often do better than a new one. I never discard a fly that's fished wet until the hook is almost bare. I've had good fishing with them when only parts of the body, hackle, and wings remain. But the hook must be kept sharp and free of rust. I touch up the hooks on a sharpening stone and oil the rusty ones lightly before putting them back in the box.

Half the fly patterns in the wet-fly boxes brought back memories, but there was one that was special. It was a fly I'd tied for Quebec brook-trout fishing with the idea that it might attract large fish. The pattern, Parmachene Belle, is an old one. However, this wasn't one of the mass-produced flies you buy for a quarter. This was a tandem fly tied true to pattern on size 4 loop-eye salmon hooks. The two flies were connected with leader material so that only half an inch separated the tail of the lead fly from the eye of the trailer.

On this particular occasion we'd fished three days with regular wet flies in sizes 4 to 10, including some run-of-the-mill Parmachene Belles. Fishing had been poor for Quebec's Laurentian region. We hadn't taken many fish and none better than 1½ pounds.

I hadn't tried my tandem Parmachene Belle during this time, partly because I felt a bit ashamed to use it when fishing with the group of old-timers I was camped with. After the third day I decided to tie on my home-brewed tandem fly and let my cronies chuckle at the experiment.

From that day on my freak tandem took more fish than any other fly our party tried. The largest trout I caught with the rig was a four-pound male brookie in full courting dress. The red coloration topping his white belly was as brilliant and deep as those shades seen in the most glorious sunset. Any artist who portrayed such a brilliant brookie would be accused of exaggerating.

I caught this prize fish near the end of our last day at the camp. All day we'd been drifting down a beautiful stream, stopping at the most likely-looking pools. We'd had good luck, too, taking at least six brookies that ran from 1½ to two pounds. I was in the lead canoe and we were getting close to camp when my guide stopped at a deep hole and suggested a cast toward a heavy stand of tangled alders.

I tossed the tandem Parmachene Belle well in under the branches that extended out over the stream. I let the fly sink a minute or two and then started retrieving slowly. Nothing happened until the fly was quite close to the canoe, and then a large fish appeared under it but sank out of sight without taking. My guide also saw the fish and became quite excited.

After that I cast and retrieved ten times without getting response. I was about ready to quit but the guide insisted that I keep trying. Ten more casts and still no response. I looked upstream and saw my wife and her guide coming along as if they'd decided to quit. I decided to make one more try before they reached us. The retrieve was about half done when the four-pounder hit. I had the thrill of playing it to a finish while my wife and the guides looked on.

There was a Coachman in my wet-fly box that brought back more memories. This wet fly, a variation of the basic Coachman pattern I've used with great success since my 'teen years, reminded me of a trip to an Eastern brown-trout stream. It wasn't a stream that looked like a producer of large fish. It seemed too small to hold whoppers. However, I'd taken some beauties from it with a dry fly on earlier trips.

On this particular outing I couldn't take any fish with a dry fly, not even small ones. I'd fished at least two miles upstream without results and was about to trudge back to the car when I thought, "Why not fish a wet fly all the way back?"

I started with a size 12 Quill Gordon wet. Half an hour went by without any action. I changed to a wet Dark Cahill, then to a Ginger Quill. By this time another hour had gone by and I was quite a distance downstream. I still hadn't caught a fish. Then I picked out a Coachman tied without tail and with white wings in size 10. Before using it I put it in wet mud for about a minute, then washed it out in the stream. I wanted the fly to sink the moment it touched the water.

The first fish I hooked on the tailless wet Coachman was a plump three-pound brownie. From then on success crowned my efforts. By the time I'd reached my car I'd hooked and landed eight trout ranging from 1½ to 3 pounds. All were taken on the Coachman.

One of the streamers I remembered as a pay-off fly was a White Marabou. The Marabou story goes back to the day when I was working a pool of a Western stream with a dry fly. I'd been twitching a large Fanwing Royal Coachman over this slow, glassy-surfaced pool and catching some trout of from ten to thirteen inches. On one retrieve, just as I was lifting the Fanwing from the surface, I saw a big trout directly under it. I cast back to the same place and he appeared again, following the fly but making no attempt to take it. The fish had a scar, a white slash, on one side of its body.

It was the last time I saw the trout during the balance of this stay at the stream, but the memory of the white-scarred lunker stayed with me all through the winter and most of the following summer—until I got back to the stream again in September. The first thing I did on my return was to head for the pool where I'd seen the big fish.

He was still there. In fact, he investigated my offering on the first cast. But that was the only time I saw him in ten days of fishing, although I probably spent twenty hours fishing the pool.

The following year I managed to get back to this stream again. The big-fish pool yielded a few ten-inchers but I didn't get a glimpse of the whopper with the scar. This was good because I figured that he wasn't there, and so didn't waste time on the pool again. Aside from the one big fish, this pool never seemed to hold anything more than a foot long, while the rest of the water produced many brown and rainbow trout weighing two and three pounds. Rainbows were especially plentiful in the stream and were taking dry flies enthusiastically. Each day I caught all I wanted, keeping only a few big ones.

Then came the last day of my stay. For the first time I'd kept a limit of rainbows to give to the rancher on whose water we were fishing. I was on my way back to camp with this catch when it occurred to me that it would take only a few minutes to make one last cast over the pool where the big trout had been. I decided to try a fly I'd never used before—the Maribou streamer. The one I chose was tied on a No. 2 long-shank hook. It was tied long and heavily dressed.

Casting this streamer to the far side of the pool I let it sink and then started retrieving. It had come back about half the distance of the cast when I saw a fish following it. Suddenly there was a swirl in the water. I felt a heavy fish take and set the hook.

The trout's first run was about thirty feet. I didn't use strong-arm tactics, but I did use all the pressure the tackle could take to tire the fish as quickly as possible. In about ten minutes the trout lay motionless on the gravel beach. It was a whopper brown trout with a long whitish scar on one side—the fish I'd been after for three years.

I didn't want to kill the fish (I already had a limit in my creel) but I did want to measure it before I released it. As the brownie lay there, partially in the water, I placed the butt of my rod at its tail and made a scratch in the rod varnish beside the trout's nose. I checked this length with a steel rule later. It was 28½ inches. As the fish was also deep-bodied, I think I'm conservative when I call it a six-pounder. It wasn't the largest trout I've ever caught, but it was one of the most interesting.

In the same tackle box was another streamer that accounted for one of my better days with smallmouth bass. This took place on an Eastern river I usually fished with hellgrammites and minnows.

The bass took these natural baits readily, and they were always available from commercial bait dealers along the river.

But there came a day when these excellent baits didn't produce. It might have been because the water was so low natural bait couldn't be fished to advantage. Anyway, I spent the best part of two days using up my bait without catching anything but sunfish and very large minnows, the type that are often called windfish. Some of these windfish ran as large as two pounds, and each one that I caught completely ruined the bait, even mangling a tough hellgrammite so badly it was useless as a bass bait.

I ran out of natural bait about three p.m. the second day. I was tempted to quit. It was a beautiful day, however, and occasionally a bass broke the surface out in water too deep to be reached with natural bait by a wading angler.

"Why not try a fly?" I reflected. I could cast a streamer the distance required.

I was fishing the natural baits with a fly rod, and there was an extra reel filled with the proper fly line in the car. So it took only fifteen minutes to change reels and tie a streamer fly to the leader. The only streamers I had with me were tied on size-8 long-shank hooks. Their general colors were white, grizzly, and brown. Without reason I decided on the grizzly streamer.

I cast it some fifty feet to a fast run where I'd seen a good bass break water. I started retrieving at once, and on the first jerk of the streamer a fish struck so hard it almost pulled the rod from my hand. After a time I landed a smallmouth bass that weighed 3½ pounds. This size smallmouth, when caught in fast water, can give you plenty to think about for some minutes. By sunset I'd caught and released six more bass that ranged from 1½ to three pounds each. It was the grizzly streamer that saved my trip.

I'm not saying that the grizzly streamer or any of the other flies I've mentioned will get sensational results all the time. They're just good, solid performers that have given me some unforgettable days in the years I've used them. I have the same kind of pets in the boxes that hold my bass bugs, spinning lures, and the various plugs and spoons used for casting and trolling.

CHAPTER XXXI

The Right Fly Leader

THE MOST fragile and vital link between a fly caster and his fish is the leader. That slender strand connecting the line and fly must be balanced to cast properly, thin enough to fool the fish in clear water, yet strong enough to hold under reasonable pressure. There's no fun in fly fishing with a leader that fails to meet all those requirements.

There's a lot of confusion about tapered leaders for fly fishing. That's understandable, because the fisherman who goes into different stores and buys a couple of nine-foot leaders tapered to 4X tips will often acquire two leaders that are quite different in performance.

Leaders of the same size and appearance are often made of different material. Size labels are confusing, too. The actual micrometer-measured diameter of one manufacturer's "4X" leader is likely to be either larger or smaller than the 4X strand of another brand. There are similar variations in leaders labeled according to breaking strength, such as "four-pound test." And tapered leaders of the same length and end size have different proportions that affect their balance in casting.

The angler wades into deeper confusion when he attempts to choose, from all the leaders available, the one that will do the best job of casting a certain size of fly on a particular kind of water that holds fish with peculiar habits.

There's no reason to get tangled up in those complications, however, for there are only three basic decisions to make in choosing a tapered leader: 1. You need the proper length and balance for the type of fishing you'll do. 2. The end strand that holds the fly must be strong enough to handle the fish, yet delicate enough so that it doesn't spook them away from the fly. 3. The material in the leader should be suitable, meaning that a thin strand should have enough strength and stiffness without being so hard and slick that you can't tie secure knots in it.

Now let's take those things one at a time, starting with leader length. I see no practical need for leaders much longer than twelve feet. A tapered leader that long is sometimes needed to cast small flies to wary trout in extremely clear and shallow water. But a twelve-foot leader is very difficult to cast, almost impossible when you use a large air-catching fly or have a stiff wind to cope with. It's better to make smooth casts with a nine-foot leader, which is long enough to suit most trout in clear water, than to get off sloppy tosses with a twelve-footer. Use a 7½-foot leader when you fish small streams or large ones that have choppy or discolored water. A six-footer is often long enough for fishing wet flies or large bass bugs.

The fly fisherman hasn't much to gain by using a leader shorter than six feet, even in small and murky streams. But don't use a longer leader where a six-footer will do. The rule is to use the shortest and sturdiest tapered fly leader that will consistently fool the fish. Short leaders make for neater casting. They're better for bucking wind and powering large and fluffy flies. They're proportionately stronger.

I use a six-foot leader tapered to 1X (.010 diameter) for unsophisticated panfish, for casting heavy bass bugs, or for offering big flies to trout in clouded or rapidly churning water. When conditions are a bit more demanding, I go to a 7½-foot leader tapered to 2X or 3X, those end strands measuring .009 and .008 inches.

A nine-foot leader tapered to 3X or 4X (.007) is my first choice for discriminating trout in clear water. When fish in a smooth, glass-clear run get downright snobbish, I tie on a twelve-foot leader tapered down to 5X (.006) or 6X (.005). That's a last resort leader—tricky to cast and so fine at the end that the landing of a big fish becomes a work of art.

In the past, all tapered leaders were made by knotting together separate strands of leader material so that a strand of 1X, say, joined a strand of 2X, which is a size smaller. And so on in sequence to produce a gradual taper from large end to small. That system of linking separate strands with knots is still the most common way of making tapered fly leaders, but you now have the option of buying a single strand of synthetic material that's drawn to a taper by machine. Good leaders are made by both systems.

Here are the general virtues and faults of the various materials used to make tapered leaders: The synthetic materials—nylon, platyl, and others—are strong in relation to their thickness, inexpensive, durable, and pliable without the need of long soaking in water. All that's to the good. The two most common faults among the synthetic leaders are a hard, slick finish that makes knots slip easily, and a tendency to float. A leader that won't soak up enough water to sink a bit at the fine end will often spook wary trout.

The so-called gut leaders are still favored by many experts. They cast beautifully, have a useful stiffness when soaked that keeps them from kinking or curling. They hold knots well and sink readily. On the debit side, gut isn't as strong as the better synthetics. It requires careful soaking before it can be used satisfactorily, and the price of fine gut is comparatively high. (Gut leaders, by the way, are not derived from intestines; they're hardened strands of the same silkworm fluid that makes silk thread.)

I prefer to use gut leaders when I need to do some delicate casting, and I often use gut for all-purpose fly fishing when I'm in a humid region where air moisture keeps the gut from drying out during false casts and rest periods. I like synthetic leaders better when I'm fishing a Western stream where the sun is hot and the air bone dry. Those conditions dry out a gut leader so fast that it loses some efficiency in the time it takes to hike to a new pool.

Like a lot of fly fishermen who broke into the sport when gut leaders were the only thing, I have some emotional loyalty to them. They were much better than the hard and springy synthetic leaders that were first put on the market. But synthetics have steadily improved. The strong and constantly pliable synthetic fly leaders offered today are crowding gut into a secondary role. The better synthetic leaders are soft enough to hold knots reasonably well, have just enough stiffness to straighten out neatly on a cast, and have a high ratio of strength to diameter. Trade names of such leaders vary widely, but you can pick out a good one by handling it.

I said tapered leaders should balance properly. By that I mean the butt end, the portion that joins the fly line, should be stiff enough to lay out the thinner portions of the leader in a straight line when you make a good cast. The whole leader should taper from butt to thin end so that it handles with the balanced flexibility of a bull whip. A weak center strand will break up this harmony. So will an end that's too heavy or too light.

A very long and light end strand, for example, often causes "wind knots" to form in the end of the leader when you cast a bushy dry fly. You need a fairly stiff end, a 2X say, to overcome the air resistance of a large spider or fanwing fly. With a tiny No. 18 fly, a 4X leader will ordinarily straighten out OK.

Dry flies as small as 18 or 20, incidentally, require leaders with end strands as fine as 4X. A thick leader will do a superb job of casting a tiny dry fly, but the bulk of the leader gives the little fly an awkward and unnatural float on the water. For wet-fly fishing, where both flies and leader are under the surface, there's seldom any point in using a leader end as fine as 4X or 5X. A 2X is adequately thin for routine wet-fly fishing.

For a 7½-foot synthetic leader I use six strands about sixteen inches long, which allows plenty of slack for secure knots. To make nine-foot synthetic leaders, use six strands nineteen inches long. A twelve-foot leader is better balanced with eight strands about twenty inches long, and its butt section should be at least .018, a bit thicker than one you'd use for a shorter leader.

I use more strands in tying gut leaders, because silkworm gut isn't available in long strands of uniform thickness. I ordinarily use seven strands of gut in a 7½-foot leader, eight strands in a nine-footer. In tying up tapered leaders to handle heavy bass bugs or to stand the fishing strain of a salmon or steelhead, you should start with a butt strand as heavy as .024 and scale the other strands down accordingly. On lots of waters you can get by with a short bass-bug leader, a six-footer made up of four strands of synthetic, for example.

For salmon or steelheads I recommend a tapered fly leader at least nine feet long. If you can handle it, an even longer leader may do better with those big fish. In synthetic material, a good nine-foot tapered leader for salmon would thin down from a butt strand about .024 to an end strand of .014 or .013. I use five strands twenty-three inches long in such a salmon and steelhead leader, scaling them down as follows: .024, .019, .017, .015, .014. You can vary the lengths and sizes a bit as long as you keep the same proportions.

I'm sure I've tied at least a hundred thousand tapered leaders for fly fishing during the many years I've been involved in the sport. My recipes for balanced fly leaders are based on that experience. Try them. They work.

CHAPTER XXXII

Hooks and Hooking

W HAT hook shall I use? It's a worrisome question for all anglers, and particularly for inexperienced ones who are understandably confused by the great variety of styles, lengths, weights, points, and barbs of hooks currently available. But the hook, of course, is the vital part of every fishing lure, artificial or natural, and the more the fisherman knows about its design and construction the better able he is to apply that knowledge to his advantage.

It might be helpful to those who don't know much about the subject to consider some basic facts about the hooks needed for various purposes. To avoid unnecessary complications, I'll limit the discussion to fresh-water hooks of the most popular designs and styles—those that are generally available either in bulk or already mounted or attached to artificial flies, spoons, plugs, bugs, or other lures. But before getting involved with specific things such as shank lengths, wire weights or calibrations, and so on, there are some things that should be considered in a general way. Let's briefly take those up first.

POINTS. Some hooks have long points on them, others have short. What difference does this make? Often it may mean the difference between landing and losing a fish. If the point of a hook is too long it may mean that you will miss rises and strikes when a fish doesn't get the hook fully in his mouth. A long point is tapered slowly, and toward the end it becomes so fine that it may bend or break, depending on how soft or hard the metal has been tempered. Often a bend or break in such a hook is so slight you can't even notice it, but it may cause you to miss many fish that take a smack at your lure. A short and quickly tapered point, provided it is sharp, will not only hook more fish, but will also hold its edge longer. A short point is less inclined to bend or break near the end, and on the rare occasions when this happens the fault can easily be seen.

BARBS. A barb is put on a hook to give the angler a better chance of holding a hooked fish in a fight. If the barb is too large it may get in the way of a fish being securely hooked, especially if the angler is using either fly or spinning tackle. If the barb is cut too deeply it may weaken the hook. A barb that is shallow may not hold a fish too well, but it is an advantage to have such hooks if you fish only for the fun of it and like to land and release your fish without injuring them. Barbless hooks are made for just this purpose. Ideally, of course, barbs should be neither too deep nor too shallow to give good performance, and they should allow for the release of small fish. But so far I've never found any hook that is a hundred percent perfect in these respects.

WEIGHTS. For best results the wire weight of a hook should be determined by the requirements of the lure. When you wish to use the most delicately tied creation and to have it float high and easy, then you need a hook of the finest wire you can get. This may be 2X Fine, but you may have to compromise on 1X Fine.

There isn't much difference between them. Only a micrometer or a wire gauge can actually tell what it is in many cases, and even then you must know just how to measure, particularly in the case of forged hooks. Forged hooks are of greater calibration from top to bottom than from side to side. A round wire hook is the same all around, or it should be.

But it isn't often necessary to use a very sparsely tied dry fly, and because of this you won't have much call for hooks of the finest weights. Standard or regular wire will serve for most purposes. Anglers who go mostly for large fish prefer a heavy and full-hackled fly to a sparse one tied on a light hook. They claim these land more fish. In many cases, however, it is just a matter of taste.

LENGTHS. The shanks of hooks come in long, short, and medium or standard lengths. The long-shanks are easy to hide and hence are used to advance when it is desirable to use very small baits. Medium or standard shanks are best for all-around use.

EYES. Eyes permit hooks to be tied directly to the line or leader. It is immaterial to me whether a hook has a turned-up or turned-down eye, but the turned-down eye is the more popular. The chief reason for this is that the average tyer of flies finds the turned-up eye more difficult to work with. Turned-up eyes, however, are well-liked for short-shank hooks and for Atlantic salmon flies.

I prefer a tapered eye for dry-fly hooks. A ball-eye hook is perhaps better, and less expensive, for wet flies, bass bugs, and similar jobs. The return or loop eye is best for salmon flies, particularly if you intend to catch heavier fish. The smoothness of the eye helps to prevent breakage of the leader. Loop eyes also help to prevent twisting of the material when tying flies, and hence make it possible to turn out a nicer head on a fly.

The loop or return eye is used only in the highest grade hooks, including the top quality long-shank streamer hooks, but in my opinion they are worth the difference in cost above the regular taper-eye hooks. Any lure that is to be used as a trailer for a spinner should be of the ringed variety—straight, not turned either up or down. These are among the cheapest eyed hooks available, but they can be had in a good grade if you look hard enough for them.

BENDS. Hooks are shaped in a wide variety of bends to suit varying conditions, but the Wide Gap, Round Bend, or Model Perfect shapes are undoubtedly the most popular dry-fly hooks being used today. Many also prefer these shapes for wet flies, though the Sproat and Limerick bends are well liked especially in long-shanked streamer hooks. The curved-in point, called by various names that suggest the claws or beak of a predatory bird, is popular among bait fishermen in some sections. Still others consider the Carlisle—an offset type—the best of all. The offset is a hook which has a point that deviates from a straight line in relation to the shank.

Except for heavy-bodied lures or flies, the gap doesn't matter too much. But where heavy cork, chenille, clipped deer hair, and similar materials are used, the wide gap gives an advantage because it allows for a fair bite. The wide gap isn't necessary in streamers, and most long-shanked Sproat hooks now come with a gap wide enough for the job. Some prefer Round or Perfect Bends for their streamers, since the gap in these runs wider than in regular Sproats, Limericks, and Snecks. Sneck hooks have a square bend. They're splendid hooks, in my opinion, but for some reason are not widely used these days. But a Modified Sneck, with a wider gap than the regular and without the offset, makes an excellent dry-fly hook. It provides a slightly longer body for the same size in a Round Bend or Model Perfect shape. Personally, I like a hook which allows room for a fair body without crowding the eye, and this shape does just that without being too long for regular patterns.

The following is a list of hooks generally used in average freshwater fishing. It is not a complete list, but it will probably serve most purposes. I have marked with an asterisk (*) those sizes which I have found necessary in my own experience.

WET-FLY TROUT. *Suggested hook styles:* Round Bend, Model Perfect, Sproat, Limerick, and Sneck.

Suggested wire weights: For still, shallow, and medium-depth water use Standard wire or the same hook as used for a regular medium-hackled dry fly. This hook does all right for fast, shallow ripples. For deep, very fast, and heavy water, or for any condition where it is necessary for a fly to sink quickly, use 2X Stout or heavier wire.

Suggested sizes: Standard shank. Average stream: 4-6-8*-10*-12*-14*-16-18. Average lake: 2-4*-6*-8*-10*-12*-14*-16.

NYMPHS. *Suggested hook styles:* Round Bend, Model Perfect, Limerick, Modified Sneck.

In some imitations a 2X Long hook is best, in others a Standard shank will do.

In some situations 2X Stout wire or heavier may be needed. Regular weight will probably be all right for general use. Since nymphs usually sink easier than wet flies, a lighter wire hook may be used to get suitable depth. Naturally the depth to be reached to interest fish, as well as the leader and line you use, also enter into the picture. Generally speaking, I'd say that a line and leader that will sink readily will carry any weight hook down with it, while a line and leader that floats will definitely resist the sinking of a fly unless the hook has considerable weight.

Suggested sizes for nymph hooks: 6-8-10*-12*-14*-16-18. Use 1X or 2X Long for long bodies, and Standard shank for regular bodies.

WET-FLY BASS. Suggest Extra Stout wire for these hooks.
Suggested sizes: 4/0-3/0-2/0*-1/0*-1*-2*.

When it is necessary to go deep for bass, I prefer to fish with natural bait or with artificials other than flies.

WET-FLY SALMON. Suggest Limerick-shape hooks and heavy wire. Sizes 2-4-6-8-10 are the most popular both in double and single hooks. Since I'm not an inveterate salmon fisherman, I haven't indicated any personal choices.

DRY-FLY TROUT. *Suggested hook styles*: Round Bend, Model Perfect, Modified Sneck.

Suggested shank lengths: For regular trout flies, including variants, Standard. For long-bodied flies, 2X Long, 3X Long, 1X Long, according to choice or need.

Suggested wire weights: For very sparsely tied, 2X Fine; for sparsely tied, 1X Fine; for regular tied, Regular or Standard; for full-hackled, 2X Stout.

Dry flies tied on 2X Stout hooks should be well fortified with stiff hackles if they are to float well. If such hackles make a fly too bushy for the conditions, then it would be best not to use them.

Suggested sizes: 6-8-10*-12*-14*-16-18-20.

In some types and patterns, such as Irresistibles, fan wings, and Wullfs, a No. 8 hook is often needed. These flies are usually obtainable only in the larger trout sizes, unless, of course, they are made privately. The smaller sizes are excellent, and the fan wings are not too bad provided you can get the wings to fit them.

For spiders I suggest Round or Perfect bend; shank length 2X Short or shorter, Standard wire. *Sizes*:   8-10-12*-14*-16*.

DRY-FLY SALMON.   (Atlantic or landlocked.) *Style*: Loopeye Limerick; either Standard or 2X Stout wire.

Suggested shank length: Either 2X Long or Standard.

Sizes: 2-4*-6*-8*-10.

These hooks are also good for some bass and trout lures. If the fish run large it is wise to use the Extra Stout wire.

BASS BUGS (cork bodies). *Style*:   Kinked, Round or Model Perfect.

Shank length: 2X Long or Standard.

Sizes: 3/0-2/0-1/0-1-2-4.

PANFISH AND TROUT BUGS (cork bodies). *Style*:   Kinked, Round or Model Perfect.

Shank length: 2X Long or Standard.
Sizes: 4-6-8-10-12.

TROUT STREAMERS. *Style:* Sproat, Round Bend, Model Perfect.
Shank length: 3X, 4X, or longer if desired.
Sizes: 4-6*-8*-10*-12.

BASS STREAMERS. *Style:* Sproat, Limerick.
Shank length: 4X, 5X, 6X, or longer.
Wire weight: 2X Stout or heavier.
Sizes: 2*-4*-6*-8.

SALMON STREAMERS (Atlantic). *Style:* Sproat, Limerick.
Wire weight: Extra Heavy.
Shank length: 5X, 6X, or longer.
Sizes: 2-4-6.
Salmon Streamers (Landlocked). Same as above, but include Nos. 8 and 10 for some fishing.

BAIT HOOKS (trout-worms). *Style:* Round Bend, Inpoint, Model Perfect, or any other shape you favor.
Wire weight: Standard or 2X Stout.
Shank length: 2X Short, Shorter, or Standard.
Sizes (approximately): For one large worm, 6; for two large worms, 4; for one medium worm, 8; for two medium worms, 6; for one small worm, 10; for two small worms, 8; for very small worm, 12; for two very small worms, 10.

I've broken this down simply to show you how to select bait hooks for any purpose. It all boils down to a matter of comparison. The same principle holds for bass fishing with worms, though you may use a larger and heavier hook all along the line if and when needed. My favorite bass-bait hook is No. 2 when using worms. Standard to 2X Stout wire is strong enough for most purposes.

TROUT MINNOWS. Hooks used for trout minnows should be small and delicate. I'd choose a No. 10 regular-weight dry-fly trout hook for all-around use, with switches to No. 12 for extremely small minnows or to No. 8 for slightly larger ones.

BASS MINNOWS. I think 2X Stout in Nos. 2, 4, and 6 about right—depending on the size of the minnows. If the minnows are fragile and die easily, then finer wire hooks would be better. The finer the wire the less injury to the bait.

HELLGRAMMITES. No. 4 Standard wire in Round or Perfect Bends are all right, but I prefer a No. 2 Sneck because the square bend holds the creatures better.

GRASSHOPPERS. Here a Standard or even 1X Fine wire might be best for surface fishing. Any hook will be all right for deep water, provided it sinks the insect. There are special hooks for hoppers and minnows, and they are very good. Crickets can be handled on the same hooks.

It is a common practice to use treble hooks on artificial lures, but in my opinion many lures would be better and it would be more sporting if single hooks were used instead.

Using these hooks properly is another matter. The way of a fish with a lure is not a cut-and-dried affair that can be set down in a formula. As in human behavior, there are many things that must be considered—such as the characteristics of the species and the size and mood of the individual fish. You must also take into account the types and sizes of baits and hooks, to say nothing of the wide variations in water conditions. I'm going to discuss now some common hooking problems, directing my remarks particularly to the person who is new at fishing or doesn't have too much time to spend at the game.

Let's start with natural bait. On the whole, game fish all take a worm in about the same manner. Because this bait has no speed in its makeup, it is likely to be taken deliberately rather than violently, unless it is being trolled or perhaps racing down a fast run. Being soft and succulent, the worm is swallowed rather quickly, so that you don't need to give much time before setting the hook; about thirty seconds is enough when the fish are hungry and take readily.

Sometimes, however, the fish will not swallow the bait at once, but hold onto the ends for an exasperatingly long time. If you miss on a quick strike, try taking a little longer. A little teasing often helps; take the worm gently away. If the fish grabs hold hard, a quick wrist movement may hook it.

When the worm is taken forcibly and a very fast run follows immediately, it usually is best to strike at the moment the available slack is used up. You will miss strikes this way, but it's better than trying to feed line until the run stops. This applies to all natural baits.

The position of the line between the rod tip and bait is most important. Unless it is reasonably direct, even a hard strike may not make the hook penetrate. This is true with any kind of bait when you are feeding line as the fish runs. The more direct the line, the less power you need to set the hook and the more likely you are to land the quarry.

In quiet or still water, unless you are in a moving boat, a slight pressure on the line is advisable. Don't let the line run out too freely, but retard it just enough so that you can feel the tugs. This calls for a nice sense of adjustment, because too much pressure will make the taking fish suspicious.

In stream fishing, where the current enters into the picture, it is particularly important to watch how you feed line. If it goes out too fast, you may have trouble taking it in to make the strike. The line may get around one rock, the fish under another, and there you are. Also, the force of the current is likely to pull at the line, making it feel as if the fish were running fast with it when really it is moving slowly. When you finally strike against the pull of the current, you put only a slight pressure against the fish— often just enough to make it spit out the bait.

If the fish does not let go after a false strike, or if it picks up the bait immediately after, take up the belly caused by the current. Do this slowly and evenly, until you are sure you know where the fish is lying. When you have a reasonably short line between the rod tip and the fish, you are ready to strike. But don't get it too taut, or the fish will smell a rat and let go. Only experience can make you skillful at this.

Often you will get your strike on the opposite side of a fast run. Since most of your line will be in the fast current, it will feel as though the fish were running downstream when it is probably moving only a short distance to some quieter place where it can swallow the food at leisure. Unless you feed line grudgingly, you will have a hard time catching the fish. Incidentally, a long rod is an advantage here, because by holding it high you can keep quite some line above the current pull.

When you fish with hellgrammites, the hooking problems are practically the same as with worms. Under similar conditions you need about the same length of time between bite and strike. However, fish are inclined to be more capricious with this bait than with worms and minnows. When they are taking well, you can strike very quickly, but often they will pick up the bait and drop it. Teasing is about the best way to handle this situation.

With minnows it is usually necessary to give extra time for the fish to get the bait far enough into the mouth for the hook to take hold. This is not true with trout, however; here it is advisable to strike very fast. Trout take worms as leisurely as other fish, but they seem to realize that a minnow is a slippery customer and must be taken on the wing or not at all.

A gang hook or minnow gang is an advantage in minnow-fishing for trout. (Don't confuse the gang hook with the treble hook; a gang is one hook following another on a snell.) You have one hook in the mouth of the bait and the other below the center of the body, which gives you a good chance of hooking the trout no matter how it manages to grab the minnow.

The stock advice on striking and hooking with minnows is to let the fish run until it stops to turn the minnow around in its mouth, then strike when it starts off again. This is fine when the fish act according to Hoyle, as many of them do. But some don't run, stop, and run again; they just run and keep running. I've had the best luck hooking these babies by snubbing tightly the moment all free line has been used up. I've also found that it is best to retard the line slightly, as when using worms.

You are better equipped to feed line fast with a bait-casting or a spinning outfit than with a fly-rod outfit, but the fly-rod equipment provides far more fun and is more efficient for much of the bait fishing in fresh-water lakes and streams.

At times fish will toy with a minnow—pick it up, mouth it a few times, and then drop it. Here again the teasing trick will work. By pulling away just as the fish drops the bait, you can sometimes induce a really savage strike.

The members of the pike family have a habit of taking a minnow crosswise in the mouth and just holding it that way. I have seen them do this for five to ten minutes at a time, often dropping the bait as a cat drops a mouse, only to pick it up again if it moves. Sometimes they kill the minnow without making any pretense of swallowing it. In such a case your only chance is to tease the fish by pulling the bait away, so that it will make a grab and get the hook in its mouth.

I've never been sure just when to strike when using crawfish. Most of the catches I've made with them have been the result of following the "run, pause, and run again" pattern. When using a bobber I've had best luck by waiting until the float went six to eight inches under the water the second time down.

Until recent years I had never used lampreys for anything except walleye pike. In such fishing I had employed them in trolling, as a bait behind a spinner attractor. When I got a strike, I either hooked or missed on contact. Then one day I thought I'd try them for bass. The bait-seller told me to give quite some time when a fish took. I did this and had one miss after another. Then I tried increasing the time, but as this brought nothing but failure I started reducing it, finally reaching the point where only a few seconds passed between the take and the strike.

With tender bait bugs such as grasshoppers and crickets, use a hook designed for the purpose and make the strike as you would in fishing an artificial. However, I see little reason for using such bait, since one can usually do as well or better with artificials.

This brings us to artificial surface lures and flies, which include surface plugs, surface bugs, and dry flies. Many anglers are inclined to strike too fast with top-water lures. They see the rise and react violently, often failing to give the fish enough time to get the hook in its mouth. With a plug in motion, of course, there is quite an element of luck involved when a fish strikes, but the many points on a plug hook take care of this quite well. All you need to do, usually, is to send the barbs home with a fairly hard strike.

Driving the hooks home at the moment of the strike is particularly important in the case of muskellunge. Once this fish clamps its mouth down on a lure, further penetration of the hooks is well-nigh impossible. After the fight has gone on for a time, the muskie opens its mouth and out comes the plug. You need a rod with plenty of backbone to send home the large hooks into the jaws of this fish.

With surface bass bugs you must take enough time for the lure to get into the fish's mouth, but not so much that the fish gets wise to the fact that it is a fake. With soft lures, such as deer hair, cork or rubber-bodies, you can be a bit slower than when using wood or plastic bugs.

This fishing calls for a fairly stiff rod, one with enough power to send home a rather large hook on a long line. Without such a rod you seem to hook fish, but after a little playing it opens its mouth and out comes the bug.

Northern pike and pickerel are readily hooked with a bass bug, but there are other difficulties. Unless you use a wire leader, which handles abominably, you are sure to lose quite a few fish and bugs. Then, too, the mouths of these fish are mostly skinlike flesh, bone, and cartilage. No matter where the hook hits, you get at least a temporary hold. If it slides down and comes to rest with the hook around a mouth bone or cartilage, then you have a precarious hold with no barb giving its vital aid. With the slightest slack the hook will fall out.

On the whole, I'd suggest hooks of heavier wire for pike than for bass, because they can be set more firmly and can often penetrate a tough bit of cartilage at the moment of the strike or at the end of a slide. Also, it helps to have hooks built for holding rather than for hooking—a bend such as the Limerick, for instance.

When it comes to dry flies, I believe that the larger the fish the more deliberate you must be in making the strike. Experienced fish become skillful in picking flies from the surface. If you use a fine leader, the slightest sudden jerk will break it. Since rather fine leaders are essential for trout under most dry-fly conditions, you must learn not to strike hard. Excessive power in the strike accounts for more losses of good trout than any other cause.

There's no need for a fast strike with a sizeable fish when you have your line and fly under control. In fact, no strike is necessary at all; you only need to take up the slack so that the fish sets the hook when it takes and noses back in the water. It takes very little pressure to set a hook in a trout's mouth, as compared with the force required to snag a bass with a bug. With salmon a definite slowness is necessary in making a strike. You usually see them when they start taking the fly, and if you are not wise to salmon you are apt to pull it away before they get it.

In any dry-fly fishing, of course, where the float must be made with considerable slack line or a decided curve in order to avoid drag, the strike must be sufficient to take up the slack. Because so many small fish rise in the course of a day's fishing, the average angler gets the wrong training for catching large fish on a dry fly. These small fish are so fast and snappy that the fisherman's nerves are keyed to this tempo. He uses the same speed and force when a large fish rises, and the result is a broken leader or a miss.

In the latter case you may get a second chance. If you didn't disturb the water too much or prick the fish, it may resume feeding. Don't cast immediately to the place where you got the rise. Take a rest and change to another pattern, meanwhile studying the situation with a view to improving your float and shortening the cast.

In fishing wet flies by the simple method of casting across and downstream, and fishing it out with a taut line, the angler has little to do with hooking a fish. It is either snagged or missed. But a bit of slack rolled with the line just ahead of the place where the strikes usually occur often produces a hooked fish. Sometimes, too, a downward snap of the rod at the instant of the strike brings good results. For this a stiff rod is best.

When you're fishing wet flies with a natural drift, however, you have a different proposition. At the slightest sign of a take you must strike and be quick about it. If you can see the fly under water, or know where it is, you often can detect a take by a slight flash or by the fly suddenly disappearing from view. When this happens you must react like a flash, or your chance will be gone. I've often heard anglers complain that they were getting no rises, when they were getting hit after hit without knowing it.

Here, as when fishing deep in quiet water, the line is a great signal giver. Keep an eye on where it enters the water. If it twitches or pauses, strike with hair-trigger quickness.

Fishing with underwater lures that are always in motion requires a quick reaction at the feel of a hit. Here again luck enters the picture, but it is essential to have speed and sufficient power to set the hook.

CHAPTER XXXIII

Winter Tackle Care

WINTER is a good time for inspecting, cleaning, oiling, and repairing tackle, for jotting down items that must be replaced because of age or loss, and for listing new tackle that you want to obtain before the next season rolls around.

Start with an inspection of your tackle box. Unless you're unusually neat, the end of the season finds it in a mess. Things have been put back carelessly, often wet and dirty; leaving them in this condition can prove costly.

When you start the job, have ready two soft cloths that are free from lint. One should be left dry, the other soaked with oil but not oozing with it. Take the items out of the tackle box one at a time and clean each one; dry-wipe the things that don't need oil and use the oiled cloth on the things that do. As you finish, arrange the items in orderly fashion so that when you return them to the box you can place them to best advantage for quick use. Put aside things in need of repair to be attended to later.

Among these latter items may be lures that are basically all right, but which lack swivels, hooks, split rings, or other parts. Wooden plugs that have taken a beating can be refurbished with a coat of clear lacquer or varnish. I have some that are at least twenty-five years old and still in good condition, though somewhat chewed up by fish and battered by rocks. If you have a lure that has produced well for you, it's wise to get a couple more like it in case you lose one. Incidentally, it's not necessary to lacquer or varnish the modern plastic lures. In fact, it might do more harm than good.

Metal spoons and spinners may have become tarnished or scratched or both, and while this dulling of metal lures may make them more attractive to the fish, there are times when brightly polished ones are best. So it's a good idea to have both in your box. Your stock of these should also be carefully checked for different sizes and shapes.

Sinkers are likely to be overlooked. These should be stocked in various styles, sizes, and shapes for various purposes. If you know certain waters well and what sinkers you'll need for fishing them, be sure you have plenty on hand. If you aren't sure about the water, provide yourself with a wide assortment so you'll be prepared for most eventualities. Your supply should include egg sinkers, dipsey or bait-casting sinkers, swivel-barrel sinkers, keel sinkers, clinch-on sinkers, and split shot. You'll need at least two sizes of split shot—BB and buckshot—so make a note to add them to your assortment.

You would be wise, if you have a lot of feathered or hair lures, to put some moth flakes in with them. Trout flies and bass bugs are also susceptible to moth damage. If you store any feathered or hair lures, or just plain feathers and hair, in metal or cardboard boxes, be sure to protect them against moths.

Before you store flies and bugs, however, straighten and clean them. Placing them in the jet of steam from a boiling kettle will fluff out the feathers and aid in restoring hair lures. Next treat the dry flies and floating bugs with a bath of silicone fly floater. In the spring you can start using these lures without any further dressing.

It's a good idea to carry an extra reel and line when you go fishing. It may save you hours of repairs. You might try dropping a hint in the right quarter that you would welcome this as a Christmas present; otherwise, winter is a good time to start budgeting for such items. Around the end of the year is a good time to pick up bargains in fishing tackle—when stores are discontinuing old models in favor of new ones. If you already have a fly or bait-casting reel, think about getting a spinning reel.

Having extra rods is another guarantee of carefree angling. If you want to go in for all three methods of fishing next season—fly casting, bait casting, and spinning—it's wise to have an extra rod for each. Again, you're not so likely to have to stop fishing to make repairs.

As for winter care of rod and reel, if your rod is made of glass it probably doesn't need any care, other than the replacement of one or more guides. The guide windings may need touching up because of cracks, or they may be badly scored from casting. Steel rods should be treated the same way and carefully wiped with an oily rag. A split bamboo rod should be varnished in its entirety, or touched up where varnish is needed. A good job of waxing with good furniture wax will insure protection for the rest of the winter and through the opening days of the season.

While you have no doubt frequently oiled and cleaned all the easily available parts of your reels during the season, it's a good idea to do a thorough cleaning and oiling job at least once a year, and winter is the best time for that. This means taking the reel apart, so you need plenty of room and a system to keep the parts in order—you have to get the reel back together without too much trouble. If you don't want to tackle the job yourself, then right now is the time to give the job to a professional, to send the reel to the manufacturer, or have your dealer do so.

Assuming that you want to undertake the job yourself, do it on a table with nothing else on it. As you take down the reel, lay the parts out in order and leave plenty of room between them so they don't get mixed up. Have the instruction and parts sheet handy (this should have come with the reel when you purchased it). When all the parts are cleaned and oiled, start putting them back together in reverse order. If any parts need replacing, now is the time to order them. If the trouble is bad, I'd suggest going to a professional repairman or sending the reel to the manufacturer.

Bait-casting reels are the most complicated and need more attention than spinning reels. However, spinning reels get out of order more often, and it's well to be equipped with spare parts for emergency repairs. The parts most likely to go wrong are the small springs and the reeling-in mechanism.

A fly reel is usually such a simple thing that you don't need instructions on how to take it apart or oil it. Most of them need only the removal of one screw or the operation of a simple locking device to take out the spool.

Fly lines made of modern materials don't need the care and attention that the old-time silk lines did, and still do. Both are subject to curling if left on the reel too long. Even during the fishing season the line should be turned around every few weeks to prevent this. In winter it should be carefully but loosely coiled and hung in a cool spot. Perhaps an easier method is to wind the line around a cylindrical object like an oatmeal box. Before storing, wipe off with a soft cloth. Fishing lines are sure to pick up dirt from the surface of the water and from contact with the earth which may shorten their lives.

If you still use a silk fly line, at the end of the season it should be carefully cleaned with mild soap and water, dried, and dressed with a good line dressing. This should be put on lightly and rubbed in with the fingers. Polish with a soft cloth, being careful not to rub so vigorously that enough heat is created to injure the line's finish. Then store as recommended for synthetic lines.

If you're a fly fisherman, how about your leader? The synthetics don't require special care, except to test for strength and to find wind knots. The fine strands at the fly end of the leader often gather simple twists from casting, which I call wind knots. They occur most often when you cast into the wind, or when you cast a leader made with very fine material. They cause the leader to break under a strain that the unknotted leader could withstand.

If you find any of these wind knots, cut and retie at such places with a blood knot or barrel knot, or replace with a new strand if it seems necessary. These knots will also occur in very fine monofilament spinning line. If this happens, break the line off at the highest knot you find. It won't be too many yards from the lure end, so little line will be wasted. But be sure to locate the *upper* knot.

Waders and boots should be stored carefully. Before storing be sure to patch any holes or leaky spots that have developed. Drying out stocking-foot waders is a simple matter. Just turn them inside out. To store, hang them in a closet or roll them up and put them in a drawer. There is the danger that rolling or folding such gear for long may cause creases that will injure fabric and the waterproofing. But if they're loosely rolled and have plenty of room, they'll be all right.

Both footed waders and regular boots are difficult to dry out properly in the foot section because they can't be turned inside out. Stuffing the foot loosely with newspaper is about the best way I know to absorb moisture. Several successive stuffings may be necessary to dry them thoroughly. I'd advise against direct heat. Even a guarded bulb may be insufficient to prevent damage from the heat, while an unguarded bulb is almost sure to injure the material.

Once footed waders are thoroughly dry, it's best to store them by hanging them feet uppermost. Good wader-hangers can be made by bending cheap wire coat hangers into a V-shape to hold the boot foot, one hanger for each boot. Of course, boots or waders should be stored away from direct heat.

Willow creels used to carry fish should be thoroughly washed with a soda solution. However, if you use your creel as a carry-all for tackle, as I've seen fellows do, there's no need to wash it. In any case, varnish the creel inside and out, working the varnish in between the willow strands. Use a good grade of varnish. For other fish carriers I recommend several thorough washings, dryings and airings.

CHAPTER XXXIV

Ray Bergman Says Goodbye

M Y ANGLING column has been in each issue of *Outdoor Life* for twenty-six years. I wrote monthly features and columns about fishing for twelve years before I became *Outdoor Life*'s angling editor. I am getting along in years. The time has come when I need to take a rest from the steady demands of writing to meet deadlines each month. For this reason I have resigned as angling editor.

It was a tough decision to make. Since joining the *Outdoor Life* staff in March of 1934 I have written for it exclusively. The association has been a happy one. Hence, I want to make it plain that, while this is my last monthly angling column, it is not necessarily the last story I will write for the magazine. I merely want to be free from a regular schedule.

I started writing simply because I loved fishing and wanted to share what I learned from my endless experiments with fishing tackle and tactics. Rather like a person airing his ideas through a letter to the editor, I typed out my first fishing story in 1921 and mailed it to the old *Forest and Stream* magazine. The story was published, and I have been writing similar stories ever since. All my writing has followed the same basic concept: to give the reader factual information gained and tested by my own practical experience, and to make it as interesting as my writing ability would allow.

I have been fishing as long as I can remember. As a child I fished with my father on the Hudson River, which runs by my home town of Nyack, New York. By the time I was ten years of age I was using a bicycle to pedal to lakes and streams near Nyack to fish for trout, bass, pickerel, and panfish. Eventually I was seeking more distant waters by train and in an early vintage automobile with blowout-prone tires mounted on those frustrating clincher rims.

Though fishing has always been my main interest, I have also written a few articles about hunting. At the age of ten, I acquired a .22 rifle (a brass-bore Hamilton) by selling magazine subscriptions. I was in the woods and hills as much as I was on the water, and I brought many a squirrel and rabbit home to add to the family larder. I have only one painful recollection of my days as a boy hunter, from when I was eleven.

Father had a double-barreled, muzzle-loading 12-gauge shotgun. He didn't object to my hunts with the .22 rifle, but he had forbidden me to use the shotgun—so of course I wanted to fire that gun the first chance I got.

Before long the opportunity came. Father was at work in the city and mother had taken a later train to go shopping there. Neither would be home until six p.m. It was a splendid setup. That day I played hooky. I gathered up the shotgun, the powder horn, a bag of shot, and the necessary firing caps. Making sure that none of the neighbors saw me, I sneaked into the woods.

I charged the old muzzle-loader with powder and shot, and began scanning the trees for squirrels. I saw one, drew a bead on it, and pulled the trigger. The next thing I knew I was flat on my back. I had put in too big a powder charge and had held the gun too loosely. Besides, I was just a small child. The tremendous recoil bruised my armpit and badly injured my right hand.

I got the gun home and put it back where it belonged, but I knew I was in for some questioning. I could get away with the bruised armpit, but I couldn't hide the injured hand. I am sorry to say that I lied about the hand. I told my parents I'd hurt it in a fall. I was guilty of further treachery at school, where I showed my injured hand and was excused from the laborious written work my classmates were doing. I represented myself as a partial invalid for as long as I could. Perhaps my punishment for these boyhood deceits came through a loss of solid enthusiasm for shotguns, which some outdoorsmen cherish as I do my fine fly rods.

I was also a trapper during my youth and early manhood. Trapping season came at a time when there wasn't any fishing. It gave me an extra excuse to explore the woods and waters. I always inspected the trout waters near my trap lines regularly during the closed fishing season—just to spy on the brook trout. This helped a lot when the fishing season opened. I knew just where to fish and how to approach the good spots without frightening the trout.

I was the proprietor of a sporting-goods store in Nyack when I was in my early 20's, but I still ran a trap-line in season. I often got up at three a.m. to run my lines before I opened the store. Routine haul from my traps at this time was a few muskrats and skunks each week, but one morning I made what I considered a bonanza catch on my eight-trap brook line. In one trap was a star-black skunk, a premium-pelt animal with only a small patch of white on its head. In another was a very dark and large northern mink, and in the very last was the largest muskrat I'd ever caught. They were all bonus-price furs.

I delayed getting back to the store until the last minute before I had to open it for the commuters to pick up their papers. I wanted people on the street to admire my catch. I stalked slowly and proudly into town at the right moment—and drove a stream of pedestrians off the sidewalk as if I'd been playing a fire hose ahead of me. Skunk trappers forget how skunks smell to persons unaccustomed to the odor. My trek through town disrupted

Nyack so much that the incident was headlined on the front page of our local paper.

It took a serious illness to get me started writing seriously. One April my doctor recommended a six- to eight-month recuperation period in the woods. We didn't have enough money to consider such a thing, but God and good fortune came to our aid. A friend connected us with a couple in the Adirondack Mountains of northern New York who had a cabin for rent at a very low fee. A family rented our own house furnished, which carried the expenses of both as well as supplying a moderate surplus.

It was a marvelous seven months. All I did was fish and hunt. I wrote a two-part article about it that was accepted by *Forest and Stream* with a request for more. Following my wilderness recuperation, I took a job with the fine old fishing tackle firm of William Mills & Son of New York. After some ten years on that job I started a one-man tackle business of my own, mostly through mail order. I have been in some phase of the fishing-tackle business all my adult life.

Between fishing for sport and working with fishing tackle, I've naturally acquired a large store of knowledge of fishing subjects. I drew on this information to write four successful books—*Just Fishing, Trout, Fresh-Water Bass*, and *With Fly, Plug and Bait*. My book *Trout*, which went through thirteen printings after its first publication in 1938, was later revised to include a section on spinning tackle.

I remember 1932 as a banner year. I had taken a leave of absence from William Mills & Son. By that time I had been writing and selling stories and articles for about ten years, and my wife and I had saved enough to finance a long fishing trip.

We began our fishing in the Catskills of New York State, then went to the Adirondacks—all familiar territory. Then we moved on to New Brunswick, Canada, fishing mostly for trout and salmon, although we took some bass and northern pike. Next we made a long trek west to Lake of the Woods in Ontario, Canada, for muskies. Ernie Calvert, now dead, gave us expert instructions on how to catch these giant members of the pike family. We also got well acquainted with northern pike.

We went from Ontario to Wisconsin, getting a variety of fishing. Then we drove down to North Carolina, where we fished for channel bass off the island of Ocracoke. Later we spent considerable time in the bayous of Mississippi and Louisiana. After that we headed north, expecting to fish the Ozarks in Arkansas and Missouri, but at Little Rock winter struck so suddenly and hard that we started home.

An ice storm plagued us for miles. By the time we reached Virginia a blizzard had taken over. We decided to keep going. We didn't make many miles that day but about dark we managed to reach a town in northern Virginia where we spent the night. Next morning we got up before daylight. It was bitter cold and the roads were snowy, icy, and slippery. Before we reached Harrisburg, Pennsylvania, in late afternoon we'd worn out two sets of tire chains. We bought another pair that didn't fit well. We had about two hundred miles to go. Being young, we decided to make for home.

The road was treacherous and the cold intense, hovering around ten degrees. The car was a five-year-old Model-A Ford, with no heater. The new chains got messed up within thirty miles. I took them off and we made out better without them. We just had to keep on going. There wasn't much else to do. That was before the days of motels scattered all along the highways, and there were few cars on the road.

Our own house in Nyack had been closed for months, so we went to my wife's parents' home. The warm greetings, the warm house, the hot tea and food were wonderful. It was a perfect ending to our first long fishing adventure. Since then we have fished in all the good fishing states and many of the Canadian provinces.

Throughout the years there have been some fishing experiences that I remember more vividly than others, and some friends who through their knowledge and helpfulness have taught me many of the secrets of successful fishing.

One of the first was an Adirondack guide named Chan West-cott, long since dead. He put me to many subtle tests before he decided I was worth helping. Then he started giving me advice on where and how to fish. He taught me much about wet-fly and bait fishing, and I was a proud young man when one day he told me I was a good fisherman. It was an honor to be accepted on even terms by those old-time Adirondack guides.

The late J. D. (Don) Bell, a lawyer in Hillsdale, New York, was the source of much inspiration and help in dry-fly fishing. Gruff, tenderhearted Don was older than I by about eighteen years, but he could wear me out on the stream until he reached the age of seventy and keep up with me until he turned eighty.

One of the English setters that were Don Bell's constant companions was forever exposing the brawny, thunderous man for the soft touch that he really was. It was common practice for this setter to splash into the trout pool Don was stalking and swim nonchalantly through the hole before the lawyer could make his first cast. Don would bellow threats at the top of his great voice, promising punishments too terrible to relate. The dog, knowing full well that all would be forgiven, would swim till it tired of the game.

Don had a weakness for dogs and dry-fly fishing. He never fished for anything but trout, and to my knowledge he never fished with anything but dry flies. I learned much of what I know about dry-fly fishing from him.

I must confess that to me the trouts are the most enjoyable fish to catch. I like them all; the rainbow as the best and most spectacular fighter, the brook trout for beauty and dogged battle, and the brown for its seeming intelligence and its first spirited runs when hooked.

I also love to catch black bass, and I must say that a small-mouth bass of equal size in the same type of water can put a rainbow in a questionable spot as to which is the better fighter. In some waters I have found the largemouth bass a very good fighter, but as a rule it doesn't have the staying power of either the smallmouth or the rainbow trout. Largemouths make up for this by their gameness in striking surface lures.

Trout and bass have held first place in my heart all through the years, but that doesn't mean I haven't greatly enjoyed fishing for all the other fresh-water fish. Muskies, steelheads, and salmon have all had a part in giving me plenty of thrills. I like fishing for pike and pickerel. I have never been enthusiastic about wall-eyes (pike-perch) though I have fished for them plenty. If they run large they'll give you a fair fight, but on the whole I think a yellow perch of equal size is as active as a walleye.

I believe the valiant fight of the common sunfish or its close relative the bluegill is as good a resistance as that shown by trout or bass of comparable size and maturity. However, it seems to me that sunfish show less intelligence in trying to escape. They simply tug and pull hard, mostly in a circular movement, whereas a trout or bass will leap and roll and tangle your line in snags.

If I had a flair for fiction, I might claim that I was charged by a huge rainbow trout I hooked while wading the Ausable River of upstate New York about twenty-five years ago. The fish took a dry fly I cast into the Slide Rock Pool and made a powerful run upstream. I was using a light 3X leader and standing hip-deep in the strong current, so there was nothing I could do but let the trout run. I saw him for the first time as he raced down-stream and leaped high in the air within five feet of me. There was no mistaking the identity or size of the fish. It was a rainbow trout that would certainly have weighed more than fifteen pounds, probably as much as twenty.

This great fish took my line far downsteam then, and I thought I'd lost him when the line went slack. A second later he was curving the slack line toward me on a sizzling upstream run. This time he was headed straight for me, and he never changed course. He struck the leg I was awkwardly balanced on with such force that I was upended in the water. The trout's mouth must have been open, for my waders were slashed as if his teeth had hung in them momentarily. Perhaps he was trying to knock off the dry fly that was stuck in his jaw. Needless to say, the monster rainbow broke off as I floundered in the water. I dropped the rod in the tumble and only managed to retrieve it because the loose line looped around my leg.

Once some disgruntled anglers at Cranberry Lake, New York, decided to have me arrested as a game hog. We were fishing where Brandy Brook flows into Cranberry Lake. On this particular evening the brook trout were exceptionally wary. Only those fishermen who knew all the tricks for this water were catching any. I was one of those in the know, having been coached by an old guide of the area.

There were eight anglers at the inlet, and this made the short stretch of shore rather crowded. Among the anglers who couldn't catch any fish was a party of three generally disliked by the local residents and an old saw filer who was sharpening saws for the Syracuse University forestry students, whose camp was at the flow of another brook.

I had caught all the fish I wanted and so had my partner. I was about ready to head for our nearby tent when it occurred to me that the saw filer fishing close to me hadn't caught a fish. He had mentioned that he'd promised the boys at the forestry camp a feed of trout.

I decided to teach him how to get these "flow" trout. It was difficult because of the darkness (night fishing was legal then) but he finally got the knack. Eventually the old saw filer got his limit of brook trout. In the meantime the three disliked big shots from the village had heard my voice in the darkness and all the splashings of the saw filer's catch. They hadn't caught a fish.

Irritated by the sounds of our success, the three luckless men decided to send one of their party to town to get the game warden. They were sure I was exceeding the bag limit. The game warden was routed out of bed and hauled six miles by boat to investigate. Our catch was strictly legal, but the sleepless warden arrested one of the three soreheads for fishing without a license. I must confess this amused me.

Before a dam put an end to long float trips on the White River in the Ozarks, my wife and I enjoyed many wonderful days on that river. We fished it so much that Jim Owen of Branson, Missouri, included our home town on a sign post in one of the restaurants. The sign showed the mileage to St. Louis, Tulsa, and other large towns within a reasonable distance of the river. Jim added

Nyack—over twelve hundred miles distant—to the list. Jim Owen introduced me to the Ozarks, something for which I have always been grateful.

My wife and I have had many excellent guides, whom we remember with fondness. We have also had some poor ones.

There is one thing I wish to press home to you about this guiding business. When a man is hired as a guide his responsibility is to see that the angler he's guiding gets the best possible service. The guide should always place the angler in the best available spot for catching fish. If fishing from a boat or canoe, the craft should be anchored or held in a place that gives advantage to the sportsman who's paying the bill. The guide should not fish at all unless the paying sportsman asks him to.

I have found the guides in the north country the most considerate of their clients. We have never had one of them who'd think of fishing himself without being coaxed to do so. Canadian guides have been outstanding in this respect.

I recall with amusement the heroic struggle described by a fisherman who lugged a big northern pike into the lobby of a resort hotel on the Canadian shore of Lake Erie. It had taken every grain of this man's strength and cunning to subdue the whopper he displayed before admiring hotel guests. I was dressed for dinner and substantially changed in appearance as I stood listening to this story. The talkative angler didn't recognize me. I had met him on the lake that day and given him the big pike to keep him from coming in fishless. I didn't bother to tell the crowd that the fish they were ogling had been boated after a rather dull tug-o'-war against the spring of my fly rod.

I have fished in some dangerous situations due to the weather, but somehow the most memorable was a windy day in Wisconsin. This wind was raging at sixty to seventy miles an hour. Trees were toppling all over the woods, some of them dangerously close to the cabin where we were staying. My wife stayed indoors and so did the owners. I went out to watch the play of the wind and got a great kick out of seeing trees gradually succumb and fall. Not.that I wanted the trees to be destroyed, but nothing could be done about that, and it was definitely exciting to be out in the blow and see things happen. The entire lake looked like froth on a glass of beer. One couldn't possibly fish it and any small boat on it would have capsized instantly or been blown against the shore.

By mid-afternoon I had become a bit bored with the play of the elements. I was about to go inside and read a book when I remembered a protected creek that ran into the lake close to our cabin. It was well guarded against the wind by banks and staunch trees. A state road culvert was at the upper end.

I decided to investigate. I took a spinning outfit and a small box of lures and was partially blown to the edge of the stream. The reasonably calm section was short, not more than 150 feet long. The wind was strong there, too, but most of it whizzed over my head and didn't disturb the creek too much. I hooked two small muskies in this stretch and was about to fish it again, having reached the culvert end. Then I heard a splash that seemed to come from the culvert.

My first cast sent the lure well inside the tunnel, perhaps a distance of fifteen to twenty feet. Because the current was coming toward me and I hadn't seen the lure hit, I started reeling quickly. A few seconds later I had hooked a fair muskie, the only decent fish we caught during our stay.

One of the greatest changes I've noticed through the years has been the continually increasing number of anglers. After each war there has been a great increase. Not too many years ago one could fish famous places and not meet more than half a dozen fishermen. Today the same places have paths worn deep along the stream banks.

When I first fished the Tennessee River in Alabama with Willie Young we could go to a spot where the fish were and have it to ourselves. Today there are many boats in every good spot. Fishing waters are becoming as crowded as our highways, and fishing has become big business.

I think too many anglers set out to catch and keep the legal limit. In some places the limit is more than one family can use. Sometimes the excess is simply wasted. Also, I've known of freezers loaded with frozen fish, many of them kept there so long that the taste is impaired.

In my opinion, fresh-water fish lose flavor and quality after being frozen. They are at their best when not frozen but kept really cold for a few days. Fish too fresh are inclined to cook poorly. Keeping the limit is fine if you can use the fish yourself or have someone who really wants them for food, but if you have caught all that you know you can possibly use and still haven't taken your limit, then put back the rest of the fish you catch.

Be careful not to injure a fish you plan to release. If you simply take an injured fish off the hook and throw it back it will eventually bloat and float to the surface. If it drifts to shore before being spoiled, some animal may come along to get it, or some bird like a fish hawk may pick it up. The only birds I've ever seen feeding on bloated or spoiled fish are crows and buzzards. If nothing eats fish that drift ashore they rot and stink up the area.

The best way to dispose of a badly injured fish that you don't wish to keep is to open up the belly so it will sink to the bottom. Then it will become food for minnows and other aquatic creatures on which game fish feed. Many anglers have the bad habit of tossing unwanted trash fish such as suckers up on the bank to rot in the sun.

I also suggest that when you give fish away you clean them first. Many folk who like fish don't care to do the cleaning. Often unprepared fish are put in the garbage pail. The best place to clean fish is right on the shore or lake where you've caught them. Then the remains should be thrown into the water where they will feed other fish and aquatic life.

There's plenty of need for improvement in common courtesy in fishing; there was even when there were only a fraction of the anglers we have now. Do not crowd any stream angler who has selected a place to fish and was there before you. Keep far enough away so that you do not spoil his fishing and perhaps yours, too. When fishing from a boat, never get so close to another angler that your lines may cross and tangle. Always apply the golden rule. Do unto others as you would have them do unto you.

I wish I could name all the fine folk who have helped me in one way or another along the road to my retirement. I trust that they will accept my sincere thanks for their generous aid.

Some of you may wonder what I'm going to do now that I've resigned from *Outdoor Life*. Candidly, I'm going to rest and do nothing except exactly what I feel like doing. What I feel like doing is some more fishing in a lazy, indolent way. I also hope to assemble all the notes I've made through the years. Then I'll write again when the urge comes to do so. Farewell for the present. I wish you all health, long life, and many tight lines.

Ray Bergman died on February 17, 1967, at Nyack, New York.